Clara Peeters

The series *Illuminating Women Artists* launches at a critical moment in contemporary culture. It marks a significant intervention within the broader movement underway among scholars, museums, collectors and the wider world of cultural heritage to make evident and contextualise historically the contributions of women artists. As such, the books, each written by a leading specialist in the field of art history, will appeal to audiences from the academic sphere to the general public. Beautifully illustrated, the volumes collectively offer an unprecedented visual contextualisation of the lives and works of their subjects, to whom in some cases a monograph has yet to be dedicated.

Books in the sub-series *Illuminating Women Artists: Renaissance and Baroque* critically reappraise the lives and works of female artists in Europe from the fifteenth to the early eighteenth centuries. Many of the women represented by the volumes were celebrated professional artists in their own eras, yet their names and works have not been passed down continually in the history of art. As the first series dedicated to correcting this omission, the books interweave established conclusions with new discoveries to reframe how women's artistic production is approached and understood.

Clara Peeters

ALEJANDRO VERGARA-SHARP

GETTY PUBLICATIONS

LOS ANGELES

IN ASSOCIATION WITH

MUSEO NACIONAL DEL PRADO

**Published in the United States of America by Getty Publications, Los Angeles
in association with Museo Nacional del Prado**
1200 Getty Center Drive, Suite 500
Los Angeles, California 90049-1682
getty.edu/publications

Distributed in the United States and Canada by the University of Chicago Press

Printed in China

ISBN 978-1-60606-950-9
Library of Congress Control Number: 2024945920

Published simultaneously in the United Kingdom by Lund Humphries
in association with Museo Nacional del Prado
Originated by Lund Humphries in association with Museo Nacional del Prado
Huckletree Shoreditch
Alphabeta Building
18 Finsbury Square
London EC2A 1AH
UK
lundhumphries.com

Copy edited by Julie Gunz
Project managed and designed by Crow Books
Set in Adobe Caslon Pro

Front cover: Clara Peeters, *Table with Cloth, Foodstufs and Other Objects*, c.1611, oil on panel, 55 × 73 cm, Museo Nacional del Prado, Madrid

Back cover: Clara Peeters, *A Still Life of Flowers in a Vase*, c.1610, oil on panel, 50 × 34 cm, National Museum of Women in the Arts, Washington, DC

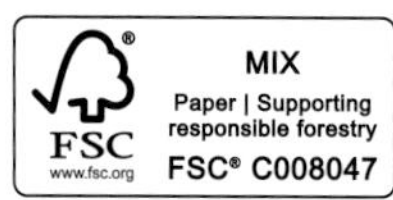

Contents

Series Foreword   6

Introduction   8

1   The Life and Context of Clara Peeters   11

2   Still-Life Painting   32

3   Artistic Production   45

4   Social Practice and Material Culture   65

5   Problems of Meaning and Interpretation   92

Conclusion: Peeters's Artistry   101

Notes   109

Bibliography   118

Image Credits   123

Index   124

Series Foreword

The series *Illuminating Women Artists: Renaissance and Baroque* was conceptualised at a pivotal moment in contemporary life, when the call to dismantle structural bias was taking on a new urgency. As social justice movements, such as #MeToo, #BlackLivesMatter, and #TransLivesMatter, exposed assumptions about gender, race, and sexual identity, academic research has been infused with a new energy around these topics. Although approaches to, and even the very applicability of, identity categories as they are defined today vary in regard to the past, early modernity and the contemporary moment share a desire to contend with the power structures that have repressed individuals and groups, albeit in historically distinct ways. Books in *Illuminating Women Artists* advance a specific aspect of this study – the feminist academic enterprise – by making evident various ways that early modern women of the fifteenth through eighteenth centuries negotiated, and sometimes resisted, structural constraints in the sphere of the visual arts.

The series is indebted to feminist art-historical studies produced from the beginning of the 1970s that aimed to disrupt the traditional academic focus on early modern male artists by writing their female counterparts into the discipline of art history. These and other scholarship also began to investigate gender norms in the Renaissance and Baroque, which created different conditions for women and men who sought to practice art as professionals or amateurs. Societal limitations disadvantaged most women (and some men) who aspired to a life in the visual arts. For example, girls were excluded from the formal apprenticeship system through which most male artists were trained, and therefore they sought informal instruction, often from male relatives. Women practitioners who married and became mothers generally experienced a lapse in artistic production while they attended to the responsibilities that came with these roles. On the other hand, fathers sometimes supportively promoted their daughters as artists, which also aggrandised the family and improved its financial standing through patronage and sales.

This series considers early modern women artists within their social, cultural, temporal, and geographic contexts. These female artmakers worked in a period when a literary defence of women's merits began to challenge the patriarchal misogynist ideas that sought to suppress women and their potential. Some women artists may have been aware of this incipient feminism or have visually voiced related issues in their art. But the female artists represented by the series also identified with the social structures of their place and time. These structures, prominent among them gender and class, contributed to shaping their identities and to forming their conceptions about others. While women challenged normative structures in important ways (some more overtly than others), they also were acculturated into dominant cultural attitudes and thus complicit in supporting social hierarchies of class and race. Renaissance and Baroque women artists themselves derived from a spectrum of social classes – artisan, merchant, professional, or patrician. Membership in these classes made it possible for some women artists to have servants or even to enslave persons who contributed to their households. This practice reduced their own domestic obligations and freed time for artmaking, but in turn contributed to reinforcing existing systems of social stratification regarded as the norm.

Some gendered conditions with which female artists contended did not necessarily impede their success, but, even when women's artistic production was critically acclaimed, it was often evaluated according to gender stereotypes. Yet, certain women independently challenged, and circumvented or broke, restrictive gender protocols to enable prolific art production. In the process, they revised those protocols and influenced the history of art. Some established their own professional studios and trained pupils, both female and male, who in turn established themselves as professionals in workshops of their own. Others produced large bodies of work as amateurs, and some rendered porous the boundaries between these two statuses by bridging them. Still others produced works for members of communities to which they belonged, such as professed nuns in enclosed convents, or for personal reasons, such as to have in their possession a portrait of a family member. Some worked under contract for patrons, producing images for prestigious European courts and churches, where their art came under the eyes of the public. These women in the aggregate produced works that varied widely in subject, including both sacred and secular themes, and in artistic media. Represented in the latter category were the familiar forms of sculpture, painting, and printmaking, and also other ways of artmaking that were valued more highly in the past than they are in the present, including papercutting, embroidery, and weaving.

Five decades of sustained research have transformed our understanding of early modern women artists. *Illuminating Women Artists: Renaissance and Baroque* takes stock of this work through books that offer state-of-the-question analyses of their subjects. These peer-reviewed volumes variously interweave established conclusions with new discoveries investigated through emerging modes of analysis to reframe our understanding of the lives, artistic production, and works of art by European women. Together the books reveal the varied ways in which women of the fifteenth through the seventeenth centuries skilfully and often successfully navigated restricting gender norms to stake out productive lives as artmakers and develop innovative approaches to the works they produced. The volumes offer an unprecedented contextualisation of the lives and works of their subjects, to whom in some cases a monograph has not previously been dedicated.

Marilyn Dunn, Loyola University Chicago
Andrea Pearson, American University, Washington, DC
April 2021

Introduction

Those who are interested in the art of Clara Peeters (probably 1587–after 1636) face a difficulty that she shares with most other women painters of early modern Europe: she has not been the focus of much scholarly attention. Despite recent research, little can be gleaned about her life or career from the scant written evidence that survives.[1] In order to learn something about the prospects that she faced as a woman artist we must make do with limited information and extrapolate from what we know about other female painters of the time, but we cannot be very specific. That this remains true approximately 50 years after the inception of feminist art history demonstrates the necessity of a book series such as *Illuminating Women Artists*. This appellation points to the goals of celebration and acknowledgement. It implies that there is a certain sense of justice in writing and publishing this text. Attention will be paid here to the limitations that Peeters encountered because of her gender and how she responded to them in her art.

We have learned in the last decades that more women painters practised in the past than had been acknowledged. A reason for this is that some were obscured behind the names of husbands, fathers and brothers, or remained anonymous because being a woman painter placed them at a grave disadvantage. An example from a different creative field and from more recent times is the famous Fortuny Delphos gown, which has traditionally been attributed solely to Mariano Fortuny y Madrazo, founder of the couture house Fortuny in 1906. In fact, it was designed by his wife, Adèle Henriette Negrin. We have also observed that scholars have not shown much interest in those woman painters who were known, for reasons of prejudice that were seen as natural in the past. The Fortuny case is, again, a telling example, as Mariano himself had acknowledged in writing that the creation was Adèle's. Historians simply did not think it important to correct the record until recently.

An opinion that I find also to be based on preconceived judgements is taking shape in our own times. It affirms that the number of woman painters active in the early modern period in Europe was not just somewhat larger than acknowledged, but much more so. To establish a realistic count, I researched how many female artists are part of the collection of Flemish paintings at the Prado in Madrid, the collection for which I have responsibility as a curator. Counting the fifteenth, sixteenth and seventeenth centuries, there are approximately 1300 paintings in that part of the museum's collection (although the numbers are not exact because of cases where the place of origin of a painting is not certain). Only six of them were painted by women: four by Clara

Peeters and two by Catarina Ykens II (b.1659).[2] It is likely that a few more have gone undetected and will eventually resurface. I have personally looked for paintings by Michaelina Wautier (1604–89), who worked for Habsburg patrons and whom I thought a likely candidate for the Prado, which is the heir of the Spanish royal collection, but unsuccessfully. Even if some works by Wautier or others are eventually identified, it is all but certain that the number will remain very small. Furthermore, I found that the numbers of works by women artists at the Prado was significantly larger for the nineteenth century. This is a period defined by a different set of social, economic and professional parameters, where the identities of those producing, collecting and writing about art had changed substantially, and bears separate analysis. The early modern period is a distinct historical epoch. The achievements of Peeters and other women artists from that time were exceptional and accomplished with difficulty. Exaggerating the numbers does not do them justice, as it minimises the extent to which they freed themselves from the norms of the societies in which they lived.

A word of warning. My first responses, many years ago, to the art of Clara Peeters were to the paintings themselves and not as much to the person who made them. This remains, by nature and by choice, my outlook as an art historian. When I stand before her paintings, or observe them in photographs, I am drawn primarily to two things: her artistry, that is, the visual language that she used to translate the reality around her into art, and the material culture that we see reflected in her paintings, which is a fascinating vehicle that speaks to us about another time. These preferences are evident in the extensive discussion of them in this book.

This is an updated revision of a work that first appeared as the catalogue of an exhibition focused on Clara Peeters that I curated at the Prado in 2016. This was the first exhibition devoted to a woman artist at the Prado, and the first monographic show on Peeters

anywhere.[3] The revision consists primarily in changing the format from an exhibition catalogue, consisting of a main essay and 16 shorter contributions on individual paintings, to one single text. A second text present in the catalogue, by Anne Lenders, is treated and cited when relevant, as are other references in this book. Where necessary, I have added or modified conclusions and cited information that has come to light since the exhibition. Comparing this book to the original reveals that some parts are very similar and others less so; that some sections have been reorganised and others have not. My decision has been not to worry about the relationship of one book to another, but to make this new project stand on its own.

One may wonder about the reasons to publish a new version of the 2016 book. It seemed logical to me to accept the generous offer of Lund Humphries primarily for one reason: to guarantee a wider distribution for a book on Clara Peeters. Catalogues of museum exhibitions have been the vehicle of some of the best art history written in the last half century, and they reach high sales numbers due to the affluence of exhibitions. But they are also notorious for their limited distribution once the exhibitions close. In the case of the Prado, this is especially so for English-language books. Reworking the original texts to adapt them to a monograph format seemed worth the effort. I am thankful to the Prado and its director, Miguel Falomir, for allowing me and the publisher to undertake this project. I also want to express my gratitude to Whitney Dennis for reading some parts of this text and contributing to making it better, and to Julie Gunz for her editing. A final word of thanks to Erika Gaffney and Andrea Pearson for their support throughout this project.

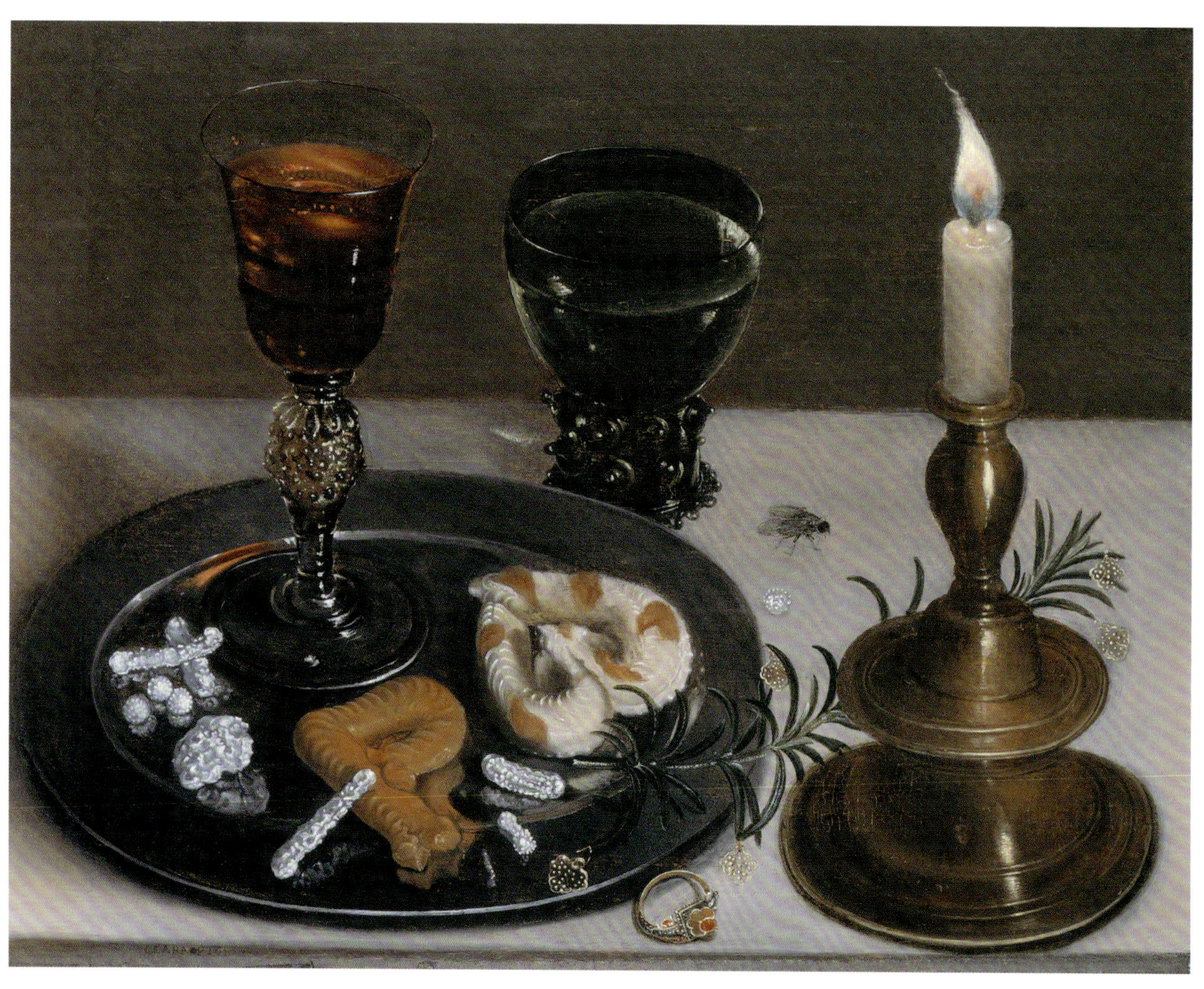

1   Clara Peeters, *Still Life with Confectionery, Wine, Jewels and Burning Candle*, signed and dated, 1607, panel, 24 × 37 cm (9 ½ × 14 ⅝ in), private collection

I

The Life and Context of Clara Peeters

Little information on the life of the painter Clara Peeters is certain. It is without doubt that she signed her first dated painting (fig.1) in 1607 and that she based her practice in Antwerp, which from the beginning of the sixteenth century was one of the main artistic centres in Europe.[1] A document from 1635 describes a picture in an Amsterdam collection as: 'a sugar banquet painted in 1608 by a woman Claer Pieters [*sic*] from Antwerp'.[2] Several of the oak and copper supports that she used for her paintings have marks from that city; she could have used these supports elsewhere, but this did not happen often as far as is known. Also, several paintings by Peeters include a silver knife with a maker's mark from Antwerp in the shape of a hand on its blade (figs 14, 33, 42, 44, 45). These knives could have belonged to someone elsewhere, but they add to the evidence.

It may seem that a problem with identifying Antwerp as the centre of Peeters's professional life is that her name is not listed in the records of the painters' guild there. Regulations did not specifically forbid women from practising, but only a few are included in the Antwerp guild documents in the early modern period. Many persons with the last name Peeters, including several painters, are

recorded in Antwerp in the late sixteenth and early seventeenth centuries. One of them was the painter Henrick Peeters, of whom hardly anything is known. He married a woman named Clara Lamberts (or Lambrechts) in the Antwerp church of St James on 27 June 1605. Even though there are no documents specifying that this Clara painted, there is enough circumstantial evidence to make a strong case for her identification with our artist: Clara Lamberts is, therefore, Clara Peeters.[3] Her marriage to a painter would explain her exemption from registering with the guild.

It was common in early modern Europe for children to follow the profession of their father. In the case of a woman who wished to train as an artist, this was nearly an imperative, because girls were not permitted to move into the household of a master painter for training, as boys did around the age of 12. The only other path that could allow a woman to become a painter was to be a member of a very high social class. Clara's situation adhered more closely to the former than the latter, as she was one in a family of painters. Her father was the painter Nicasius Lamberts, who is documented in the Mechelen Guild of Saint Luke in 1581. Her paternal grandfather was Peter Lamberts, also a painter in the same city (we do not know any paintings by either of them). Clara's mother was Clara Moreels. Her brother Maurus was a painter active in Mechelen, whose son Maurus Moreels II painted as well. The elder Maurus was married to a sister of the renowned Prague court painter Pieter Stevens (c.1567–after 1626), the only one of these artists who has retained some notoriety. The older sister of Clara Lamberts, Agneete, married the landscape painter Laureys vander Veken II in Antwerp in 1604.

Nicasius Lamberts and Clara Moreels had several children. The names of six of them are documented, but none of these are called Clara. However, the records of the christening of their second child, born in Mechelen and christened in August 1587, are no longer legible because the materials have deteriorated. This could be our painter. Shortly after this date the family moved to Antwerp, where Nicasius was admitted to the painters' guild in 1589. He continued to work as a painter, as we know that he took on apprentices in the following years. Two of them, Hans Vervoort and Hans Wichters, of whom we never hear again, began to work with Nicasius in 1605 and 1607. These dates suggest that they may have shared their apprenticeship with Clara Peeters, who signed her first painting in 1607, as mentioned.

As we have seen, Clara Lamberts married the painter Henrick Peeters in June 1605. If born in August 1587, she would have been 17 at the time, a plausible age for marriage. We have some additional but scant information on her adult life. A son of hers was baptised in Antwerp in June 1608, and a daughter (also named Clara) was baptised in December 1611. By then she was signing some of her best works as Clara Peeters. In 1609, Henrick Peeters purchased a house in Antwerp which he mortgaged the next year and later transferred to his creditor in 1621. Clara Peeters is next documented (as Clara Lamberts) in 1630, still in Antwerp, when she acted as godmother to one of her nephews. Finally, in January 1636 she and her husband are both documented as living in Ghent, where she transferred her inheritance to two of her siblings in exchange for a financial settlement. We do not know her death date.

It is significant that Clara Peeters practised her art primarily in Antwerp. From the early sixteenth century, the city had grown into one of Europe's main commercial and financial centres (fig.2).[4] The German artist Albrecht Dürer (1471–1528) – in the diary of his journey to the Netherlands in 1520–21, when he made Antwerp his base for nearly a year – described many objects and products that speak of the material wealth of the city, which was the result of processes of exchange such as foreign trade and of colonialism. Among the gifts he received were not only paintings but many imports, such as French and Portuguese wine, preserved sweets, including a box of sugar candy and barley sugar, marzipan and sugar canes 'just as they were harvested'.[5] These types of luxury products were characteristic of a city that was one of Europe's gateways to the world. They continued to arrive, and to impress, for over a century, to judge from their presence in the still lifes of Peeters.

In the early sixteenth century paintings were among the speciality products of Antwerp's thriving economy. In 1515, over a hundred painters were registered in the painters' guild in the city, not counting itinerant artists and apprentices. By then it had superseded Bruges, Brussels, Ghent and other cities as the main urban centre for painting in the Southern Netherlands (roughly equivalent geographically to the modern nation of Belgium). The success of painting in Antwerp resulted from new approaches to artistic quality and from streamlining production. For example, the landscape painter Joachim Patinir (c.1480–1524) and other leading masters were pioneers in creating paintings through collaborative activities between two or more prestigious artists with different areas of speciality. This was not the same as a painting made by a master

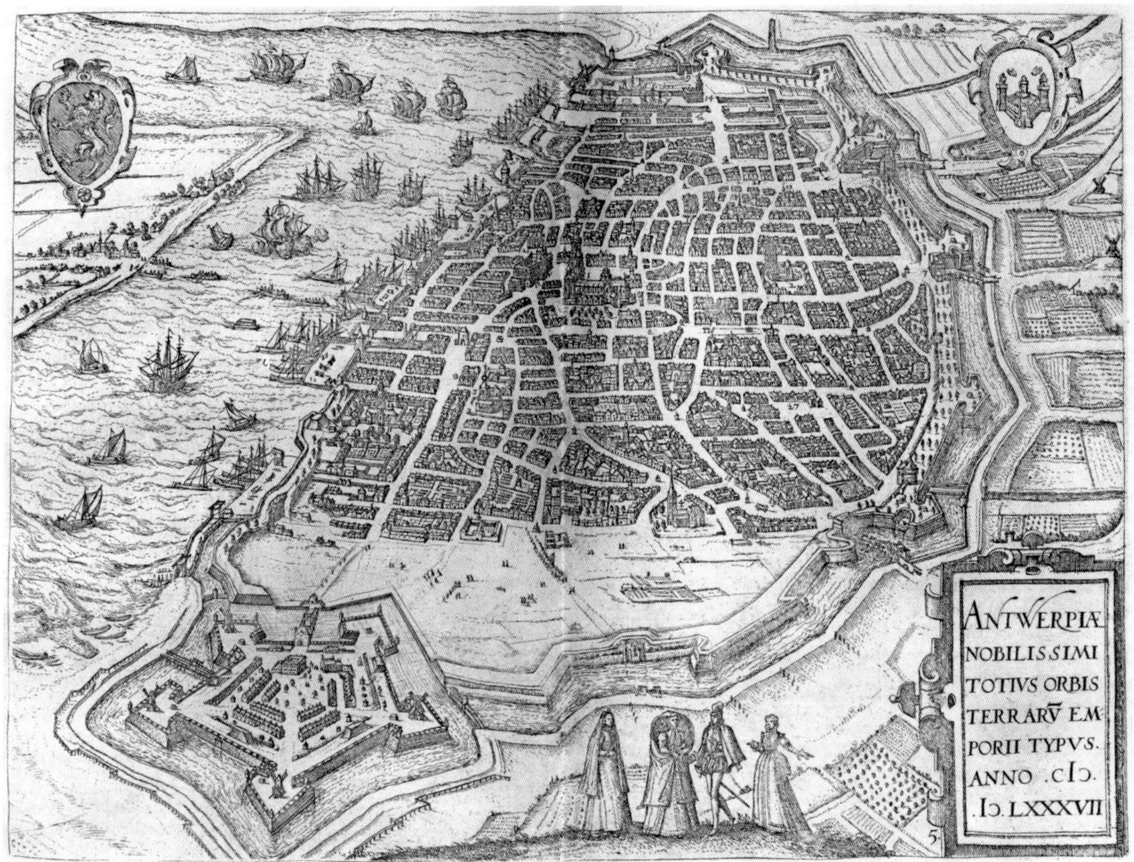

2　View of Antwerp, from Lodovico Guicciardini, *Descrittione di tutti i Paesi Bassi*, Antwerp, W. Silvius, 1567

with the help of his assistants since the pairing of two well-known masters implied a more exclusive product. An early example of this practice is a painting by Patinir and another Antwerp painter, Quentin Massys (1466–1530), called *Landscape with the Temptation of Saint Anthony* (Museo del Prado, Madrid) from *c*.1520, which was acknowledged as made by the two artists in the Spanish royal inventories in the late sixteenth century ('las figuras de mano de Maestre coyntin y el paysaje de Maestre Joachin').[6] Karel van Mander, in his biography of the Antwerp painter Joachim Beuckelaer (*c*.1534–*c*.1574/5), provided another example when he wrote that

Beuckelaer 'painted clothing in portraits' by the famed portrait painter Antonio Moro (1516/21–1576/7).[7] The most famous examples from Antwerp, however, are more than 20 made jointly by Jan Brueghel the Elder (1568–1625) and Peter Paul Rubens (1577–1640) about a century later.

Clara Peeters and other Antwerp painters also benefitted from innovations in the marketing and dispersal of artworks. Although Peeters probably made some of her paintings on commission from patrons, like most artists in the city from the beginning of the sixteenth century, most of her work was probably created for the market. Here again,

Antwerp led the way. In 1540, a permanent art gallery opened in the city, the first in Europe. This meant that paintings were not only sold in annual markets or made on commission, as had been the case in the past, but also were produced, increasingly frequently, on speculation. Furthermore, the flourishing printing industry in Antwerp contributed to the fame of painters by disseminating their designs and, in the case of Peeters, exposing them to images by other artists from which they could draw inspiration. Hieronymus Cock (c.1510–70) and Volcxken Diericx (1525–1600), founders of the publishing house Aux Quatre Vents, were among the most important printers in the city at the time. They published engravings and woodcuts after works by Hieronymus Bosch (c.1450–1516), Dürer and Pieter Bruegel the Elder (c.1525–69) among others. By mid-century, Antwerp was producing more prints than any other city in Europe. Just short of a century later, engravings after designs and paintings by Rubens and Anthony van Dyck (1599–1641) were made in large numbers and widely distributed on a world scale. Contemporary prints that reproduce paintings by Clara Peeters are not known, but, as we will see later, she took some figures, flowers and other elements of her still lifes from engravings.

More important for Peeters's self-promotion, however, was her understanding of, and responses to, the culture of painting in Antwerp. As discussed in detail in the following chapters, she may have known works by the most important painters of the previous century, including Patinir and Massys, whom Dürer mentioned in his discussion of the art of Antwerp in his travel journal. Another possible reference for Peeters is the artist Susanna Horenbout (1503–54), from whom Dürer purchased a miniature painting of a *Salvator Mundi*; she was the daughter of the famous Ghent miniaturist Gerard Horenbout (1465–1541). Jan Gossaert (c.1478–1532) also worked in Antwerp before his death in 1532, and later in the century Marinus van Reymerswale (c.1489–c.1546) and Pieter Bruegel

based their studios there, as did Jan Sanders van Hemessen (active by c.1524–d.c.1564), Pieter Aertsen (1508–75), Joachim Beuckelaer, Frans Floris (1517–70) and Maerten de Vos (1532–1603), among other leading painters of their time on a European scale.

SOCIO-POLITICAL CHALLENGES AND RECOVERY

Prosperity in Antwerp during the sixteenth century was accompanied and eventually thwarted by conflict that affected the lives and careers of artists. In the 1520s a small group of followers of Luther in the city was confronted by authorities with the cruelty typical of law enforcement in early modern Europe. Some were forced to recant; a few others left the city or were burned at the stake. This was but a very small precedent of the conflict to come. In August and September 1566, a violent episode of iconoclasm destroyed many works of art in the city's splendid and recently finished cathedral and in other churches and buildings. In 1581 another episode followed, led by the city's new Calvinist council. Memory of this destructive event would last. Karel van Mander (1548–1606), an influential painter and writer who emigrated from the Southern Netherlands to Haarlem, wrote in 1604 in his *Het Schilder-Boeck* (*The Book of Painters*) that 'In Antwerp in the Onze Lieve Vrouw Church there was a *Palm Sunday*, very artfully painted by [Beuckelaer], which was smashed to pieces during the second iconoclasm.'[8] Just a few years earlier, in 1576, Antwerp had joined a rebellion that had begun in the previous decade. It pitted a part of the nobility of the Netherlands and Protestant religious authorities against the Habsburg monarchs who had inherited the rule of the land from their Burgundian ancestors in the late fifteenth century. Eventually, the city was definitively taken for the Habsburg King of Spain, Philip II, in 1585, together with the rest of the Southern Netherlands. The northern provinces of Holland, Zeeland and several others attained de facto independence.

In the history of art this political shift marks the beginning of a new period, one with revised geopolitical terminology that has sometimes led to confusion about the origins and contributions of Clara Peeters. Earlier, the term 'Netherlands' was used for the entire Netherlandish region, both South (roughly the modern nation of Belgium, including Antwerp) and North (the present-day Kingdom of the Netherlands). However, from the last years of the sixteenth century onwards the term 'Flemish' was used for the South and 'Dutch' for the North. Confusion around these terms led to cases in which Peeters was erroneously described as a Dutch rather than a Flemish artist, despite her origins and residence in Antwerp. The mistake of considering Flemish practices as characteristically Dutch is repeated often enough for it to be labelled as a case of art-historical appropriation. One example is the renowned book *The Embarrassment of Riches*, where historian Simon Schama mentions Peeters as an example of such supposedly Dutch traits as 'creating much from little' and of the essentially descriptive nature of Dutch art.[9] Others have fallen into this same error.[10] This kind of Dutch exceptionalism is at odds with the facts. Implicit in these mistakes is a connection between Peeters's art and the social and economic model of the Dutch Republic. In fact, as we have seen, Peeters based her practice in Antwerp, and her art is firmly rooted in the context of that city and the Southern or Spanish Netherlands.

Clara Peeters initiated her career in Antwerp in a period of urban recovery with a potential to significantly advance the professional lives of artists. Before her birth, Antwerp was transformed by war and exile from one of the busiest commercial centres in Europe, with a population of roughly 100,000, to a city half that size. While many artists remained, others fled to the North. The Southern Netherlands recovered part of its prosperity after 1599, under the government of Isabel Clara Eugenia, daughter of Philip II, and her husband and cousin

Albert VII of Austria, son of Mary, one of Philip's sisters. The Archdukes, as they were known, signed a 12-year truce with the Northern Provinces in 1609, which led to a period of expansion. The goal of the Archdukes was to rebuild their territories along the ideals of the Counter-Reformation and of aristocratic society, with loyalty to the King of Spain. Antwerp's population grew again, and the city recovered part of its commercial pulse. Luxury industries thrived in this period of the city's history, which has been seen as an era of conspicuous consumption. To our eyes today, the art of painting is the best expression of this second Antwerp boom, of which Peeters was a part. This was also the time of Jan Brueghel the Elder, son of Pieter (father and son spelled their last names differently), and of his friend Rubens, of Frans Snyders (1579–1657), Jacob Jordaens (1593–1678), Van Dyck (figs 3–5) and David Teniers (1610–90). They were all cosmopolitan painters, who worked locally but also extensively for export, who were sought by foreign courts and who reached the highest level of recognition on a continental scale.

The ambition and cosmopolitan outlook that defined painters from Antwerp is also apparent in the art and career of Peeters. Yet, two very different social ideals coexisted in the city, inspired by local customs on the one hand and the cultural interests of the new governors on the other. Wealthy citizens embraced the commercial culture that had made the city the most modern economy in Europe in the preceding decades. Simultaneously, they adopted many of the traditional aristocratic customs and cultural interests that the government of the Archdukes promoted. Rubens, who was probably some ten years older than Peeters, embodies this paradox. He was a savvy businessman who created one of the greatest workshop systems in the history of European art; he profited from real-estate investments and by negotiating the reproduction rights of his works. He built a palatial home when he returned to Antwerp after living in Italy for eight years, he dressed and lived in an

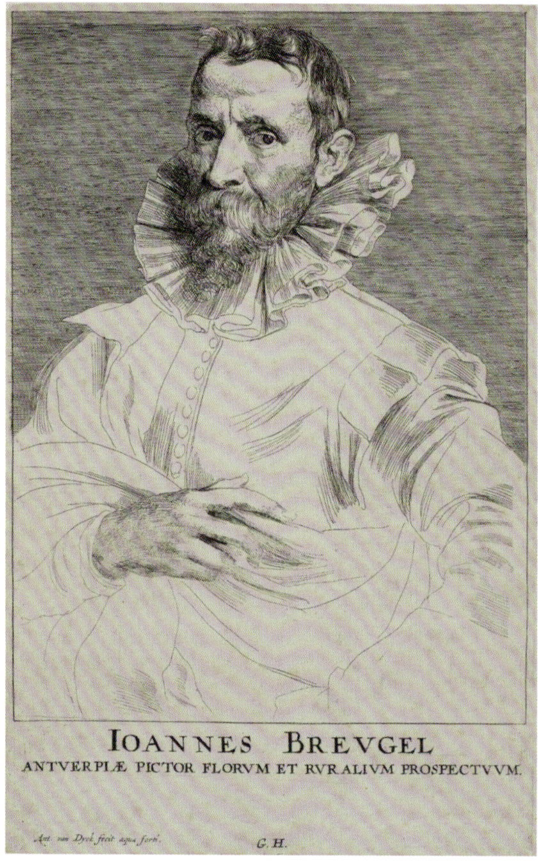

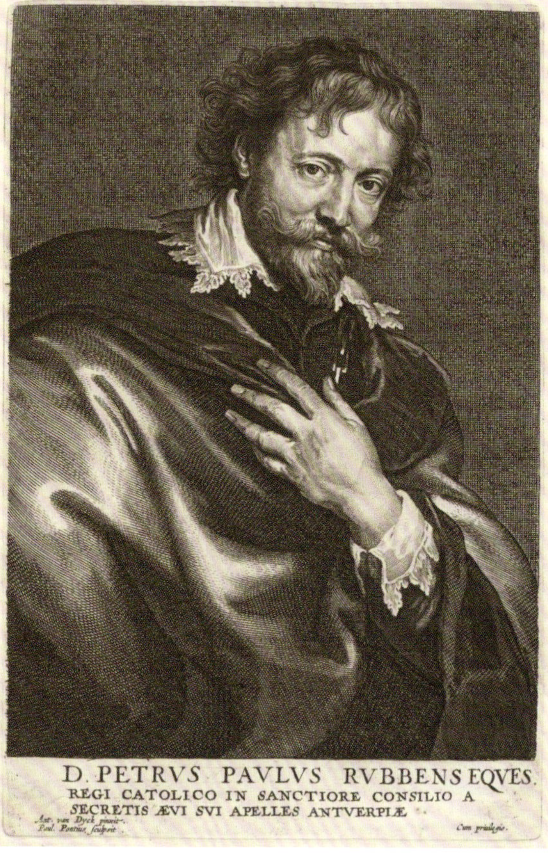

3 Engraved portrait of Jan Brueghel the Elder, from Anthony van Dyck's series *The Iconography*, 1st edn, 1632

4 Engraved portrait of Peter Paul Rubens, from Anthony van Dyck's series *The Iconography*, 1st edn, 1632

aristocratic fashion, and he sought acceptance in the highest echelons of court society.

The paintings of Clara Peeters reflect this dialectical tension. Her still lifes display objects associated with traditional social habits, such as the elitist activities of hunting and collecting items that proclaimed distinction, including raptors used in falconry, porcelain made in China, exotic shells, gilt cups, Venetian-style glassware, imported wine and other products. These are the same types of objects that we find in many paintings by Jan Brueghel, an artist who epitomises the sophisticated taste of the wealthy elite of the time. A comparison between paintings by Peeters and Brueghel (fig.43) is revealing. While many of the same objects appear in the work of both artists, it is striking that they are presented in such different manners. Brueghel's presentation, with its saturated colours and miniaturist handling of the brush, is rooted in the aesthetic of fifteenth-century Netherlandish painting, and more

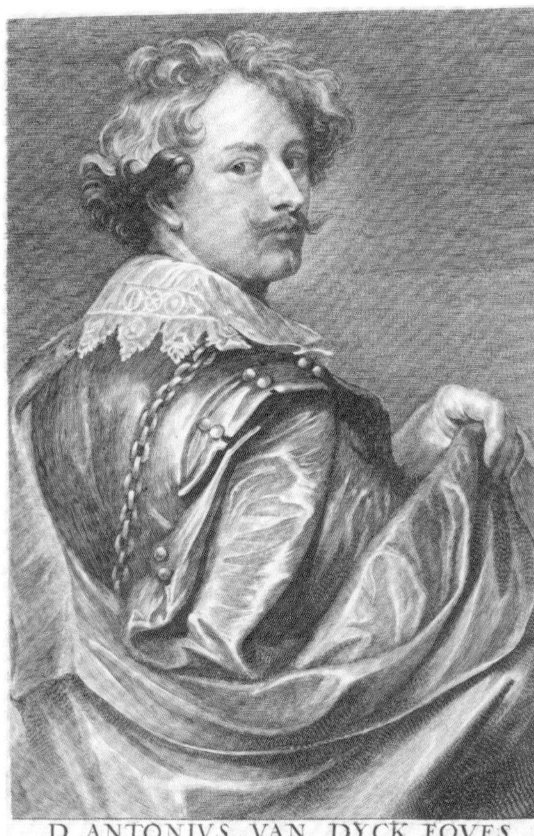

5 Engraved portrait of Anthony van Dyck, from his series
The Iconography, 1st edn, 1632

specifically in the art of miniature painting. Peeters, by contrast, addressed the collecting habits of her elite contemporaries in the appearance of the latest, more realist artistic fashion. This approach implies a forward-looking, entrepreneurial mentality.

POSSIBILITIES AND LIMITATIONS FOR A WOMAN ARTIST

In the sixteenth and early seventeenth centuries, widespread and long-standing prejudices kept women away from many paths of life that men could follow, including artistic professions. The fact that women were considered intellectually and physically inferior to men had been seen by most as a part of the natural order of things for centuries, a status quo that was hard to change. An example pertaining to a female artist is Dürer's proclamation in his journal about Susanna Horenbout: 'It is very wonderful that a woman can do so much.' Thus, even as Dürer appreciated and purchased a painting by Horenbout, he was surprised at its quality given her gender. Women, furthermore, were bound by strict norms of conduct that upheld modesty and chastity as defining virtues. Books on morals such as the widely read and translated *De institutione feminae*, by Luis Vives, first published in 1523, *Philothea* (or *Introduction to Devout Life*) by Saint Francis of Sales in 1609, and *The Book of Matrimony*, of *c.*1562, by the Protestant priest Thomas Becon, described the desired behaviour for women. In these accounts, the home was seen as their appropriate place, with fathers or husbands acting as their guardians and responsible for their actions, keeping them subordinate in all orders of life.

It is important, however, to distinguish between these ideals of behaviour and the realities of life in this period. In Flemish paintings made at approximately the same time as Clara Peeters's works, women are frequently portrayed outdoors. This reflects a social reality grounded partly in class. Caring for the house, for example, included washing and bleaching outside the home. Activities and labour that complemented those of the husband were permitted. In the countryside of the Southern Netherlands this might mean dairying and contributing during the harvest or collecting fruit. In the cities, women also worked out of the house as seamstresses, servants and as street vendors and market-stall attendants. The diary of an English woman named Lady Margaret Hoby, from around 1600, describes supervising the sowing of wheat, measuring the corn, gathering fruit and honey, fishing and making candles all as part of her daily activities.[11]

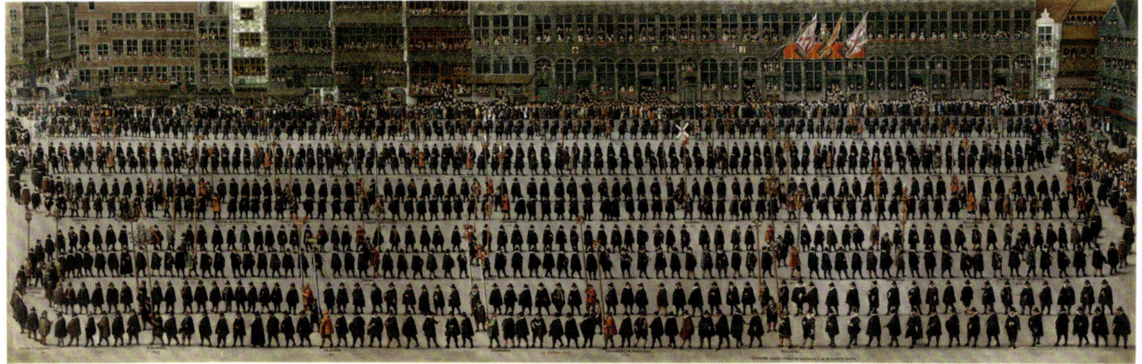

6   Denis van Alsloot and Antoon Sallaert, *The Ommegang in Brussels: Procession of Guilds*, 1616, oil on canvas, 131 × 383 cm (51 ⅝ × 150 ¾ in), Museo Nacional del Prado, Madrid

In the case of artists, we know of women who advanced their artist-husbands' careers or posthumous reputations. An example is Mayken Verhulst Bessemers (1518–96/9), who was the wife of the prominent artist Pieter Coecke van Aelst (1502–50). She was responsible for the posthumous publication of her husband's design *The Customs and Fashions of the Turks* as a woodcut in 1553.[12]

Some paintings from this era show women involved in various public activities. Paintings, of course, transform reality rather than replicate it, but they are based on what painters saw and knew. In several large canvases painted by Denis van Alsloot (*c*.1568–1625/6) and Antoon Sallaert (1594–1650) in 1616 (fig.6), hundreds of men are shown marching in the parades in Brussels in 1615 as members of religious orders and professional congregations, but no women are involved. Amongst the public and the attending authorities, however, we see many women of all classes. Some watch from windows, but many are out on the street. A few women are shown cleaning, caring for children and delivering food: in one painting from the series, *The Procession of Our Lady of the Sablon* (Museo del Prado, Madrid), a woman carries a tart like ones in Peeters's still lifes. Most women in these scenes simply observe the events and mingle with other onlookers, and they had been part of the crowds that witnessed similar events for centuries. Women who watched also had the power to influence men, as discussed in recent scholarship.[13] According to a contemporary written account, when Isabel, daughter of King John I of Portugal, travelled from Lisbon to Bruges in 1430 after her marriage by proxy to Philip the Good, she was met there by many representative figures (among them 'a great crowd of lords, knights, squires and gentlemen [. . .], many prelates, bishops, abbots, priests and clergymen, the mendicant orders, nuns, beguines, [. . .] governors and prominent bourgeois'), and by large crowds of more common welcomers, both men and women ('It is not necessary to mention the people of all classes, men and women, that, both on the streets and at the windows, witnessed the arrival').[14]

Even though custom and law did not favour women's integration into the professional world, there were ways to circumvent these limitations. Class could make a difference, and accidents of life such as noble birth, or family circumstances such as an absent husband due to war, could make women take on some business responsibilities or aspire to move out in some way from the constraints imposed on them by the culture of their time and place. The personality of an individual could also be a factor and some entrepreneurial women could make inroads into different kinds of activities. The opportunities for a woman to become a professional in the sixteenth and seventeenth centuries were rare, but not unheard of. A growing number of women managed to work, including as painters. In the first edition of Giorgio Vasari's famous *Lives of the Most Eminent Painters, Sculptors, and Architects*, which appeared in 1550, only one female artist is mentioned, the sculptor Properzia de' Rossi (*c.*1490–1530). In the edition of 1568, the number had grown to 13. We also find women artists listed in Ludovico Guicciardini's *Descrittione di tutti i Paesi Bassi* (*Description of all the Netherlands*) of 1567, and in *Het gulden cabinet van de edel vry Schilder-Const* (*The Golden Cabinet of the Noble Liberal Art of Painting*) by Cornelis de Bie, of 1662, where Peeters is mentioned briefly. The number of women artists was very small compared to men, however.[15]

Although little documentary evidence about Peeters is available, we can build a meaningful context for her career as a woman painter by examining the situations of other early modern female artists. Four such women from the Southern Netherlands appeared in Guicciardini's *Descrittione di tutti i Paesi Bassi*: Catharina van Hemessen (1527/8–after 1567), Levina Teerlinc (1510–76), Anna de Smytere (*c.*1520–after 1566) and Mayken Verhulst. Teerlinc, a renowned miniaturist, was the daughter of the celebrated Simon Bening (1483–1561), and Verhulst, married to Pieter Coecke van Aelst, was the grandmother of a generation of painters from the Brueghel family, including Jan Brueghel.

Van Hemessen is the best known of these artists. Like Peeters, she practised in Antwerp, where she was born to the painter Jan Sanders van Hemessen. Her father's profession allowed her to bypass certain restrictions that she would have encountered otherwise; Peeters may have had similar opportunities in the studio of her father Nicasius Lamberts. The training of female artists indeed differed from that of most male artists in early modern Europe, who received their practical formation in the workshop of a master. This implied moving out of the family home at about age 12 to 14 to reside in the master's household. Apprentices would work in one shop or transition to others for three to four years. For a woman to do so, however, meant losing a hand at home at a time when house chores and caring for the family were activities assigned to girls. It also placed their virtue at risk.

Similarly, women who pursued a professional life in the visual arts would have received little instruction in the depiction of human anatomy, given the perceived impropriety of women's exposure to nude models. The importance of anatomical study is evident in numerous testimonies. The English miniature painter Edward Norgate (1581–1650), a contemporary of Peeters, wrote, in jest, that artists learned to draw in places where models 'stand or hang naked sometimes in a posture for two or three hours'.[16] In Italy there were places for study known as 'academia del nudo' and 'studio del nudo'.[17] In Antwerp, Rubens and Van Dyck followed similar practices when Peeters was active in the city. For artists across Europe, mastering anatomy was an important qualification for making historical paintings, which occupied the apex of the hierarchy of genres. History paintings were multi-figure compositions that showed historical themes, or stories from ancient mythology or Christianity. They derived their prestige from the link to the great books and authors of the past, including the Bible, Homer, Virgil and Ovid, and from the moral teachings that could be derived from them. Painters aspiring to the highest level in the profession understood the importance of producing history paintings, which depended on the accessibility of life drawing. Testimonies of this artistic ideology are abundant.

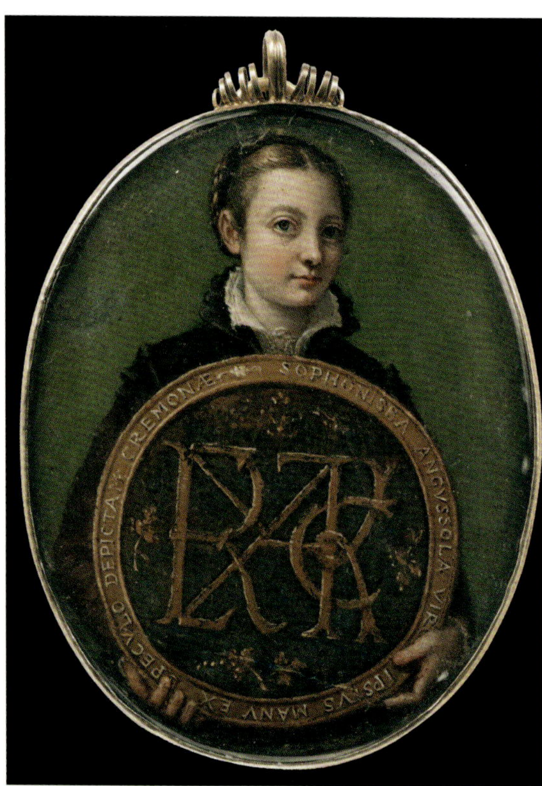

7 Sofonisba Anguissola, *Self-Portrait Holding a Medallion*, *c.*1556, watercolour on parchment, 8.3 × 6.4 cm (3¼ × 2½ in), Museum of Fine Arts Boston, MA

By contrast, Clara Peeters, Catharina van Hemessen and most other early modern women artists were dedicated to genres of painting that their contemporaries considered relatively modest. Trained informally, some perhaps ascribed to Van Mander's assumption in *Het Schilder-Boeck* that a painter, 'If not adept in figures and histories, [...] may paint animals, kitchens, fruit, flowers [...].'[18] Van Mander described still-life painting as having little intellectual worth, which therefore made it trivial in status. Later in the century, when ideas about art became more clearly codified, a book by the influential Samuel van Hoogstraten (1627–78) equally placed still-life painting at the bottom tier of themes for painters; it was work for 'common soldiers in the army of art'.[19] Still life provided an opening for aspiring women artists. A more positive light can be cast on these facts, however. Despite opinions stated in writing at the time, the large number of still-life paintings produced in Europe during the seventeenth century demonstrates that demand for the genre was high and that prejudice against it was waning.[20] Yet, it remains likely that Peeters's singular speciality in this type of painting was partly a consequence of the restrictions of gender.

Portraiture was also a viable speciality for women artists. Most of the few paintings that are known by Van Hemessen are portraits. Especially noteworthy is a small image of her in the act of painting made in 1548, when she was only 20, that she inscribed with her name and the date. Likewise, for the Cremonese painter Sofonisba Anguissola (1532/5–1625), whom Vasari called the best woman artist of her age, portraits dominated. Like Peeters, Anguissola painted self-portraits: 12 are known (fig.7). In a world shaped not only by gender but also by class – Anguissola came from a noble family – an elite heritage allowed her not only the freedom to practise as an artist but provided the time and social connections for her father to vigorously promote her, including through her self-portraits, albeit with the overarching objective of the family's advancement. Notably, Anguissola painted portraits for Elisabeth of Valois, third wife of King Philip II of Spain from 1559, and after her death attended to Elisabeth's two daughters, one of whom was the aforementioned Infanta Isabel Clara Eugenia, who later ruled the Southern Netherlands and was an important patron of Rubens. As a courtier in Madrid, her artistic talent was a plus. She sometimes received clothes and jewels for paintings, and she gave lessons to Isabel too, but she was not paid a salary as a painter or teacher.

Even as artists like Peeters, Van Hemessen and Anguissola produced paintings with subjects that responded to the gendered conditions of their training, other women resisted these restraints. Artemisia Gentileschi (1593–after 1654), one of the most successful female artists of early modern Europe, was one such painter. Close in age to Peeters, she was born in Rome as the daughter of the famous painter Orazio Gentileschi (1563–1639). Unlike Peeters, however, she made still life a limited part of her career.[21] Evidence from the trial for her rape by the painter Agostino Tassi (1580–1644) reveals that she had few connections outside her family circle in her youth. This suggests that her early artistic formation was somewhat isolated from the world of young male artists who were meeting at the academies in Rome.[22] Yet, she specialised in history painting, which we have seen is the type that occupied the apex in the hierarchy of genres at the time and was practised largely by men like her father, who could instruct her.

Another example is Michaelina Wautier, who found success with elite patronage and with her dedication to large multi-figure paintings of grand themes from history, albeit she also painted portraits, genre paintings and flower garlands. She was born near Antwerp, in Mons in the province of Hainaut, and worked in Brussels, sharing a studio and quarters with her brother Charles. Particularly noteworthy among her works are a majestic self-portrait painted in the 1640s (fig.8) and a large *Bacchanal* that also includes a self-portrait (Kunsthistorisches Museum, Vienna).[23]

Most early modern women artists knew they occupied a vulnerable place in contemporary society. The correspondence of Gentileschi demonstrates aspects of this situation. She complained in a letter about a patron, Antonio Ruffo, who had given a drawing of hers to another artist: 'If I were a man, I cannot imagine it would have turned out this way.' On another occasion she wrote to Ruffo, 'a woman's name raises doubts until her work is seen'. And again: '[. . .] I will show your Most Illustrious Lordship what a woman can do'.[24] This kind of

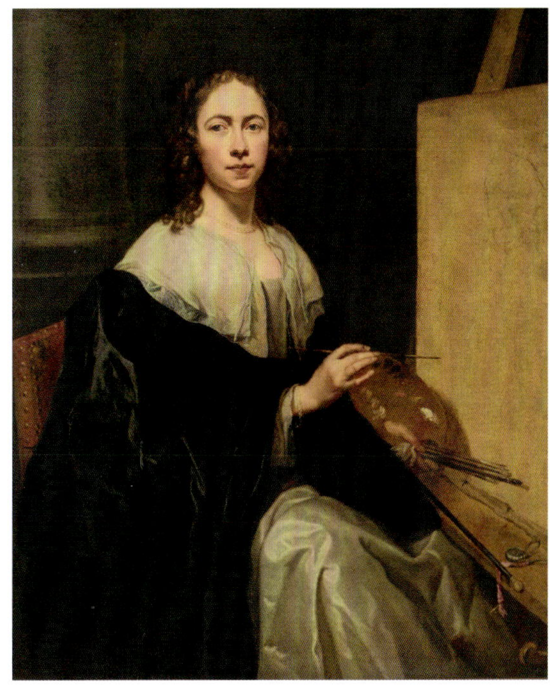

8   Michaelina Wautier, *Self-Portrait*, 1649, oil on canvas, 120 × 102 cm (47¼ × 40⅛ in), private collection

rebellious self-confidence is not an exception. The Mechelen sculptor Maria Faydherbe (1587–after 1633) complained in 1632 to the city authorities and the sculptors' guild about the discrimination that led to her receiving less important commissions than her less talented male colleagues.[25]

Clara Peeters shared with other artists a desire for social recognition, as demonstrated by the constant assertion of her authorial identity in the form of signatures and the innovative self-portraits included in her paintings. Because of her gender, Peeters had an added cause for affirmation in a professional world that hardly made room for women.[26] Portraits in general had multiplied in the second half of the sixteenth century, a situation to which Paolo Lomazzo bore witness in his *Trattato dell'arte della pittura* of 1584. To this point, he stated that anyone with a little talent could paint these images. Examining one's physiognomy in a mirror, as artists did when they produced self-portraits, was a way for painters to study features and expressions.

ARTISTIC SELF-CONSCIOUSNESS AND THE REFLECTED SELF-PORTRAITS OF CLARA PEETERS

The self-portraits of Peeters reveal her capacity for invention and innovation, for they are not direct representations as are most other portraits of the kind by early modern artists, including Van Hemessen and Wautier (fig.8). Rather, they appear as reflections in metal objects, small in scale and difficult to detect. Peeters included these representations in at least eight of her paintings, starting with her first known work of 1607, *Still Life with Confectionery, Wine, Jewels and Burning Candle* (fig.1).[27] In this picture, a few touches of the brush hint at a face and a garment reflected in the lower part of the candleholder to the right. In later paintings her presence becomes more prominent, never as much as in *Still Life with Flowers, Gilt Goblet, Eatables and a Pewter Flagon* (fig.9), where she included seven reflected self-portraits, and *Still Life with Flowers, Gilt Goblets, Coins and Shells* (fig.10), where there are six or seven. Some are so small that it is hard to tell if they are portraits or reflections of something else. In other paintings we rarely see more than one self-image, located on the metal lids of jugs.

The very small size of these self-portraits – the faces measure only 3 mm or so in their vertical dimension – demands close looking if they are to be discerned. Yet, they are not without details that reveal something of the painter's time and place. In one painting already discussed (fig.9), Peeters shows herself wearing a high headpiece, a large, thin collar and a dress with high shoulders. These garments are similar to those displayed in images of urban women from the Southern and Northern Netherlands at this time, which show collars and headpieces of different sizes, as in the painting by Van Alsloot and Sallaert mentioned earlier (fig.6). Beyond that, what we see of her outfit does not allow us to place her socially. In another case (fig.10, 11), she shows herself painting, with a palette in one hand and brushes in the other – she is right-handed, as is also indicated by the light that enters her paintings consistently from the left, thus avoiding a bothersome shadow. She wears a thin collar, and her head is uncovered. She looks young, but exactly how young it is impossible to say.

The revelatory nature of these self-portraits by Peeters suggests a certain social tension. They are nearly concealed by their size and their reflected nature, making them seem made by someone who is simultaneously hiding and wanting to be seen. We can consider this as a metaphor for how she reacted to the limitations imposed on her by the world she lived in. She was discreet, which she may have considered a necessity in a professional field overwhelmingly dominated by men. But she was also a confident pioneer who wished to be seen and acknowledged. Furthermore, her self-portraits demonstrate her skill at illusionistic painting: what is reflected is the image of someone plausibly standing in the place that we now occupy as viewers.

Peeters also likely knew that important precedents existed for the type of self-portraits she painted, thereby defining herself through their production as a participant in a consequential historical discourse on representations of the kind. Vasari wrote in the 1568 edition of his *Lives of the Artists* about Parmigianino's *Self-Portrait in a Convex Mirror* of 1524 (Kunsthistorisches Museum, Vienna), which he praised for the 'subtleties of illusion' and the 'strange effects' of the distorted reflections. Painting reflections was singled out and valued by writers at the time. Vasari, in his reference to Parmigianino's picture, applauded 'the luster of the glass, the reflection of every detail, and the lights and shadows, all so true and natural [. . .]'.[28] Van Mander also described what he called '*reflexy-const*', or

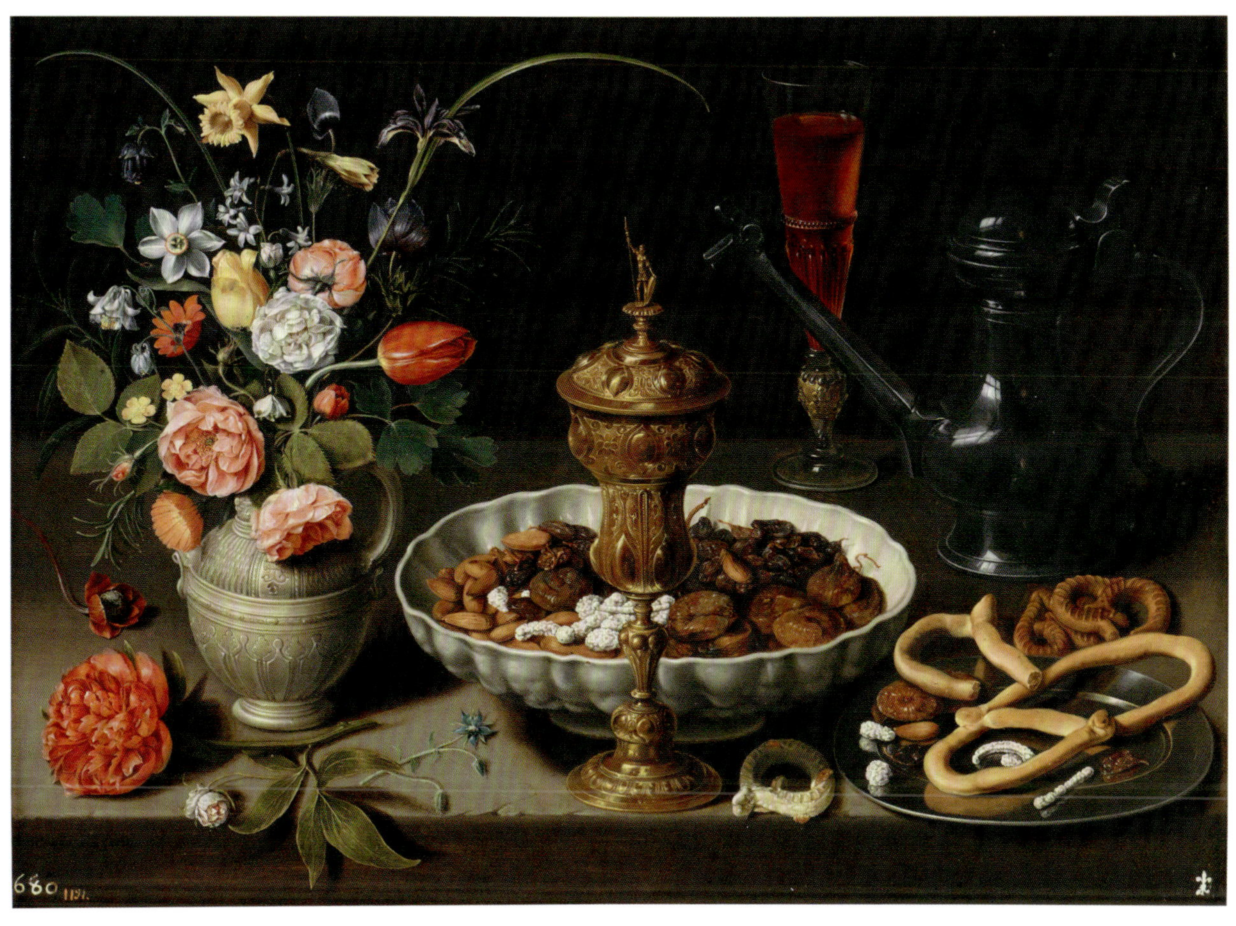

9   Clara Peeters, *Still Life with Flowers, Gilt Goblet, Eatables and a Pewter Flagon*, signed and dated, 1611, oil on panel, 52 × 73 cm (20 ½ × 28 ¾ in), Museo Nacional del Prado, Madrid

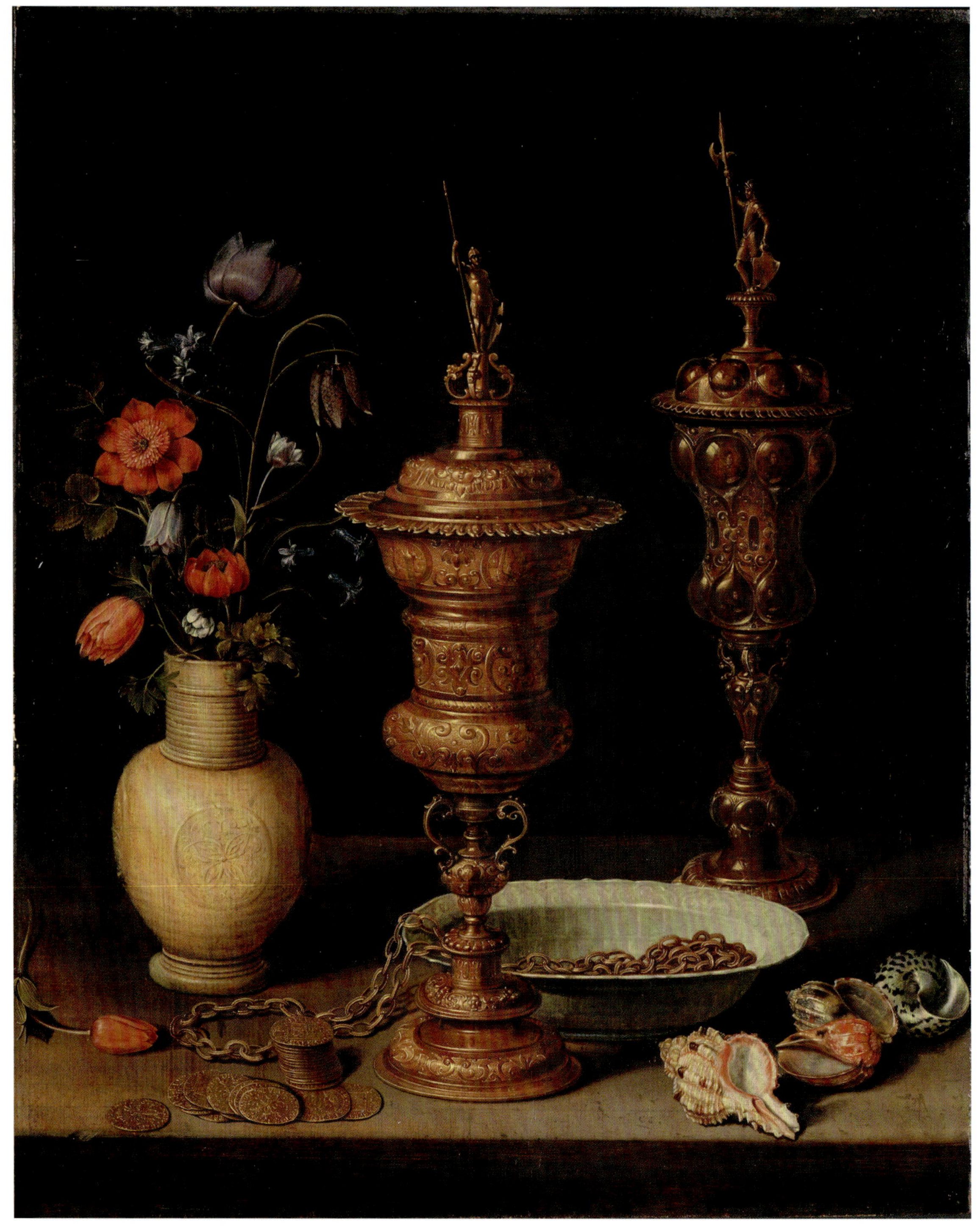

10 Clara Peeters, *Still Life with Flowers, Gilt Goblets, Coins and Shells,* signed and dated, 1612, oil on panel, 59 × 49 cm (23 ¼ × 19 ¼ in), Staatliche Kunsthalle Karlsruhe

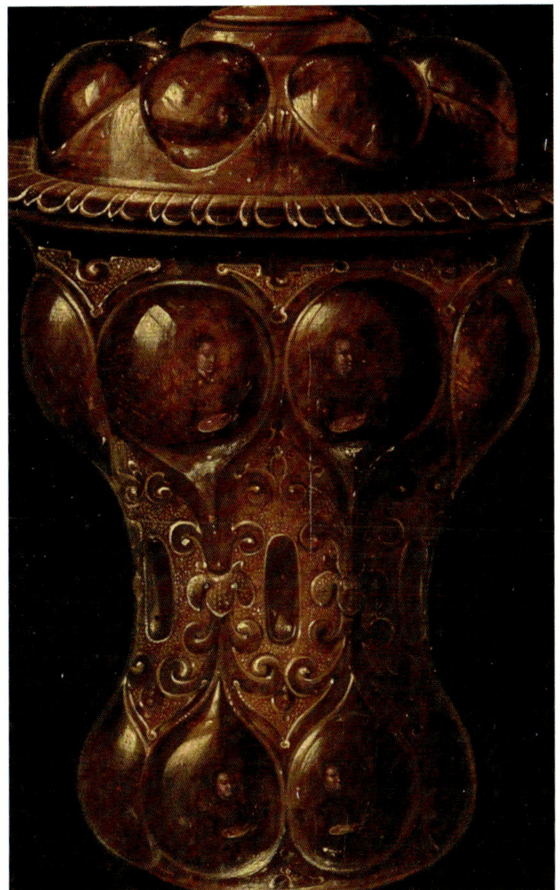

11 Detail of fig.10 showing self-portraits

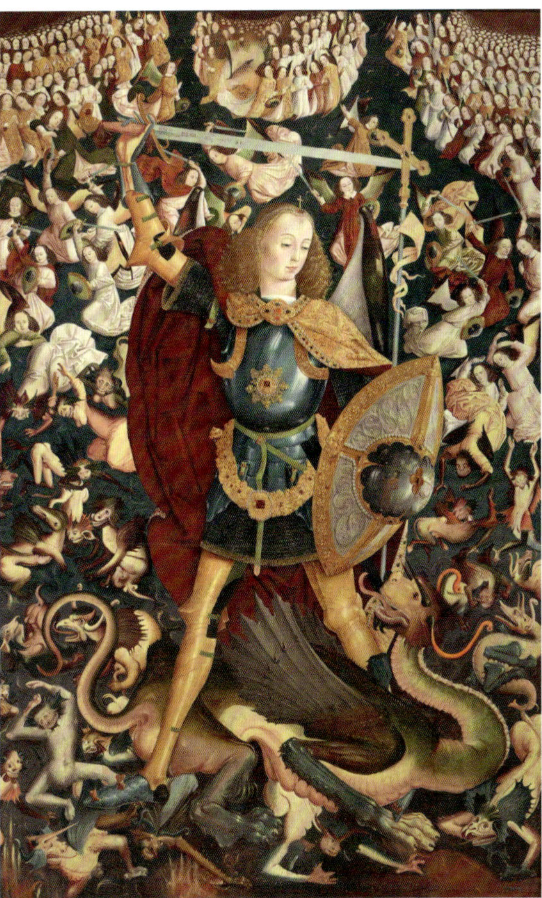

12 Master of Zafra, *Saint Michael*, c.1495–1500, mixed
method on panel (transferred to canvas), 242 × 153 cm
(95 ¼ × 60 ¼ in), Museo Nacional del Prado, Madrid

the art of reflection, as an important skill for painters.[29]
The texts by Vasari and Van Mander were known by
professional painters, as was likely the case with the
reference to a self-portrait of a woman painter, Iaia,
by Pliny the Elder in his *Natural History*, and to an
ancient sculpture by Phideas mentioned by Plutarch
in *Life of Pericles*. The artist, it was said, had sculpted
a figure of Minerva that included a representation of
himself carved on the shield of the goddess.[30] Socrates,
via Plato, used the reflective self-portrait as a metaphor
for self-knowledge. In a statement to the Athenian

statesman and general Alcibiades, Socrates compared
the eye to a mirror: 'And have you observed that the
face of the person who looks into another's eye is
shown in the optic confronting him, as in a mirror, and
we call this the pupil, for in short it is an image of the
person looking?'[31] The Greek philosophers are telling
us that we know ourselves because we are in the sight
of others.

Perhaps inspired by these ancient models, and
incorporating self-images in ways more like Peeters, is
the case of Jan van Eyck (*c*.1390–1441), who included

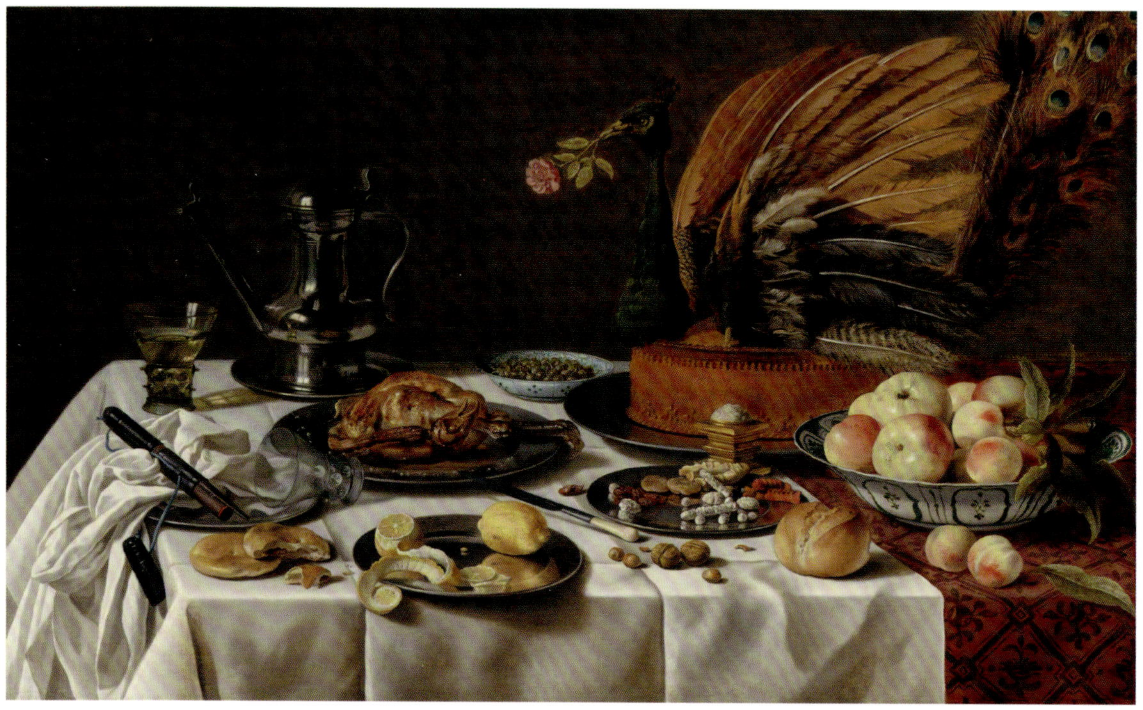

13 Pieter Claesz., *Still Life with Peacock Pie*, 1627, oil on panel, 77 × 129 cm (30 ⅜ × 50 ¾ in), National Gallery of Art, Washington, DC

a very small reflection of two figures in his *Arnolfini Portrait* of 1434 (National Gallery, London). They are represented frontally, reflected in the convex glass mirror on the background wall. They are so small that they cannot be seen in discernible detail, but they stand where the painter would stand to reproduce what we witness in the scene. To make the point of his presence stronger, an inscription on the frame of the mirror reads '*Johannes de eyck fuit hic*' ('Jan van Eyck has been here'). There is also a very small, reflected self-portrait in another picture by Van Eyck, *Virgin and Child with Canon van der Paele* (Groeningemuseum, Bruges), which was finished in 1436. It is in the curved surface of the shield of Saint George and is very hard to see.

Although it is not clear to what extent these two tiny self-portraits were recognised as such, Van Eyck was a celebrated artist and the two paintings mentioned were highly regarded. Both had been accessible for at least some viewers, the former in Mechelen (in the collection of Margaret of Austria, regent of the Netherlands) and the latter in Bruges (installed in the church of Saint Donatian). Dürer mentions seeing them in the diary of his travels in the Netherlands in 1521.[32] By the time of Clara Peeters, the *Arnolfini Portrait*, where the self-portrait of the artist is easier to see, had been sent to Spain as a gift. Other paintings made under the influence of Van Eyck in the fifteenth and sixteenth centuries include similar mirrors and reflected portraits.[33] Among them is a *Saint Michael* (Museo del Prado, Madrid) by an anonymous artist known as the Master of Zafra. Painted at the end of the fifteenth century and showing knowledge of Flemish art, it includes an image of the artist reflected on the saint's shield, with a brush and palette in hand (fig.12).

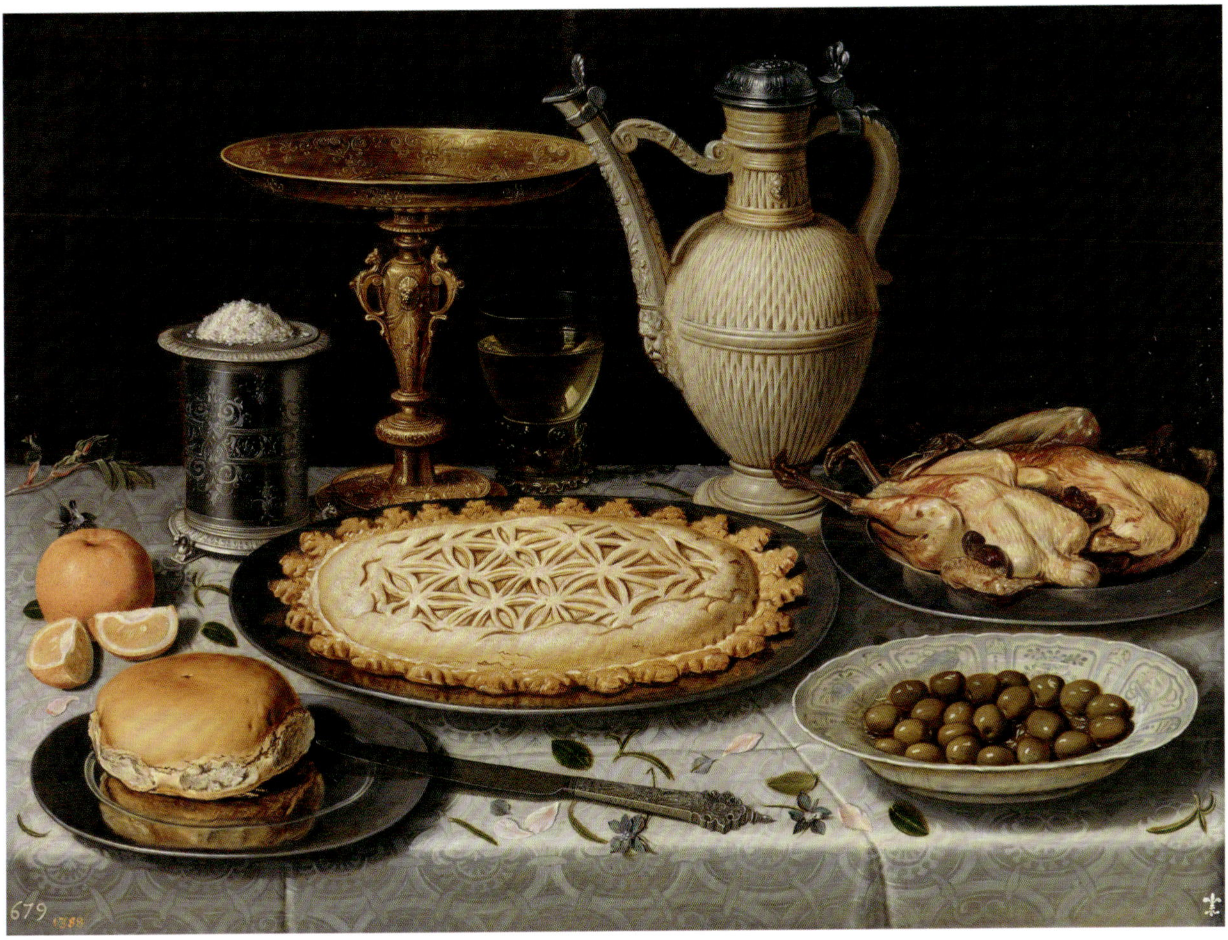

14 Clara Peeters, *Table with Cloth, Foodstuffs and Other Objects*, inscribed with the artist's name on the knife, *c.*1611, oil on panel, 55 × 73 cm (21 ⅝ × 28 ¾ in), Museo Nacional del Prado, Madrid

15 detail of fig.14 showing inscription on the handle of the knife

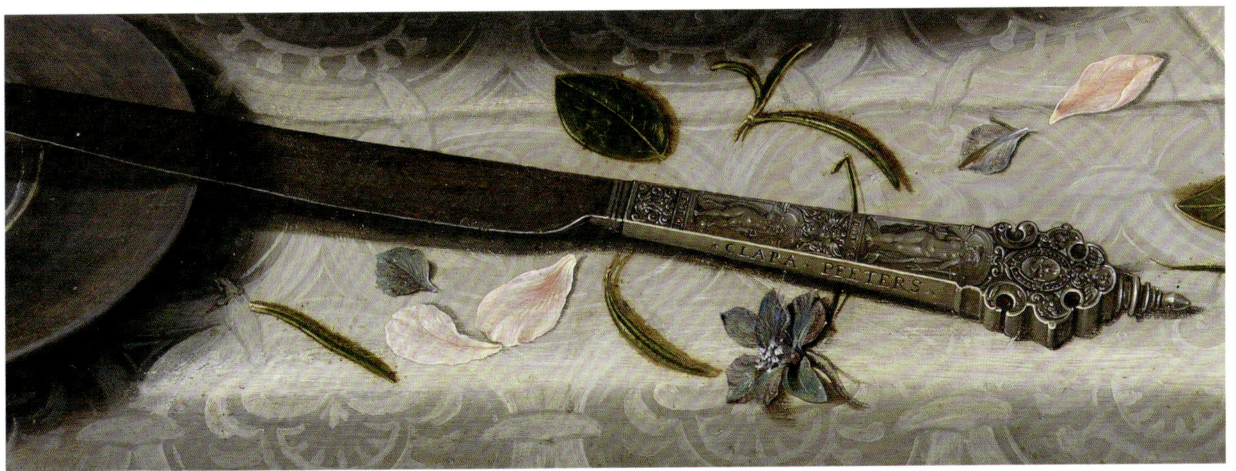

Examples of painted reflections of portraits are more common than of reflected self-portraits. In a painting by the Master of Moulins (plausibly identified as Jean Hey) of about 1495 (Kelvingrove Art Gallery and Museum, Glasgow), showing a donor and a military saint, a reflection of the former is carefully rendered on the armour of the latter; depictions of metal surfaces lend themselves well to these displays of skill. Even if we consider paintings made after Peeters's time, reflected self-portraits remain rare. Pieter Claesz. (1597–1661), a Dutch specialist in still-life painting, portrayed himself reflected on a glass ball in *Still Life with Crystal Ball*, a painting dated *c*.1628 (Germanisches Nationalmuseum, Nuremberg). Around the middle of the century, Abraham van Beijeren (1620–90) portrayed himself reflected on a silver jug in *Banquet Still Life* (Mauritshuis, The Hague). In 1668, Maria van Oosterwijck painted herself reflected in a glass flask in one of her sumptuous, allegorical still-life paintings (Kunsthistorisches Museum, Vienna). With some effort, we can see her reflection as she sits behind an easel, holding a palette. However, most painters avoided including their own reflections in their works. In his painting *Still Life with Peacock Pie* (fig.13), Claesz. included a flagon to the left with reflections of foodstuffs and other objects. He could have easily chosen to add his own image there but did not. Why so, when reflective surfaces abound? If one stands in front of a shiny metal surface, a reflection does indeed appear – it will be more or less evident depending on the surface and the level of its polish. The likely reason for this absence is a kind of imposed modesty. For the most part, painters did not think it proper to show themselves in their work, unless they had been specifically asked by a patron to do so.

Be this as it may, the fact that so few artists used this form of self-portraiture, and that Peeters did so often (even several times in a single painting), demonstrates, by contrast, her understanding of art history, her innovative responses to historical works,

and her independent spirit. Many of Peeters's still lifes include additional self-references that attest her careful construction of a personal and professional identity. Some of these references are in the form of a signature or an inscription with her name; the signatures are placed either on the ledge on which objects rest or on the surface of plates, and the inscriptions on the edge of the handle of a knife (fig.14, 15). These knives were carried by guests when they were invited to dine at someone else's table, and they were also used as wedding gifts. The knife in the paintings by Peeters (see also figs 33, 42, 44, 45) could be a souvenir from her own wedding, which is otherwise not documented. Given the artist's inclination to leave her personal marks on paintings, other elements in them were likely self-referential. The biscuit in the form of a letter 'P' in some of her paintings (figs 1, 31) is also likely a reference to herself, given the first letter of her last name. Like the reflected self-portraits, these details subtly advance the notion of artistic ingenuity while also preserving modesty.

AN INTRIGUING PAINTING

Another work by Peeters, one that combines still life with a probable portrait, engages many of the issues addressed in this chapter. It shows a young woman, elegantly dressed, sitting at a table (fig.16).[34] She holds in her left hand a small box with a glass lid that appears to contain a mussel. A bubble floats next to her; on it is the reflection of a window. On a table next to her are objects like those in many of Peeters's still lifes, such as flowers, an expensive standing cup, a gilt goblet, coins, jewellery and, unusually, two dice. The apparent symbolism of these objects is unusual in Peeters's paintings. Bubbles of glass or soap were used in paintings as symbols of the temporary nature of all things, and dice could refer to the arbitrary nature of fortune, or perhaps to gambling and excess. The jewels and coins support the latter idea. Together, the objects

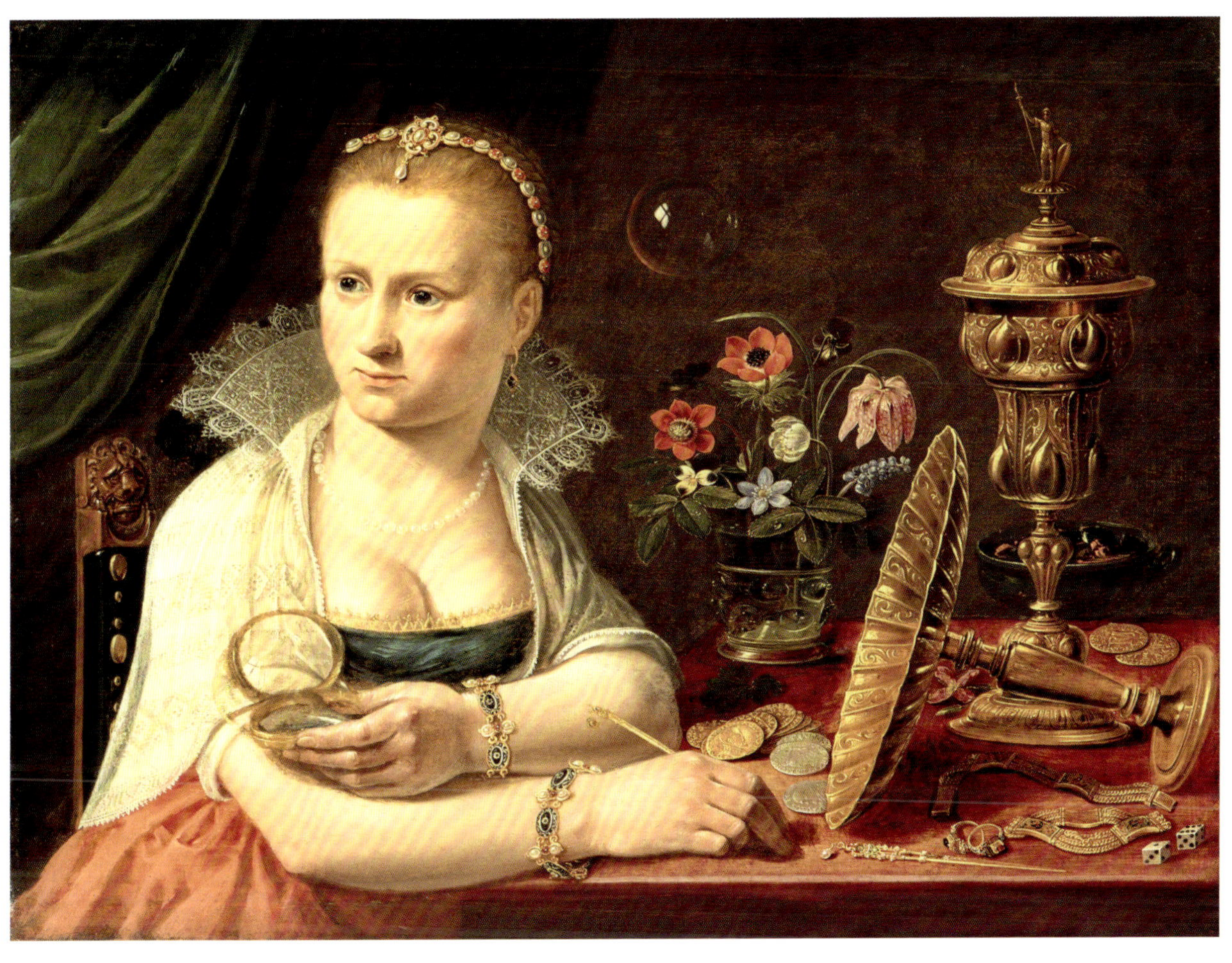

16 Clara Peeters, *Woman Seated at a Table with Precious Objects*, *c.*1607–11, oil on panel, 37 × 50 cm (14 ⅝ × 19 ⅝ in), private collection

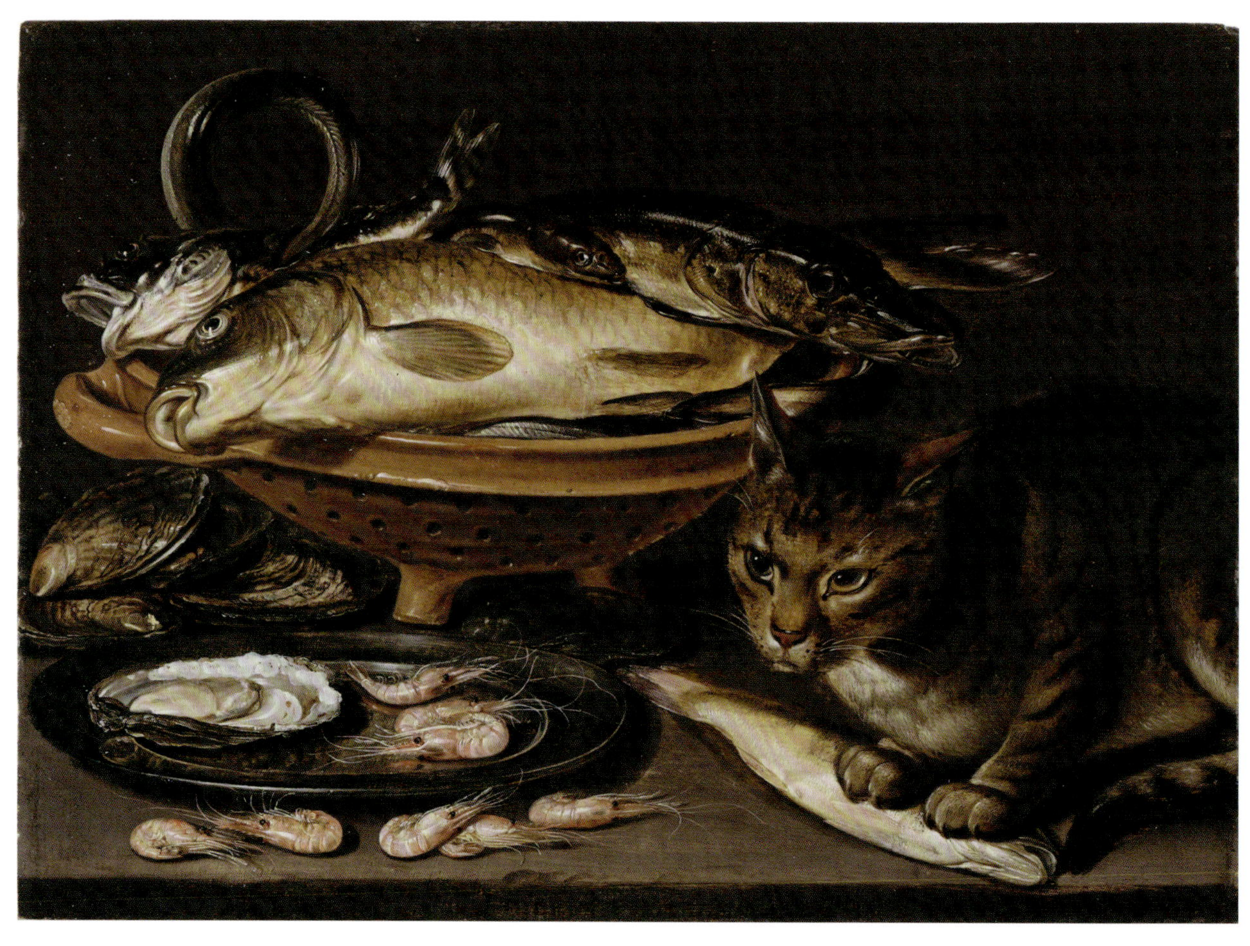

17 Clara Peeters, *Still Life with Fish and Cat*, c.1610–20, oil on panel, 34.3 × 47 cm (13 ½ × 18 ½ in), National Museum of Women in the Arts, Washington, DC

appear to refer to human vanity, a common theme in paintings of the period and especially in still-life paintings. The low-cut dress the woman wears shows off her cleavage. Could this also be a reference to excess, perhaps her own, or of those who look at her? This kind of meaning makes sense in the context of the *vanitas* theme in seventeenth-century painting and culture.

The woman represented in this painting is generally identified as a self-portrait, but this premise is uncertain. She does not look like the figure in the diminutive, reflected self-portraits that exist in other paintings, which admittedly are so small that they do not provide good comparative material. Neither does she make eye contact with the viewer, a feature of many self-portraits made with the use of a mirror. Furthermore, the tool she holds in her right hand does not appear to be a brush, as one might expect given her profession, for it is golden in colour and has hangings on its visible end; it is also like another object on the table next to her hand. Furthermore, there are problems of execution in this work, both in the still-life elements, which lack the detail and convincing illusion of foreshortening that we see in Peeters's best works, and in the portrait, for the facial features and breasts of the woman are excessively schematic. These visual effects, uncharacteristic of Peeters, can be explained either because this is a painting by an assistant or follower of the artist, or if it is an early work, perhaps made somewhere in between the signed paintings of 1607 and 1611. This seems likely, but it is impossible to ascertain until the painting is better known and studied.

That a painting as intriguing as this remains out of sight in a private collection is not uncommon for works presumably by women artists who have remained somewhat or fully obscured for centuries. The difficulty for the artist of rendering the human form is revealing of restrictions in training confronted by women painters, as already mentioned. In other paintings by Clara Peeters that include human figures

or other living creatures we find similar problems that we do not see in the objects that populate her still lifes. This is an indication that her training had some limitations, which are also suggested by *Still Life with Fish and Cat* (fig.17), where Peeters complemented the still-life elements that she shows us on a ledge or table with the presence of a cat. The cat seems alive, but its anatomy is painted somewhat awkwardly. Its paws and the shape of its head are formulaic, as are the eyes and the whiskers. The Spanish writer and painter Francisco Pacheco (1564–1644) explained in his book *Arte de la pintura* (finished by 1638 and published posthumously in 1649) that it was easier to imitate dead fish and birds than live ones because of the need to make the movements of the latter seem natural.[35] The skills necessary to paint inanimate objects are not sufficient to paint living creatures, especially the human form. Peeters's ability to paint vessels, fowl, dead fish, fruit, cheese and other such items demonstrates that she had the potential to develop as a painter of living creatures. It is likely that the societal limitations imposed upon the training of women artists limited her ambition and precluded her from doing so fully.

2

Still-Life Painting

When Antwerp became the leading art centre in northern Europe in the early sixteenth century, painters in the city were spurred to innovate by a competitive environment. Also important for the new developments was the growing hold of materialism and naturalism on European culture, which gradually undermined the need to see and think of things exclusively in terms of the supernatural and the ideal. In ancient Greece and Rome and again in the Renaissance, the primary goal of art had been to confront viewers with images that would make them experience a higher, more beautiful realm. In contrast, and more so than in other types of painting, the focus of Clara Peeters's preferred genre of still life in its early stages was the representation of tangible objects without idealisation. The objects portrayed in these images were selected in part to satisfy an expanding art world hungry for novelties, which found support in ancient precedents mentioned by writers of classical antiquity, such as Pliny the Elder and Philostratus the Elder, as described by Karel van Mander in his *Het Schilder-Boeck* of 1604.[1] Peeters's art reveals that she was deeply engaged with these developments. The present chapter investigates her understanding of and responses to still-life precedents likely known to her, before analysing her paintings and their innovations in the chapters that follow.

The precise origin of the still-life genre is hard to pin down, for Antwerp was but one of several cities in Europe where it was being practised by the end of the sixteenth century.[2] There, pictorial genres and their relative value were subject to experimentation and revision in the period prior to Peeters's lifetime. The Antwerp painter Joachim Patinir, for example, created the artistic speciality of landscape painting in the two decades before his death in 1524. Importantly, he reinvented earlier approaches by reversing their iconographical hierarchies: where in earlier works landscapes had simply served as backgrounds for religious scenes, he made paintings where the natural setting was more prominent than the figures within it, thereby elevating landscape as an important if not necessarily the primary subject. Similarly, certain objects selected for representation in still lifes can be traced to a new interest in what had earlier been comparatively underemphasised. Paintings showing kitchens and markets laden with foodstuffs by Pieter Aertsen and his nephews and pupils, the brothers Joachim Beuckelaer and his brother Huybrecht (1535/40–after 1605), made in Antwerp from the 1550s and until still life emerged as a dedicated genre, contained many such objects. They were a part of larger allegorical and religious scenes where they contributed to forming meaning around the

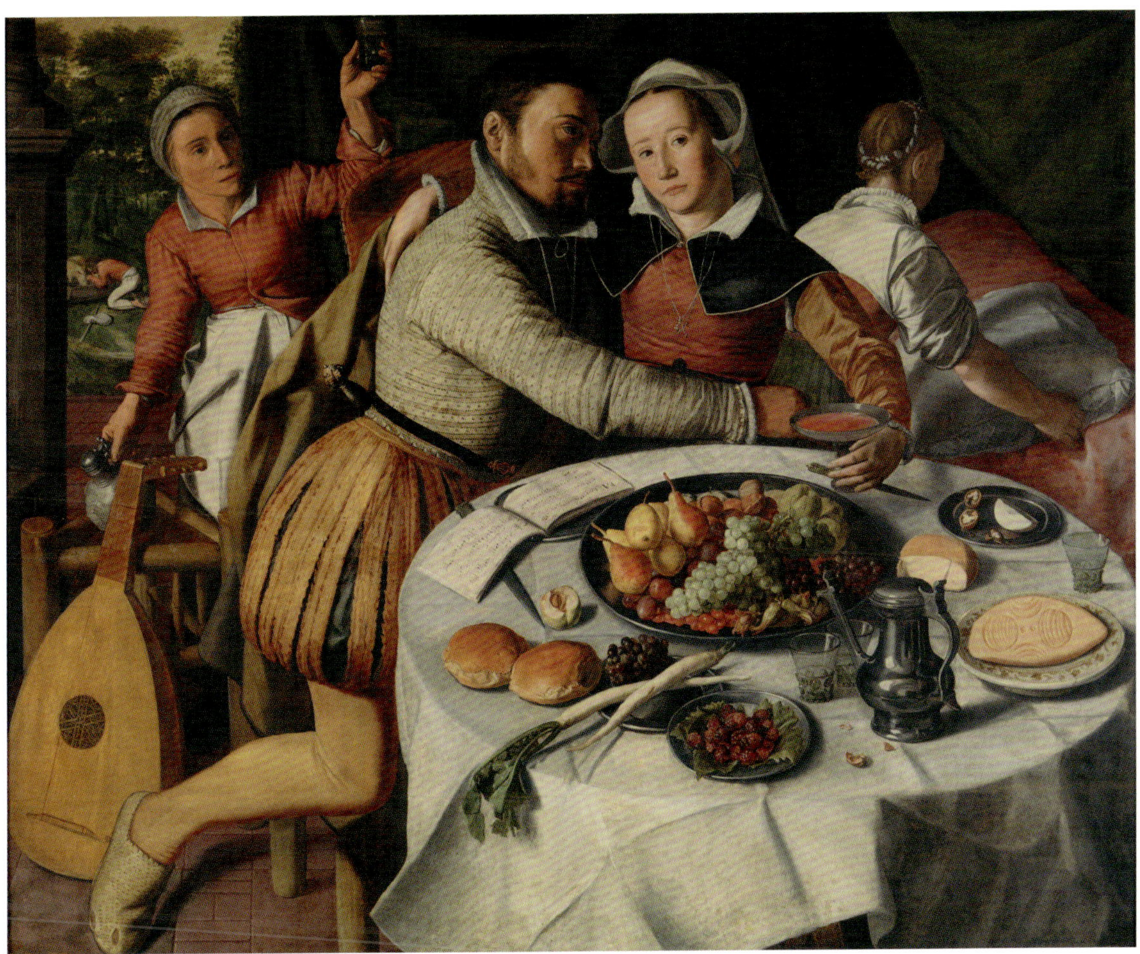

18 Huybrecht Beuckelaer, *The Prodigal Son*, c.1565, oil on panel, 127 × 155 cm (50 × 61 in), Royal Museums of Fine Arts of Belgium, Brussels

main subject. In *The Prodigal Son* (fig.18) painted by Huybrecht Beuckelaer, for example, the abundant objects displayed on the table in the foreground, including fruit, meat, tankards and other vessels, stand for excess and thereby emphasise the squandering actions of the errant son.

Void of such references, still-life painting rose to greater prominence over time, with examples entering major European collections at an increasing rate. Its desirability in the first decade of the seventeenth century is attested in a new type of painting created in Antwerp by Frans Francken the Younger (1581–1642) and Jan Brueghel and made in the following decades by many other artists: the collector's cabinet or *constkamer*. These paintings show contemporary collections of artwork and other luxury objects, often with elegant observers looking on (fig.19). Among the pictures that can often be seen within these images, hanging from the walls of elegant rooms, are still lifes like those painted by Peeters. The appearance of such works in paintings of this type reveals that they were sought by leading collectors and displayed alongside

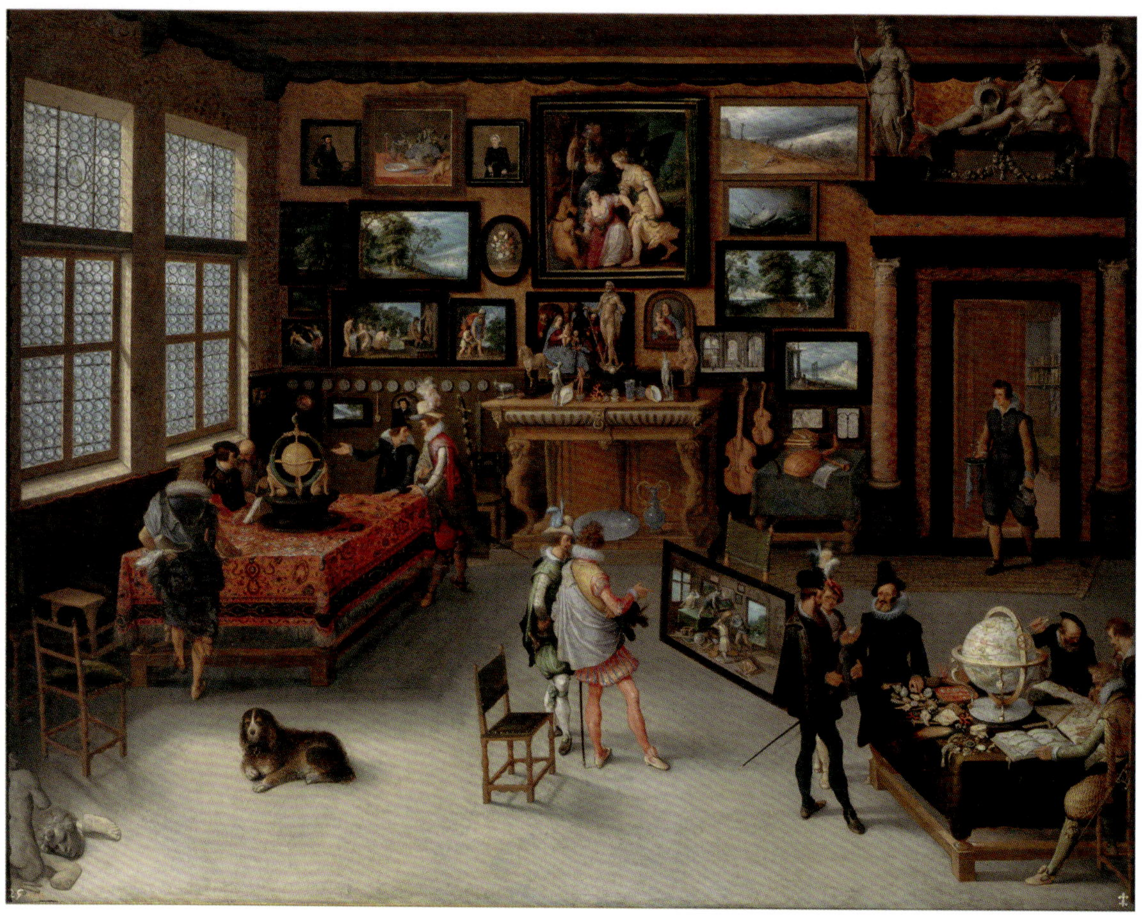

19 Adriaen van Stalbent, *The Sciences and the Arts*, c.1650, oil on panel, 90 × 117 cm (35 ⅜ × 46 ⅛ in), Museo Nacional del Prado, Madrid

other works by artists they appreciated. Even with these developments, however, in Antwerp the term *stilleven* (still life), which specified that a new pictorial genre had taken root, was not used until the mid-seventeenth century. Before then, such works were described in documents simply as paintings of the objects displayed in them: paintings of flowers, fruits or animals, kitchen scenes, *vanitas* (paintings that refer to the transience of life through symbolism), banquets or breakfast pieces. These last two terms were used interchangeably and referred to paintings of food displayed on a table.

The paintings of Clara Peeters reveal that she was engaged with the major trends of her preferred genre. Works she made approximately half a century after Beuckelaer's include some of the same objects, foregrounded emphatically and shown from a high viewpoint. Beuckelaer was not the only point of reference, however; Peeters's realistic style, which she laboured to achieve, recalls the approach of early still lifes from Antwerp (fig.20).[3] However, sometimes Peeters chose to revise the approaches of her predecessors even as she retained others. This is the case with Frans Snyders, the most elite

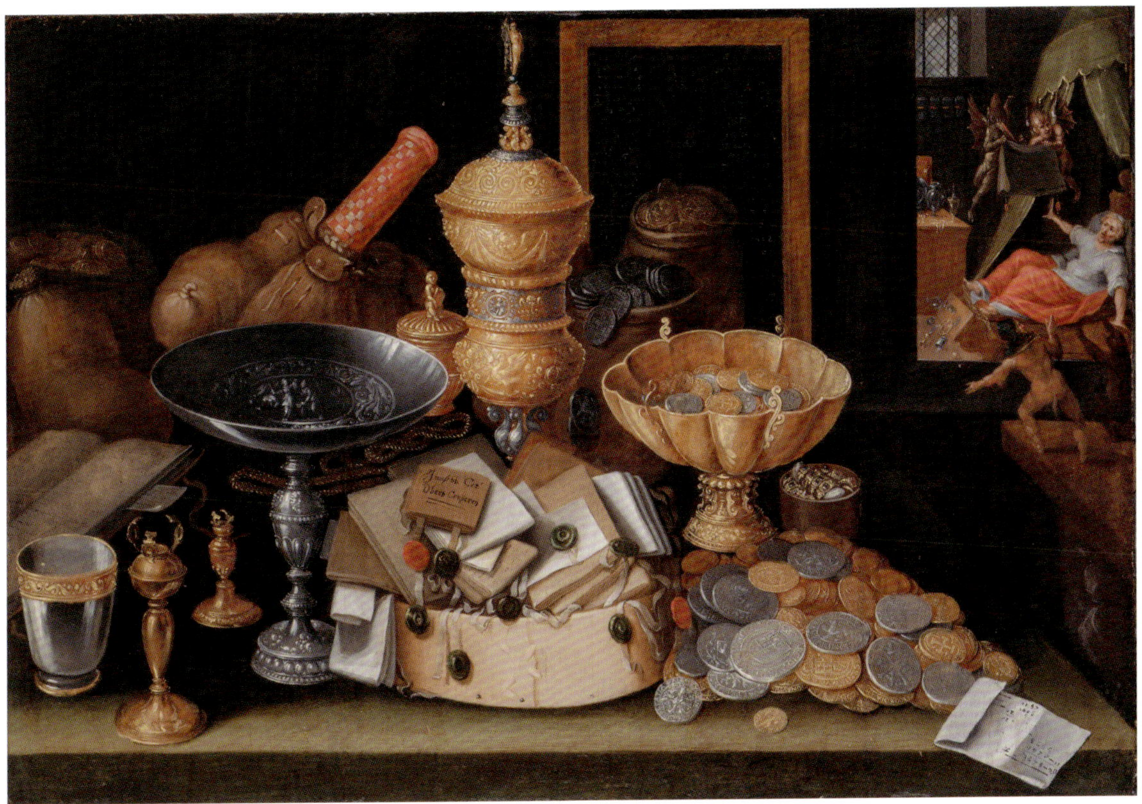

20 School of Frans Francken the Younger, *Allegory of Worldly Riches*, 1600, oil on panel, 50.8 × 74.3 cm (20 × 29 ¼ in),
Wadsworth Atheneum Museum of Art, Hartford, CT

painter of still lifes in Antwerp in terms of clientele. Snyders entered the painters' guild in 1602. He later travelled to Italy and, upon his return in 1609, often collaborated with Peter Paul Rubens. Peeters's still lifes show similarities and differences with the paintings by Snyders (fig.21). Both often include the same types of objects, among them the same fruits and animals, Chinese plates and bowls, and gilt standing cups. But Snyders painted in a more idealised and robust style than Peeters did. Works by Snyders are often seen hanging in the back walls of paintings of collectors' cabinets, an indication that they were a common presence in elite collections in Antwerp. Snyders indeed painted for the highest level of patron: Rubens owned four still-life paintings by him, and Diego Mexía, the Marquis of Leganés (*c.*1580–1655), one of the most important European collectors of the century as discussed below, owned over 50, many of them large animal paintings and hunts, but also kitchen scenes of various types, and still lifes.[4] Importantly, Mexía also owned two paintings by Peeters. The appearance of paintings by Snyders and Peeters in such an elite collection is informative about her status. Although a few artists in Antwerp had more prestige than her, she was clearly part of the upper tier of the art market.

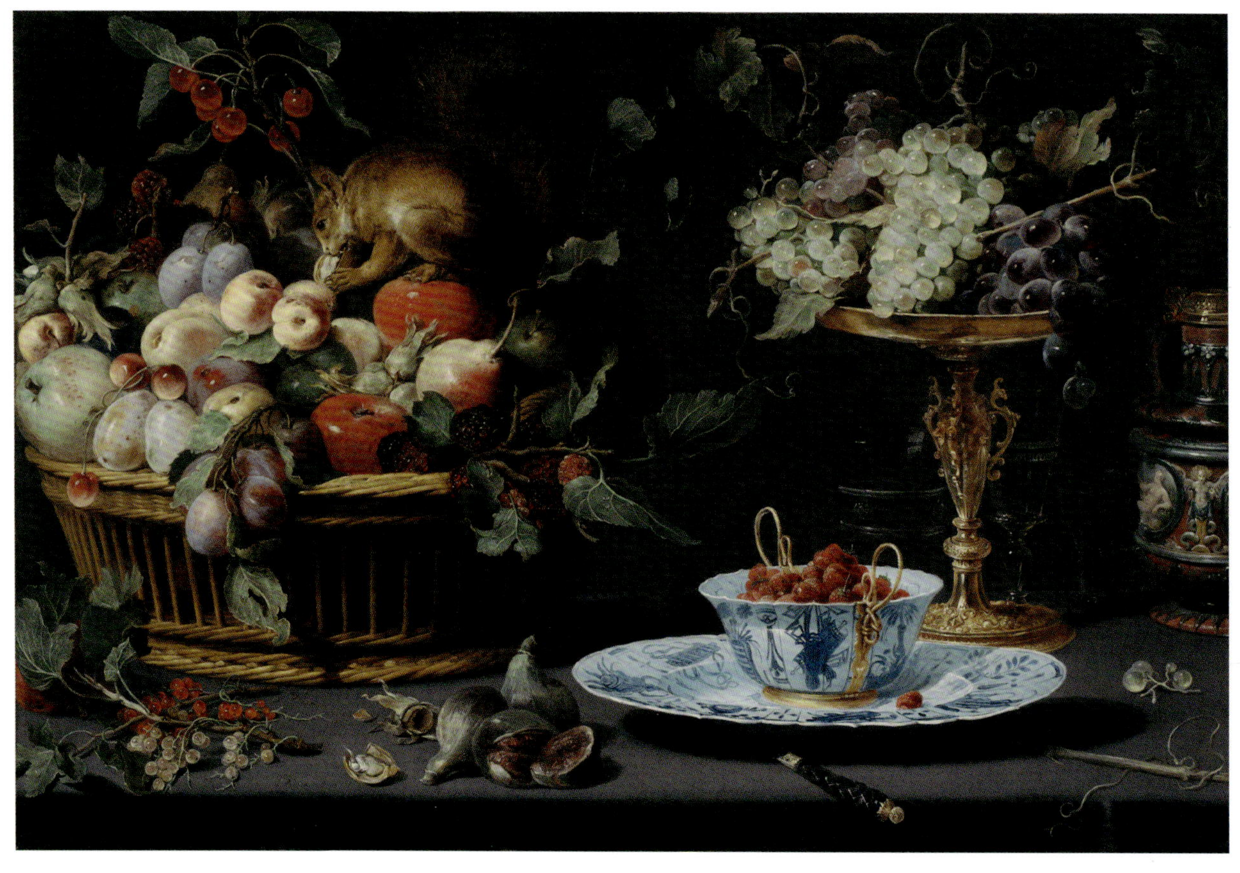

21 Frans Snyders, *Still Life with Fruit, Wanli Porcelain and Squirrel*, 1616, oil on copper, 56 × 84 cm (22 × 33 ⅛ in), Museum of Fine Arts Boston, MA

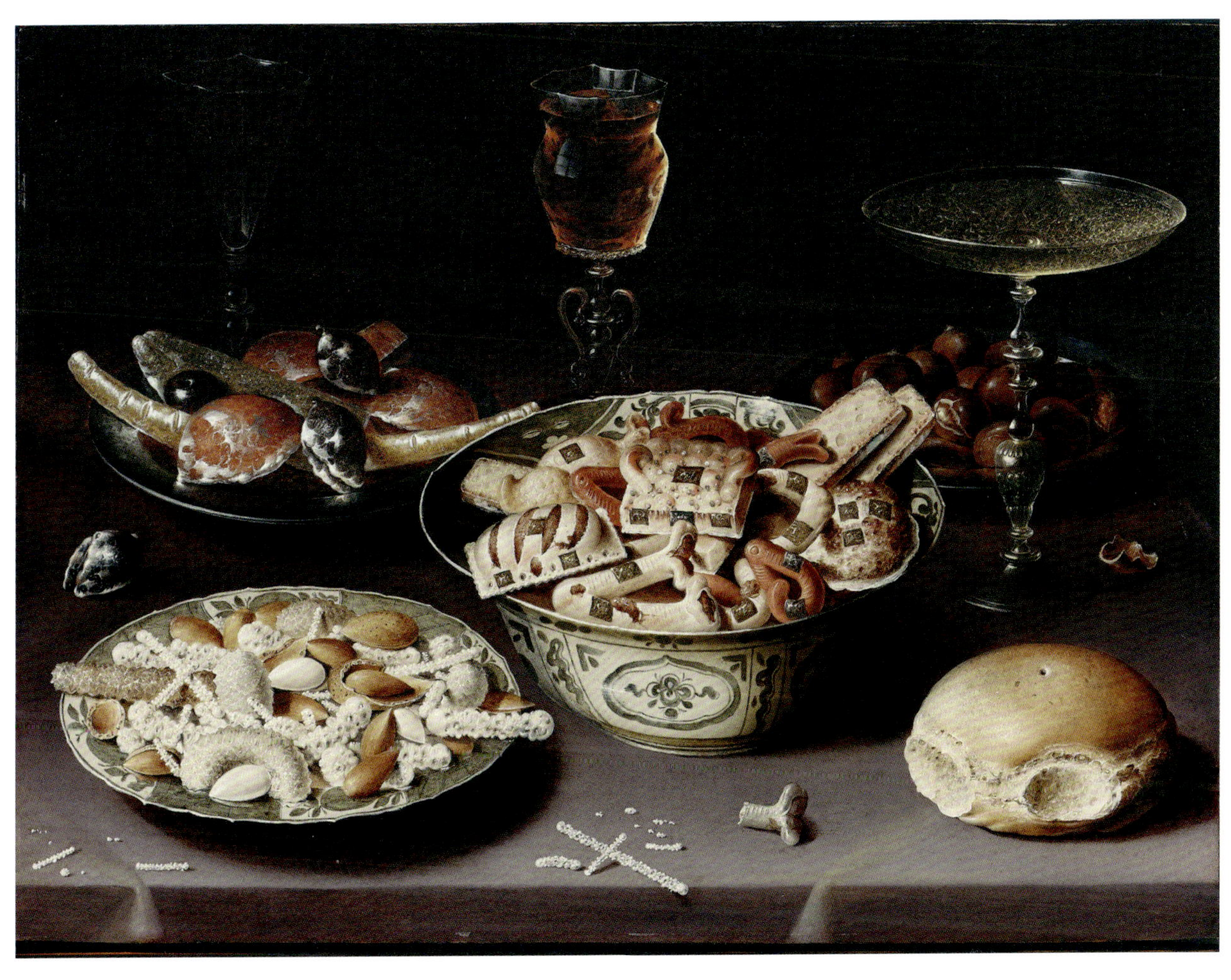

22 Osias Beert, *Still Life with Porcelain Vessels, Glassware and Eatables*, c.1610, oil on copper, 50 × 68 cm (19 ⅝ × 26 ¾ in), Sotheby's New York, 26 January 2012, lot 43

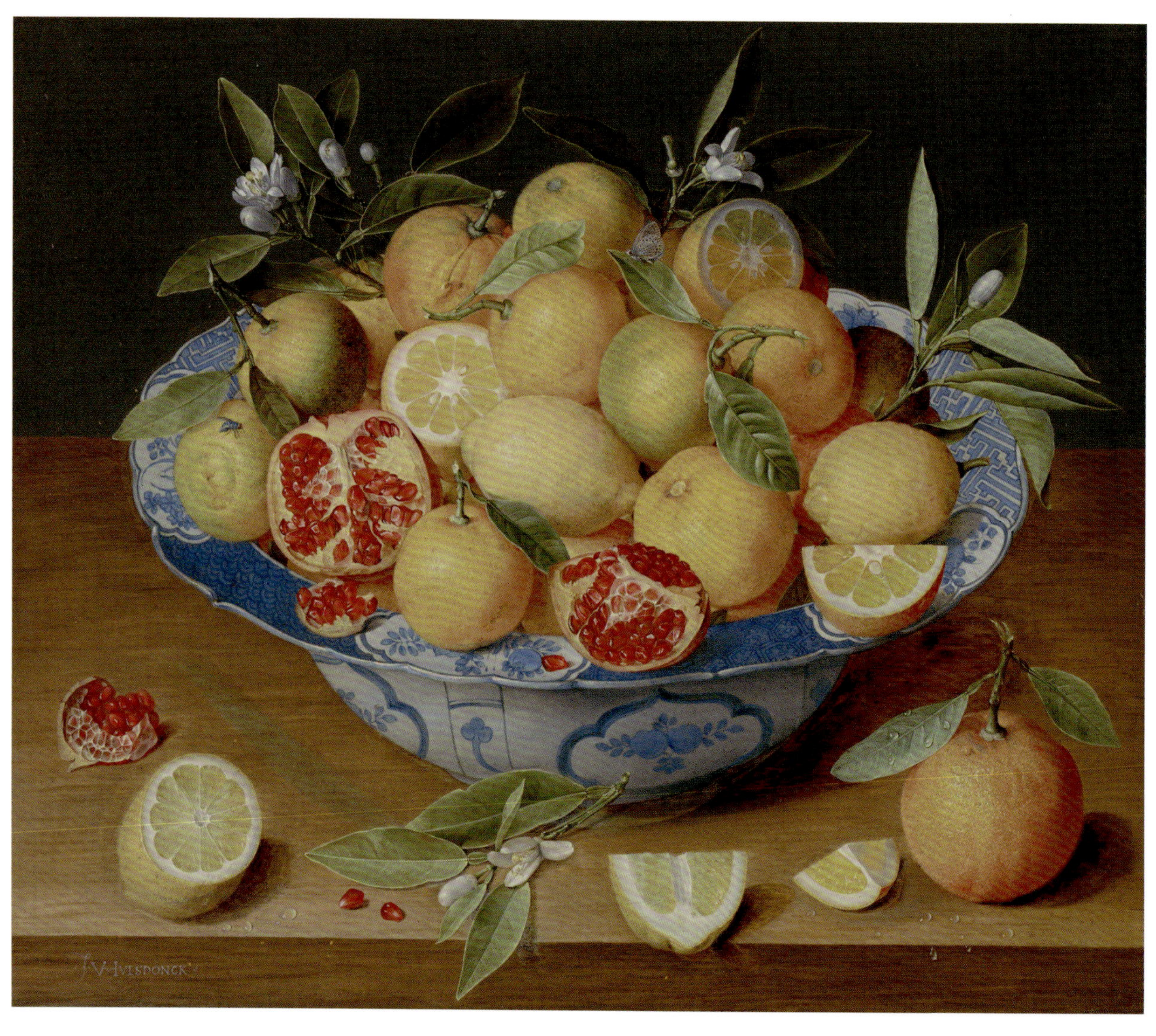

23 Jacob van Hulsdonck, *Still Life with Lemons, Oranges, and a Pomegranate*, c.1620–30, oil on panel, 41.9 × 49.5 cm (16 ½ × 19 ½ in), The J. Paul Getty Museum, Los Angeles, CA

The place of Peeters in the Antwerp art world also can be contextualised through Osias Beert (1580–1623), who worked in the city throughout his life.[5] Beert entered the painters' guild in 1602, five years before Peeters's first dated painting, and several of his works can be dated to 1603 and shortly thereafter. His still lifes (for example, fig.22) are like Peeters's in their precision and in the careful disposition of the objects so that we have an unobstructed view of them all. They are different in other ways. The objects in most paintings by Peeters are depicted from a lower point of view than in Beert's, contributing to a greater sense of reality, which also makes her art seem more forward looking. And Beert's works display a greater sense of abundance, with numerous *façon de Venise* glasses (fine blown glass in a Venetian style), porcelain dishes and plates overflowing with fruits, oysters and sweets. The impression of luxury of these paintings is emphasised by the rich glow of his heavily glazed surfaces, and the bulging forms and sinuous contours that he favoured. Beert collaborated with Rubens in the painting *Pausias and Glycera* (*c*.1615, John and Mable Ringling Museum of Art, Sarasota). This connection with Rubens who was the dominant figure in Antwerp from 1608 – when he returned after an eight-year stay in Italy – until his death in 1640 is not known in the case of Peeters. She seems to have been less well connected than some of her peers.

Peeters's paintings suggest that she may have responded not only to Beert but to other artists in Antwerp as well. A painter of still lifes whose works are more like Peeters than Beert is Jacob van Hulsdonck (1582–1647). He was born in Antwerp and, after spending time in Middelburg in the Northern Netherlands, joined the Guild of Saint Luke in his hometown in 1608; he remained in Antwerp until his death. Van Hulsdonck painted fruit baskets, tables laid with fruits (fig.23) and a few flower pieces in a style marked by the careful description of textures and a peculiar modesty; they do not call attention to style or design. Because Van Hulsdonck and Beert were

both probably slightly older than Peeters and because of some similarities with her manner of painting, it seems reasonable to speculate that they may have encouraged and influenced her during her formative years. Also reminiscent of Peeters is Jan Lambert. He is known only as the signatory in 1613 of a painting documented today through an old photograph that shows a work comprising a large table laden with food and vessels.[6] The descriptive and precise nature of his style, and the composition that positions the objects to allow a full view of each, is similar to Peeters's works. What is curious about this artist is the proximity to Peeters not only in his approach to painting, but also in date and family name. Alas, we do not know if there was a relationship between the two and, even then, whether potential influences were directional, mutual or a combination of both, presuming the kind of exposure that would enable such practices. Even less is known of the painters that, according to documents, worked as apprentices to Clara's father Nicasius Lamberts after he settled in Antwerp, and to her husband Henrick. Not a single painting can be assigned to these young men who probably accompanied Clara as she grew into the artist that we know from her paintings today.

Clara Peeters was part of a generation of artists who shared a general knowledge of developments in the field of still-life painting beyond the cities where they lived and worked. She was likely aware of approaches to it even outside the Southern Netherlands, as suggested by close parallels to her naturalistic style in the work of painters such as the Czech-born Georg Flegel (1565/6–1638), Jacques de Gheyn II (1565–1629), Jeremias van Winghe (1578–1645), Floris Claesz. van Dijck (*c*.1575–1651) and Nicolaes Gillis (active by 1612–32). These painters also probably had at least a general notion of each other's works, perhaps through networks of painters who had connections to the Southern Netherlands. De Gheyn, for example, moved from Antwerp to Haarlem in 1581.[7] Since he was a Catholic, he probably did not move north because of

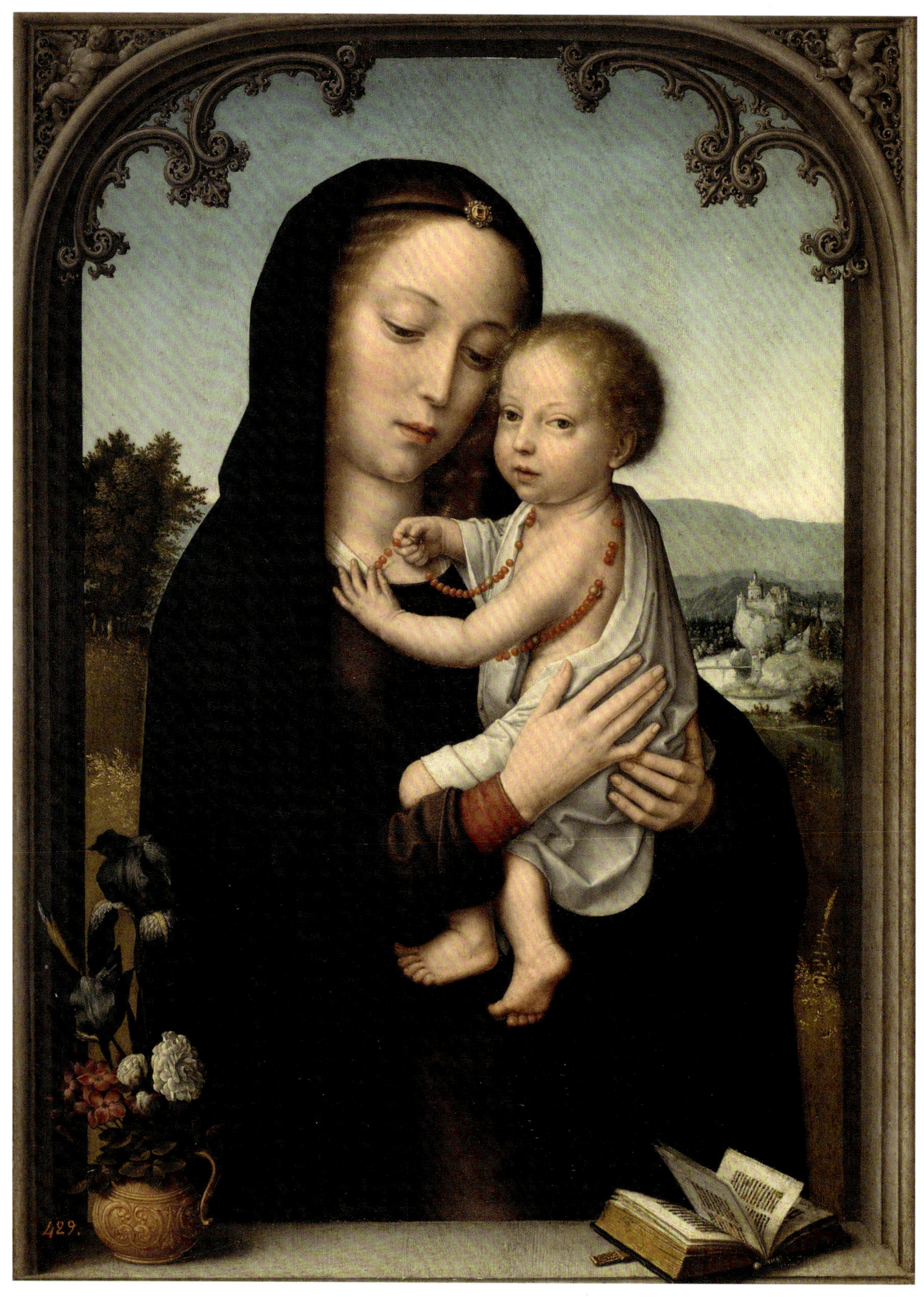

24 Gerard David (?), *The Virgin and Child*, c.1520, oil on panel, 45 × 34 cm (17¾ × 13⅜ in), Museo Nacional del Prado, Madrid

religious persecution, and may well have maintained ties with his home town, acting as a conduit for ideas. Gillis was born in Antwerp at an uncertain date and was in Haarlem by 1615. His early pictures date from the first years of the century and may have been painted in Antwerp. Van Winghe came from a Brussels family that had moved to Frankfurt. Van Hulsdonck, as mentioned, moved back and forth between Antwerp and the nearby city of Middelburg, at the mouth of the River Scheldt, which was controlled by the Dutch, and which had received many emigrants after the religious troubles discussed in the first chapter. Despite the war, the border between the Southern and Northern Netherlands was permeable. Jan Brueghel travelled to Middelburg at least five times in the years 1596–1612 and sold paintings there.[8] Ambrosius Bosschaert the Elder (1573–1621), who left Antwerp when he was 14 or 15 and who trained Balthasar van der Ast (1593/4–1657), later a leading Dutch flower painter, is known to have dealt in paintings between Antwerp and other cities in Europe.

Like Van der Ast, Peeters had an affinity for painting flowers (see figs 36, 52, 53). Flower paintings had antecedents in the fifteenth century, where blossoms had secondary roles and often symbolic meanings in imagery. An example from the early sixteenth century is a painting of *The Virgin and Child* (fig.24) probably made in Antwerp by an artist working in a style close to Gerard David (1460–1523), perhaps Simon Bening, where the blossoms suggest qualities of Mary and Christ, such as modesty and purity, through their symbolic associations. A new interest in the natural sciences in the next decades brought about a market for scientific illustration, as studies moved beyond ancient sources such as Aristotle's *History of Animals* and the works of Theophrastus, Dioscorides and Pliny the Elder which had inspired artists of earlier generations. Contemporary naturalists revisited the works of these authors, bringing their fields up to date through empirical observation. Artists provided illustrations

for the most distinguished scientific books of the period, such as Leonhart Fuchs's *De historia stirpium commentarii insignes* (*Notable Commentaries on the History of Plants*) of 1542; Pierre Belon's *L'histoire naturelle des estranges poissons* and *L'histoire de la nature des oyseaux*, of 1551 and 1555, respectively; Guillaume Rondelet's *Libri de piscibus marinis* of 1554; Conrad Gessner's monumental *Historia animalium*, published between 1551 and 1558; and the *Natural History* by Ulisse Aldrovandi, published in 13 volumes from 1599 until 1668, long after Aldrovandi's death.[9] These images were usually schematic, offering the most objective and complete view of a specimen. They had one main purpose: to provide information to the viewer.

The drawing and painting of plants and animals gradually became a speciality for Antwerp.[10] The cartographer and geographer Abraham Ortelius (1527–98) and other members of the city's elite encouraged the work of artists such as Joris Hoefnagel (1542–1601), who was based in Antwerp until the 1570s; Lambert Lombard (1505–66), illustrator of some of the animals included in a work known as the *Spanish Album*; and Hans Bol (1534–93), who, while working in Antwerp, made three watercolour albums devoted to quadrupeds, fish and birds. Adriaen Collaert (*c.*1560–1618), one of the most prolific engravers in Antwerp at the end of the sixteenth century, made and published several series devoted to plants and animals that were very influential and helped to normalise the representation of these subjects in art. The earliest, descriptive drawings quickly evolved into more artistic images, with a greater sensitivity to aesthetic qualities. Hoefnagel is especially important when considering how this hybrid moment of transition took place. In the 1570s, while still in Antwerp, he began a series of watercolour and gouache drawings that would be collected in four volumes devoted to the four elements: *Animaliarationalia et insecta* (fire), *Animaliaquadrupedia et reptilia* (earth), *Animaliaaquatilia et cochiliata* (water) and

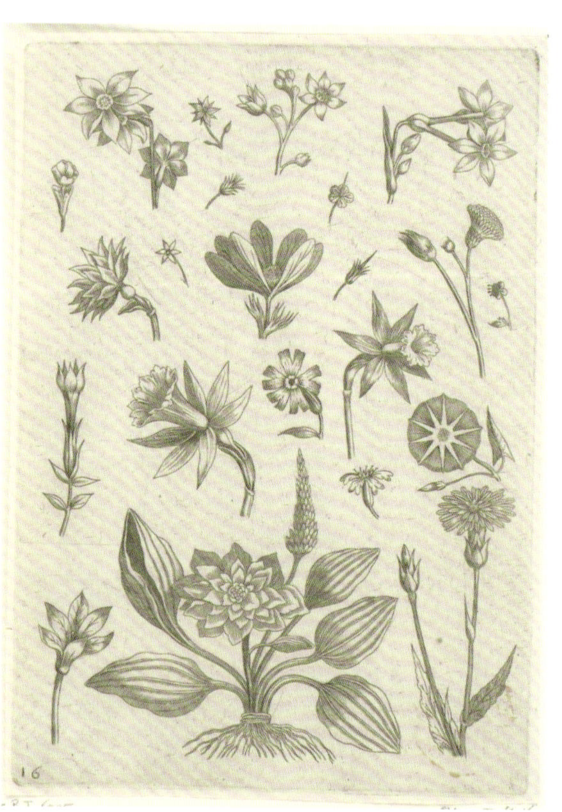

25 Adriaen Collaert, *Daffodils*, 1587–9, engraving, from the series *Florilegium*, Antwerp, 17.8 × 12.7 cm (7 × 5 in), Rijksmuseum, Amsterdam

26 Jacob Hoefnagel, after Joris Hoefnagel, *Archetypa studiaque patris Georgii Hoefnagelii ('Delectasi me Deus in factura tua . . .')*, 1592, engraving, 15.5 × 21.1 cm (6 ⅛ × 8 ¼ in), Rijksmuseum, Amsterdam

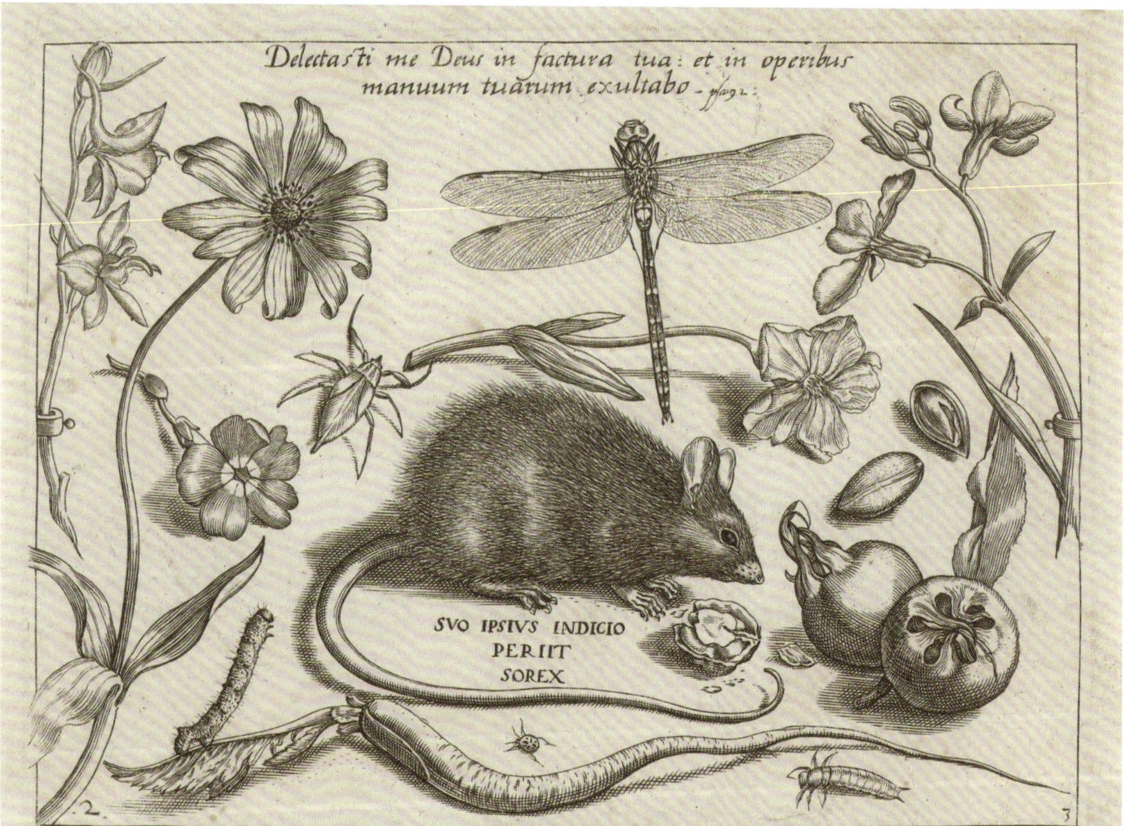

Animaliavolatilia et amphibian (air).[11] They include images of flowers, plants, fruits, insects, seashells and small animals, all represented in a highly detailed and descriptive manner; clearly one of their functions is didactic. From an artistic standpoint, these are also extraordinary images. There is a strong emphasis on highlighting design and on creating formal patterns. The concern with symmetry highlights artifice as opposed to nature and brings the images closer to the realm of art than most other scientific illustrations of the time. Hoefnagel's images are hybrids of science and art; they document the appearance of things, but they also display the ability of the artist to emulate reality skilfully and to design compositions that have harmony and beauty.

The earliest dedicated flower paintings emerged from a confluence of these interests, remaining reliant on earlier trends in certain ways. The first examples were made when Peeters was probably a young apprentice, just before the turn of the century, by Ambrosius Bosschaert, Roelant Savery (1576–1639), Jacques de Gheyn and Jan Brueghel (until then Brueghel had mainly painted landscapes). All four artists use a pictorial language that is conspicuously stylised, characterised by luscious colours and a mannered grouping of elements. In the paintings of Clara Peeters, we find many objects that appear to be carefully observed from life, but also some animals and flowers that were probably inspired by Collaert and other printed repertoires of images. A daffodil at the apex of a flower bouquet in Peeters's *Still Life with Flowers, Gilt Goblet, Eatables and a Pewter Flagon* (fig.9) is so similar to one of the flowers included by Collaert in his series of engravings *Florilegium* (fig.25), published in Antwerp in 1587–9, that it may have actually been inspired by the engraving. Formal similarities between the images by Hoefnagel and the paintings of Peeters suggest that they were sources of inspiration for her. Although access to Hoefnagel's drawings was limited, bringing into question whether she knew them, he had an international reputation

made possible in large part by the publication of his images. Many were available in the book *Archetypa studiaque patris Georgii Hoefnagelii*, published in Frankfurt in 1592 by his son Jacob Hoefnagel (1573–1630). A comparison of one of Hoefnagel's designs (fig.26) with Peeters's *Still Life with Flowers, Gilt Goblet, Eatables and a Pewter Flagon* (fig.9) reveals that the two compositions share a strong central axis and framing of elements at the right and left. More importantly, in both images the artists attempt to display the clearest possible view of the objects, while at the same time making the scenes look natural by overlapping them (this is especially notable in the flower arrangement). In later still lifes by Peeters a more natural overlapping is evident, which obscures certain elements of the composition. However, in their realism, the paintings by Peeters are more attuned in style to the artistic trends of the early seventeenth century than to earlier botanical works, whether by Hoefnagel or others.

If being a woman placed Clara Peeters at a professional disadvantage, the fact that she was from Antwerp played in her favour. After the troubles of the late sixteenth century, and especially during the peaceful years of the Twelve Years' Truce, from 1609 to 1621, the city managed to regain its privileged place as one of the most productive and innovative art centres in Europe. Painters could sell their works to an important elite of local collectors, and they also exported them so that they were collected by leading amateurs abroad. Due to its artistic importance, Antwerp was at the forefront of innovations like the emergence of the genre of still-life painting. In fact, the specialisation of local artists in scientific illustration must have prepared painters and collectors for the new genre. Workshop practices that were developed in the city from the early sixteenth century – from the time of Patinir and Quentin Massys, among others – were in place when Peeters began her career. We recognise them in the way she made her own paintings, which is the subject of the next chapter.

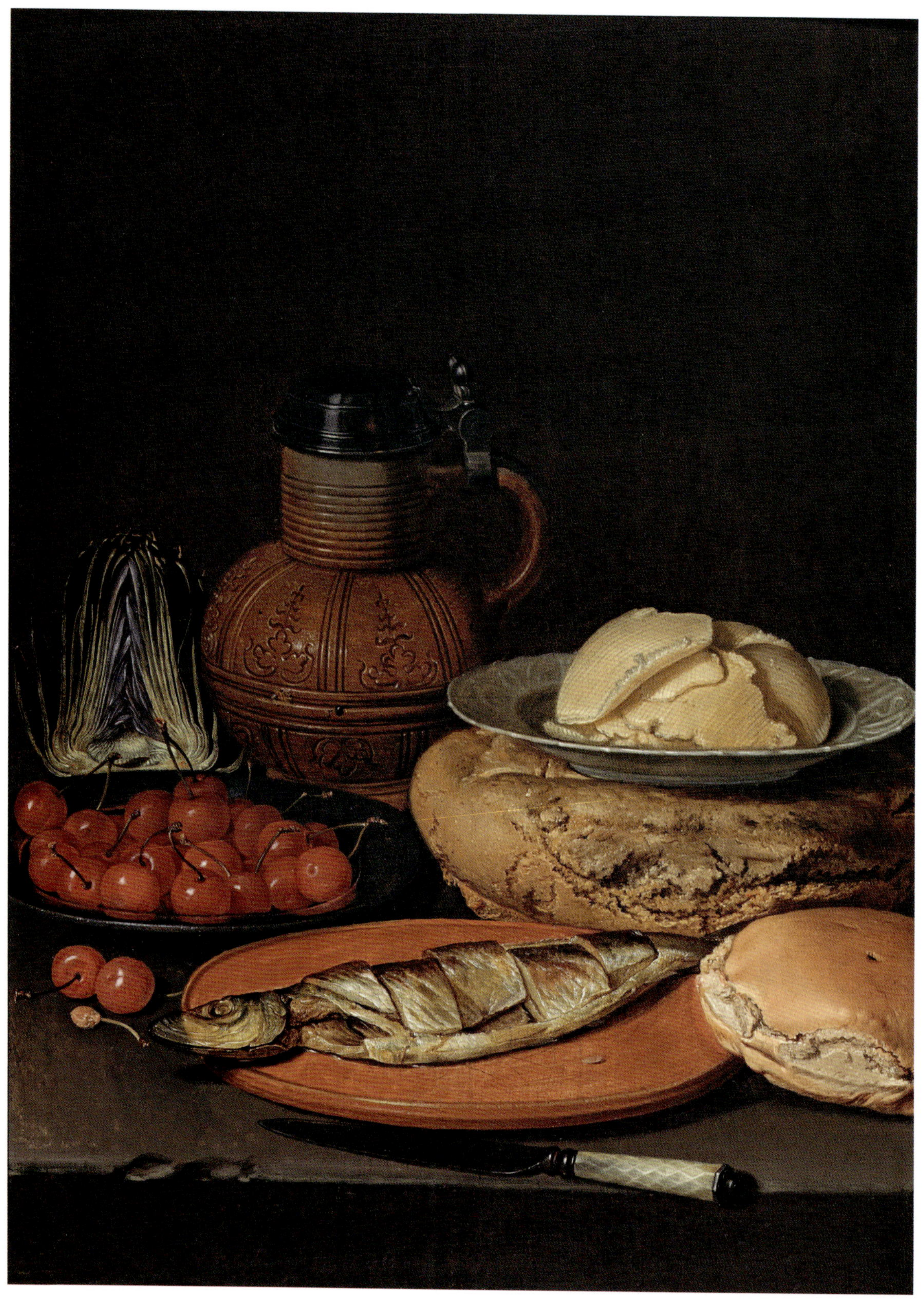

27 Clara Peeters, *Still Life with Herring, a Porcelain Dish with Butter and Other Eatables*, signed and dated, 1612, oil on panel,
45 × 33 cm (17 ¾ × 13 in), private collection, Spain

3

Artistic Production

The fact that Peeters specialised in still-life painting was probably at least partially a consequence of her gender. Her practice was similar to that of elite professional male painters in Antwerp and other leading artistic centres in Europe, even as fewer works can be firmly attributed to her than to most of her contemporaries. This chapter assesses Peeters's approach to art-making, including matters of style, materials and process, her command of the workshop she oversaw, and the dissemination and reception of her paintings. A skilled artist and strategic entrepreneur, Peeters built a reputation that attracted a broad spectrum of clientele from the local to the international.

STYLISTIC EVOLUTION AND RECEPTION

There are currently 39 known paintings bearing the signature or an inscription with the name of Clara Peeters.[1] A few unsigned works can also be plausibly attributed to her, bringing the number of works to approximately 45, a relatively modest production for the period. A partial chronology for Peeters's works can be constructed through the 11 known paintings by her that bear dates. The two earliest are from 1607 and 1608, eight are from 1611–12 and the next is from 1621. This is the only firm evidence available to determine

her evolution as an artist. Documentary evidence, albeit scant, suggests the desirability of her works among collectors.

The two earliest paintings already show many of the objects that Peeters painted throughout her career: a salt cellar, drinking glasses, foodstuffs of different kinds, a knife and pewter plates, all set on a table or a ledge against a dark background.[2] She would later add game, fish, some live animals and arrangements of flowers. The painting from 1607 (fig.1) already includes one of the most characteristic features of her still lifes: her reflected self portrait, examples of which are discussed in Chapter 1. In both paintings the foreshortening of the objects is not fully resolved; they tilt upward and tend to merge with the picture plane. This is especially noticeable in the pewter plate and the lower section of the candleholder. Also, some objects appear as if seen from a different viewpoint than others. These unresolved passages bespeak the production of these works early in her career, when her skills were under development.

If Peeters was born in 1587, as it seems, she was 19 or 20 years old when she painted these two scenes. The very fact that she signed the paintings suggests that she felt that her art was ready for a stage beyond her studio and deserving of recognition. A few years later she may have thought differently about these early paintings, for in the works dated 1611 and 1612 her skill at creating an illusion of three-dimensional volume and spatial depth – the litmus test for painters from the Renaissance until the nineteenth century – has greatly improved. At this point she was an artist in full control of her skills.

The differences between the two paintings of 1607 and 1608 and those of 1611 to 1612 are not only a matter of technical ability. In the former, the tables and objects displayed are painted as if seen from a high vantage point. This viewpoint lowers somewhat in 1611, as can be seen in her *Still Life with Flowers, Gilt Goblet, Eatables and a Pewter Flagon* (fig.9) and even more so in pictures dated 1612, such as *Still Life with Flowers, Gilt Goblets, Coins and Shells* (fig.10) and *Still Life with Herring, a Porcelain Dish with Butter and other Eatables* (fig.27). The tables and ledges on which the objects rest are now portrayed as if from a lower vantage point, and they occupy a smaller portion of the compositions. This lowering of the horizon line follows a trend seen also in landscape painting in Europe throughout the sixteenth and the early seventeenth centuries. Within the world of pictorial convention, a lower vantage point was seen as more realistic than a higher one, a quality that artists at the time generally strived for. A progression in that direction is logical for Peeters, who certainly was aware of, and presumably wanted to capitalise on, new trends in painting.

After 1612, Peeters's next dated work is *Garland of Flowers with a Madonna and Child* which she signed in 1621 (fig.28).[3] This is also her last known dated work. Its flowers are like others that she painted but it is exceptional in its miniature scale (15 × 13 cm), and in that it is her only known garland. The idea of making paintings showing a garland of flowers or fruits surrounding an image of the Virgin Mary was first conceived jointly by Jan Brueghel the Elder and his patron Cardinal Federico Borromeo from Milan, for whom he worked in Rome and Milan,

and also from the Southern Netherlands after his return there. Brueghel painted his first scene of this type around 1606, and several followed. They were meant to celebrate the worship of the Virgin Mary, which had special meaning in the Catholic, Southern Netherlands because many images of the Virgin were damaged or destroyed in the iconoclastic violence at the end of the sixteenth century. The garland by Clara Peeters is thus a typical product of this Counter-Reformation culture promoted in the Southern Netherlands during the rule of the Archdukes Isabel Clara Eugenia and Albert VII of Austria, proponents of Catholicism who ruled the Habsburg Netherlands at the time.

Peeters's garland is one of only two paintings by her that include human figures, other than those that incorporate her self-portraits in reflections. In the garland painting they are the Virgin Mary and the Child Jesus, inspired by Raphael's famous tondo *Madonna of the Chair* which she must have known from a print. Because it was common practice in Antwerp to have different artists paint the figures and the garlands in a single painting, it is not impossible that the same happened here. We saw earlier that Joachim Patinir and the figure painter Quentin Massys collaborated on a painting, and Jan Brueghel often enlisted his friend Peter Paul Rubens to paint figures in his pictures (the *Five Senses* series at the Prado is an example of this practice; fig.43). A division of labour depending on the speciality of painters had been in place in studio practice since the fifteenth century. The only available comparative material that we have for Peeters as a figure painter is in *Woman Seated at a Table with Precious Objects* (fig.16). The flowers in this and the garland painting, which are painted in similar size, are alike in the manner of handling the paint and in the placement of the flowers in relation to the picture plane. Differences in texture may be explained by the different surfaces of the two pictures; the garland is painted on copper, the other on panel. But the faces

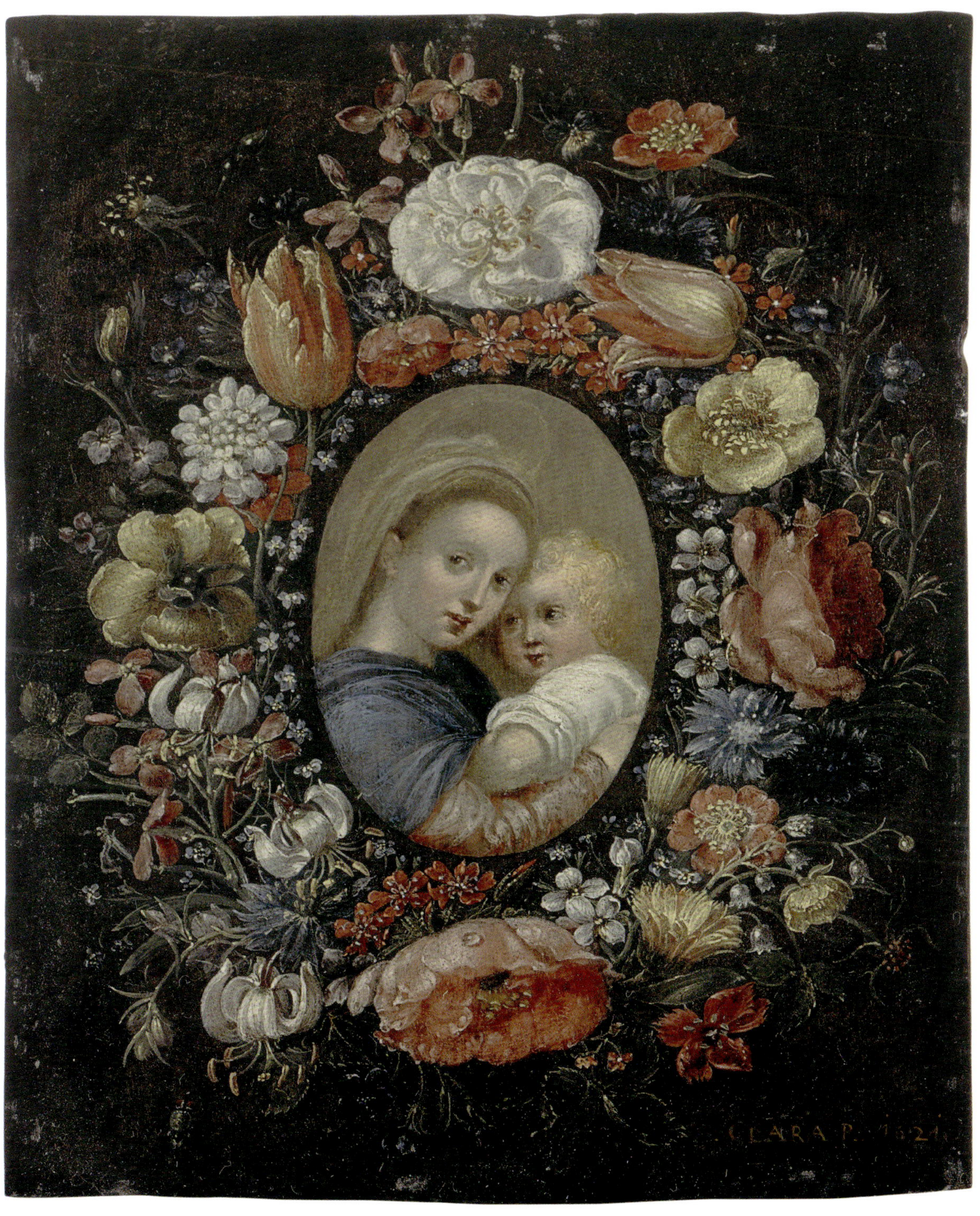

28 Clara Peeters, *Garland of Flowers with a Madonna and Child,* signed and dated, 1621, oil on copper, 15 × 13 cm (5 ⅞ × 5 ⅛ in), private collection

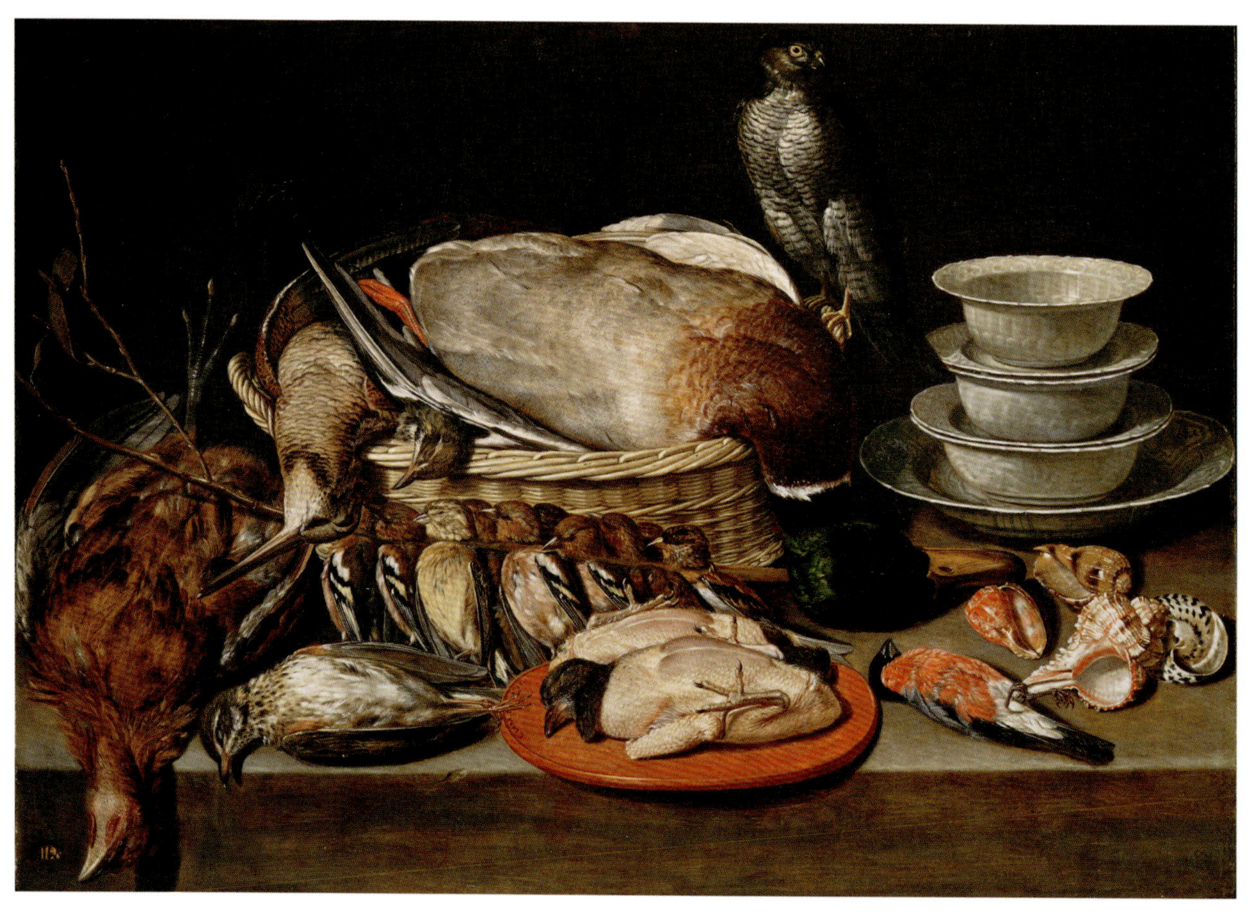

29 Clara Peeters, *Still Life with a Sparrow Hawk, Fowl, Porcelain and Shells*, signed and dated, 1611, oil on panel, 52 × 71 cm (20 ½ × 28 in), Museo Nacional del Prado, Madrid

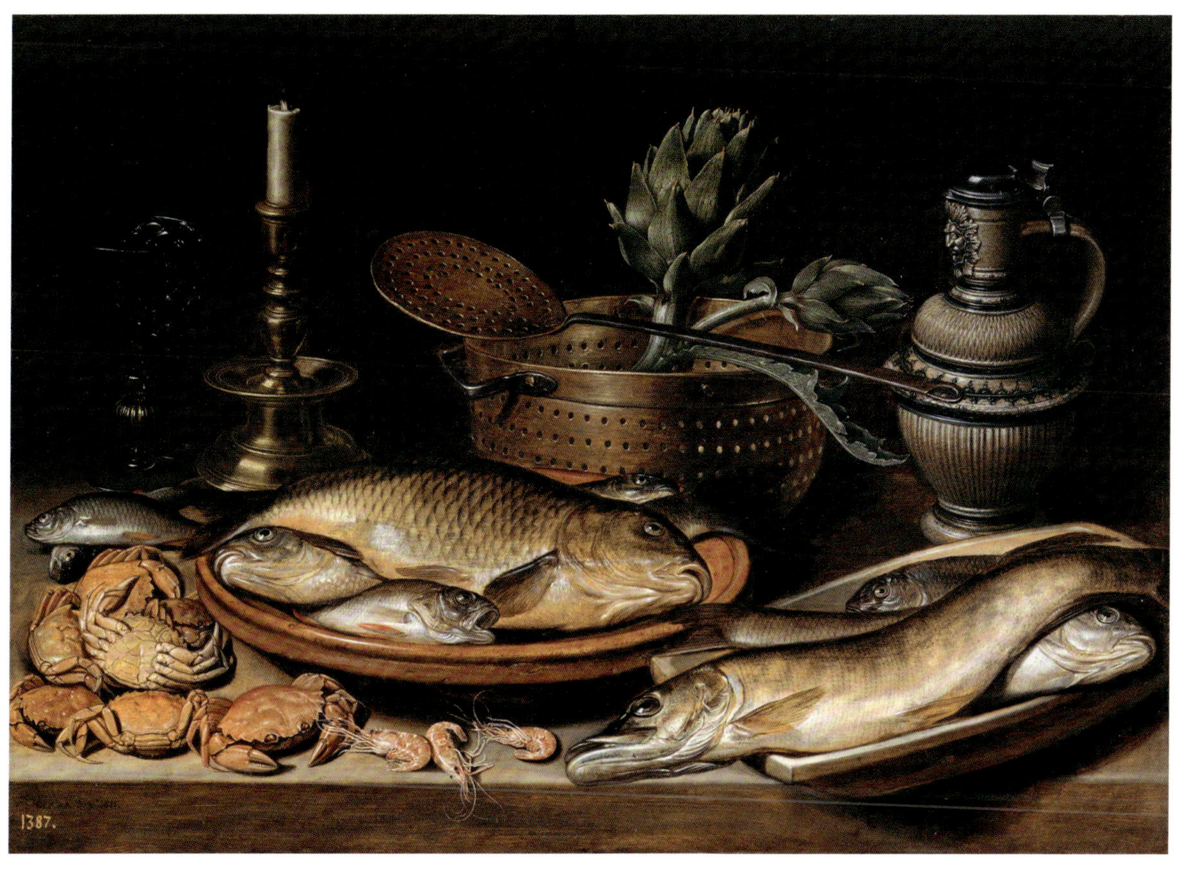

30 Clara Peeters, *Still Life with Fish, Candle, Artichokes, Crabs and Shrimp*, signed and dated, 1611, oil on panel, 50 × 72 cm (19 ⅝ × 28 ⅜ in), Museo Nacional del Prado, Madrid

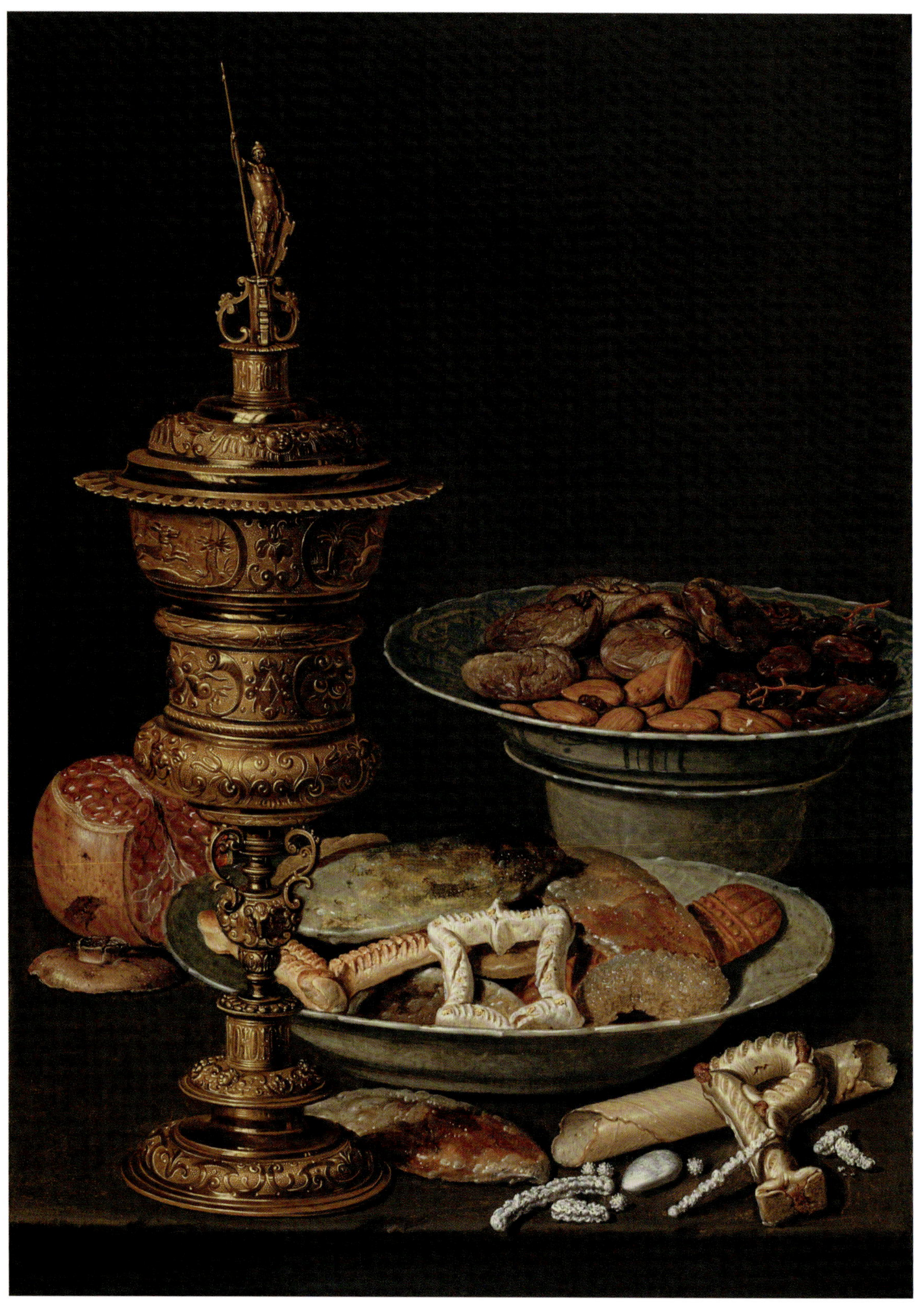

31 Clara Peeters, *Still Life with Gilt Goblet, Porcelain and Eatables*, oil on panel, signed, *c.*1612, 45 × 33 cm (17 ¾ × 13 in), private collection, Spain

are of such different sizes that the comparison is not useful. Common sense would dictate that for such small figures it was not necessary to enlist outside help, but this is not certain.

The stylistic evolution of Clara Peeters from 1607 to the group of paintings dated in 1611–12 is logical in terms of technical skills. The long hiatus between these years, in what presumably would have been a productive period, and the next signed painting of 1621 is puzzling. Peeters may not have painted at all after completing *Garland of Flowers*; no paintings are dated later and no written records refer to a painting by her after 1621.

Early documents suggest that Peeters had some name recognition in the Northern Netherlands in the first decade of her artistic production. Her name first appears in a document regarding her art in 1627, when a painting described as 'fish after Clara Pieters' is listed as part of the property of a woman named Lucretia de Beauvois from Rotterdam, wife of the landscape painter Herman Saftleven.[4] As we saw in Chapter 1, a painting by Peeters was listed in 1635 in a collection in Amsterdam, where it was dated to 1608.[5] Somewhat later, in 1685, another painting by her is documented in a collection in Haarlem.[6]

Written sources also speak of an elevated status for the paintings by Peeters in Spain. Two such references appear in the 1637 and 1655 inventories of the collection of Diego Mexía in Madrid; the current whereabouts of these paintings is not known.[7] Mexía, who became Marquis of Leganés in 1627 and is generally known by that title, was a military commander and courtier of the government of Philip III and Philip IV of Spain, and of the Archdukes in the Southern Netherlands. He was also one of the most important art collectors of his time, a man whom Rubens described in a letter of 1628 as 'among the greatest connoisseurs [of painting] in the world'.[8] Rubens drew and painted portraits of him. Leganés built his collection by purchasing paintings in the Southern Netherlands, Italy and Spain. He owned many important Flemish paintings and was

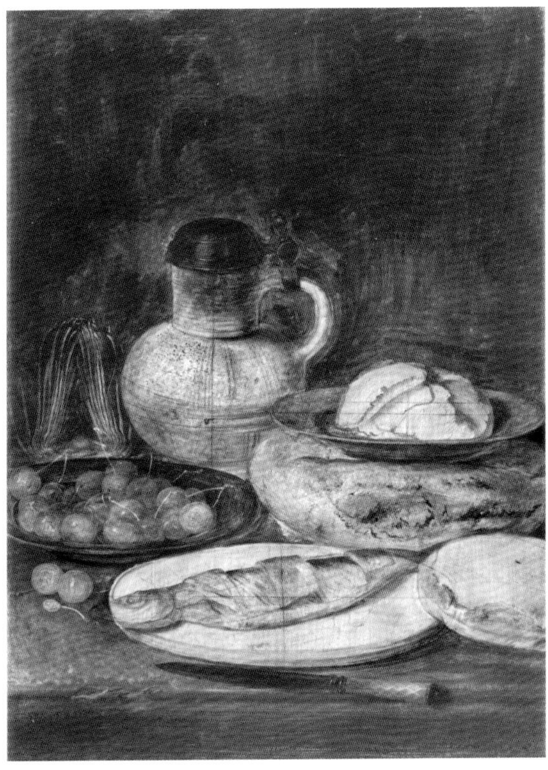

32 Detail of infrared image of a section of fig.27

also a collector of still lifes. That two pictures by Peeters were in this collection, one of the largest in Europe – in 1642 he owned more than 1200 paintings – is a testament to their desirability outside the Netherlands.

Also telling of the appreciation of still lifes by Clara Peeters in the seventeenth century is the fact that two of them were in the royal collection in Madrid at this time. This was very likely the largest collection of paintings in Europe during this period and certainly one of the most prestigious.[9] The paintings are *Still Life with a Sparrow Hawk, Fowl, Porcelain and Shells* (fig.29) and *Still Life with Fish, Candle, Artichokes, Crabs and Shrimp* (fig.30). They are listed anonymously in an inventory of the royal collection of 1666 but are ascribed to Peeters by name in the eighteenth century. The fact that her paintings were in some of the most important collections not long after their production is a sign of Peeters's ambition and professionalism and of her recognition as a skilled and desirable artist by her contemporaries.

MATERIALS AND PROCESS

Peeters can be further understood as a painter through the materials she used and her working methods. Studies conducted by certain museums provide us with interesting clues and confirm what is already apparent by observation: Peeters shared the professional culture and financial means of elite painters of her time. Most of the materials that conservators have detected in her paintings were standard in Antwerp, where a highly organised painting industry had existed since the early 1500s. A few materials are noteworthy. In at least one painting, namely *Still Life with Gilt Goblet, Porcelain and Eatables* (fig.31), she added a few touches of shell gold to one of the biscuits in the scene, a white one with a nearly square shape. Shell gold – so named because it was usually kept in mussel shells – is gold ground into powder and mixed with a medium so that it can be used as paint. It had been common in manuscript illumination and was sometimes used for highlights by European painters such as Andrea Mantegna (1430/31–1506) and Giovanni Bellini (c.1431/6–1516). The Antwerp still-life painter Osias Beert used a similar gold leaf on the surface of some of the sweets in his paintings. The reason Peeters used this material probably has to do with her ambition to paint lifelike images, a quality enhanced by it. In addition to the visual effects it enabled, gold increased the monetary value of the painting, thereby raising its appeal among connoisseurs.

For at least one painting Peeters used another expensive material, ultramarine blue, obtained from the precious stone lapis lazuli, for the colour of a porcelain plate (fig.33). Lapis was imported from mines in what is now Afghanistan. European painters traditionally used this material in small quantities; its use implies a high-end product. Peeters painted the exact same plate in several paintings but seems to have used lapis only in this one. In other porcelain plates she used the less costly cobalt blue pigment, which has faded over time and now looks nearly grey (figs 14, 29 31). Surprisingly, some of the paintings where this happened are very carefully made and of a very high quality. The reasons for choosing one type of blue pigment over another must have been influenced by availability or by the demands of a patron.

There are other signs of the care with composition that went into the best paintings of Clara Peeters, such as in *Still Life with Fish, Candle, Artichokes, Crabs and Shrimp* (fig.30). Infrared images have revealed that Peeters moved the eye of the fish closest to the lower right corner down slightly from its original position, elevating our viewing point. She also changed the original position of the holes that dot the copper skimmer, next to the stem of the artichoke, during a second stage of production. This type of small adjustment, which is best seen in an infrared image of the painting, a technology that reveals underdrawing beneath the paint layers, shows the exacting standards of the artist. To place the objects in her carefully planned and executed paintings, Peeters drew axis lines over the preparation layers of her paintings, which are again visible to us thanks to infrared technology. An infrared image of the picture *Still Life with Herring, a Porcelain Dish with Butter and other Eatables* (figs 27, 32) shows lines she drew with black pencil to mark different vertical and horizontal axes. These lines served as aids to paint the objects; similar lines are visible in other examples of her work. In this and other paintings we can also see freehand underdrawing beneath the preparation layer. The artist combined this with some marks that

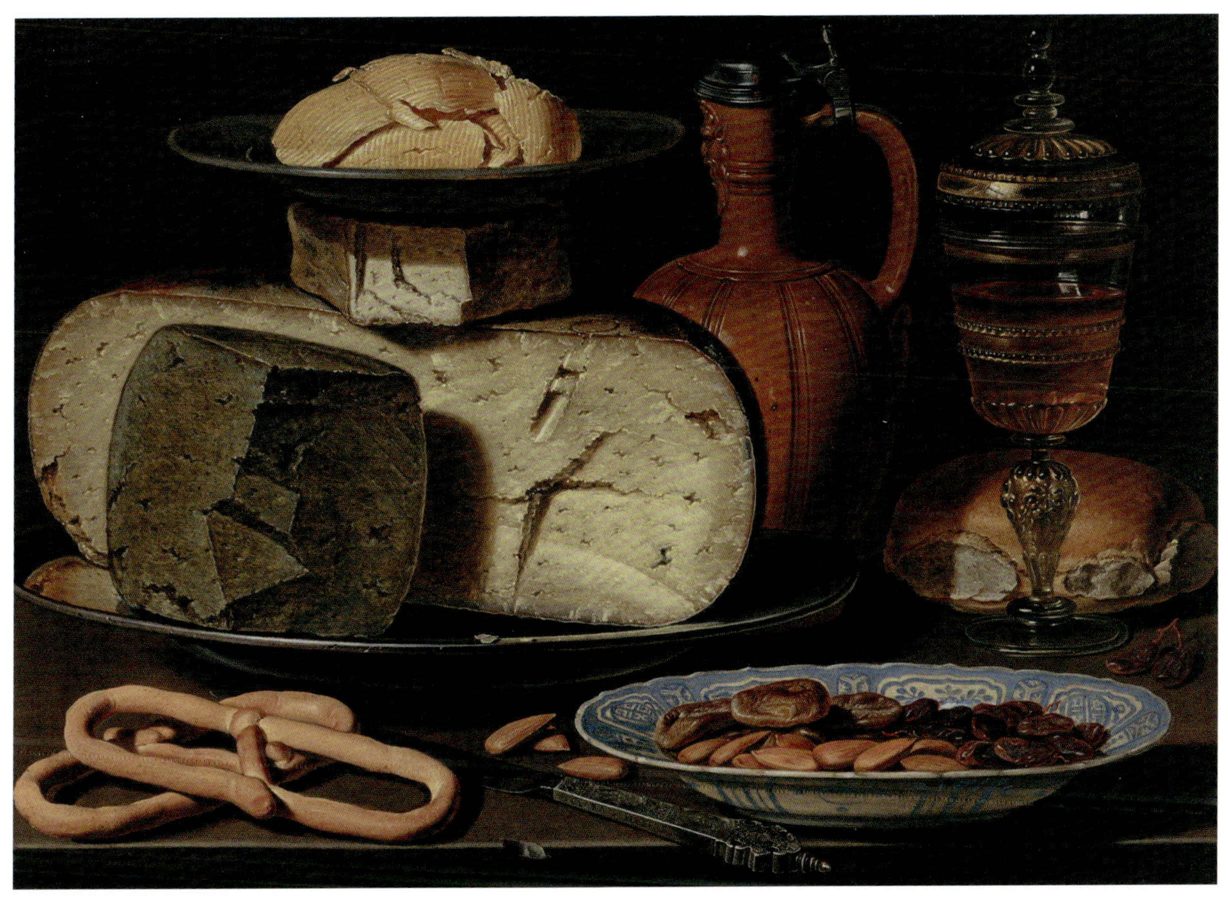

33 Clara Peeters, *Still Life with Cheeses, Almonds and Pretzels*, inscribed with the artist's name on the knife, *c*.1612–15, oil on panel, 34 × 49 cm (13⅜ × 19¼ in), Mauritshuis, The Hague

coincide with the contours of the plates, suggesting the use of a stencil or another mechanical aid.

Peeters created in many of her works subtle visual effects that reveal her understanding of the properties of paint and her skill with its application. In many of her paintings the light brown base used under the paint layers, known as *imprimatura*, shows through as a luminous glow. This is most visible in the section of the ledges on which objects rest that is closest to the bottom of the paintings. In *Still Life with a Sparrow Hawk, Fowl, Porcelain and Shells* (fig.29) we can clearly see this effect, which wisely adds to the visual elegance of the scene. The strokes of a wide brush loaded with dark brown paint have been applied with a horizontal movement of the hand, from left to right and from right to left. This dark tone mixes in our vision with a lighter tone that is simply the *imprimatura* layer showing through. In the clay plate on which two plucked pigeons lie the artist has applied the reddish paint unevenly. In some areas the light underpaint of the *imprimatura* layer again shows through, adding to the variety of texture and tone. The idea of using the tone of the preparation layers in the final appearance of a painting had gained momentum in the sixteenth century, as can be seen in works by Pieter Aertsen, Joachim Beuckelaer and many others. Peeters, like Rubens and other painters of her generation, further developed this technique.

In the same painting just mentioned, there are also some corrections (known to art historians by the Italian term *pentimenti*) of the kind referred to in the description of *Still Life with Fish, Candle, Artichokes, Crabs and Shrimp* (fig.30) above. In this case we see the corrections along the contours of the left wing of the mallard where it overlaps with the rim of the basket. The wing was initially larger; a dark tone reveals its original limits. The head of the bird that emerges from under the same wing (a woodcock) was added after the basket had been painted. Corrections of this type are common in paintings from the time, yet Peeters was more careful than most in revising even the finest details.

Clara Peeters often repeated the same objects in different paintings, combining them in a variety of ways. This is the case with a salt cellar, gilt goblets and cups, some fruits and other objects. The mechanical reproduction of certain items or designs was standard practice and a well-known method of increasing production and profit for painters in the Southern Netherlands, as well as in other artistic centres in Europe, from the fifteenth century onwards. The repetition of so many elements indicates that Peeters must have kept stencils in her studio and drawn or painted models of the type that we know from other painters. For example, close to her time, Aertsen repeatedly painted the same large fruits, as did other artists such as Ludger Tom Ring (1522–84), who was active in Antwerp in the mid-sixteenth century, and also Jan Brueghel. By repeating elements, artists not only could save time, but also create a brand of sorts in the form of a set of objects that could be identified with them. Sometimes Peeters painted the same objects in different sizes, or from a different point of view. On other occasions she repeated them precisely. A salt cellar of the same size and shape is repeated in several of her paintings (figs 14, 34, 35), occupying different places in the compositions. Also repeated in her paintings are a pewter plate, a porcelain plate, a *roemer* glass with white wine, an ornate gilt standing cup and several other objects. The gilt goblet in the painting in Karlsruhe is the same as one in a private collection (figs 10, 31). When two images of the soldier that tops the cups represented in these two paintings overlap, they are nearly identical, indicating that some mechanical device was used to paint the figure. Peeters must have owned this object or had the opportunity to make a sketch of it for use in her studio. By combining the objects in different ways, however, she avoided the impression of excessive repetition that could lead to paintings being considered as versions rather than distinctly different works of art.

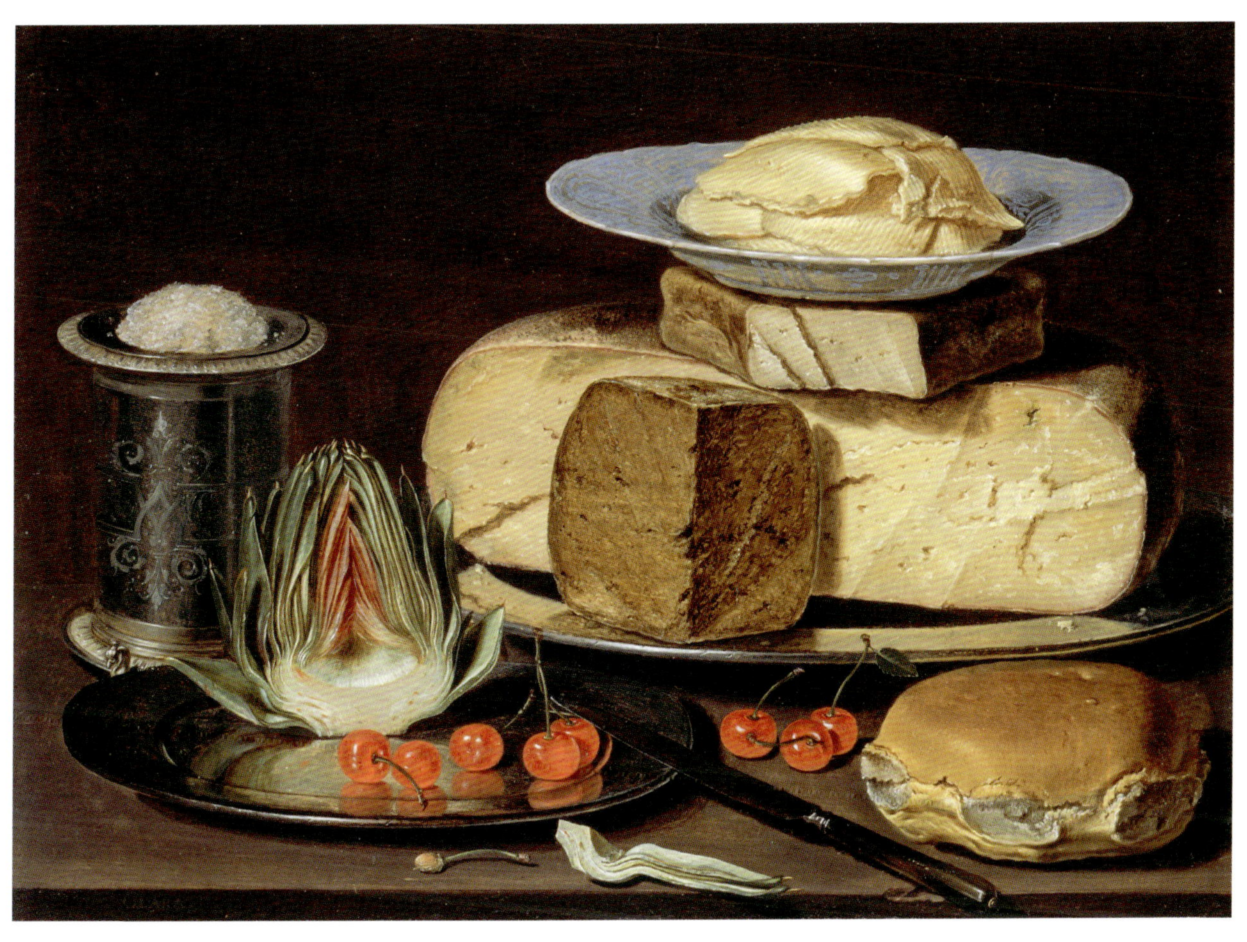

34 Clara Peeters, *Still Life with Cheeses, Artichoke, and Cherries*, c.1625, oil on panel, 33 × 47 cm (13 × 18½ in), Los Angeles County Museum of Art, CA

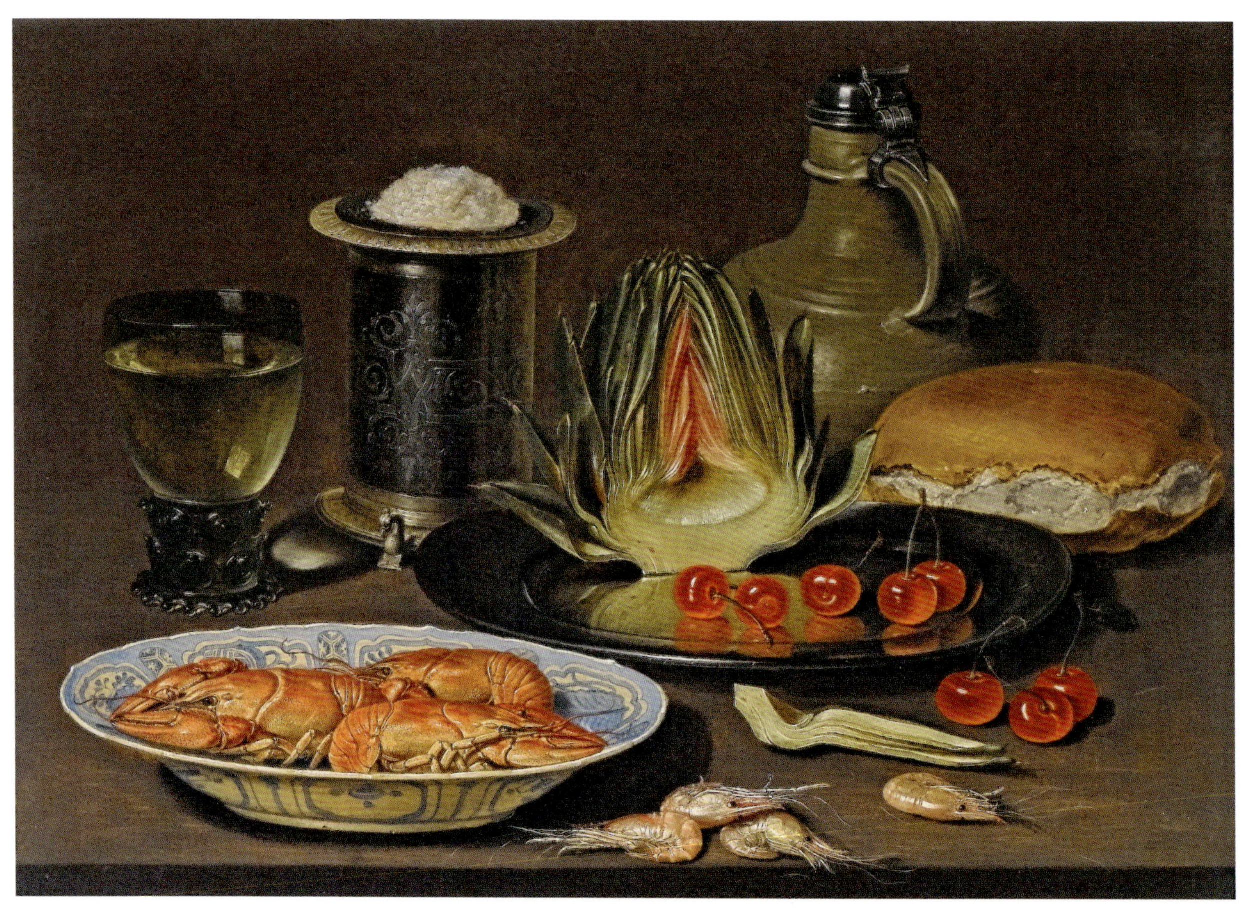

35 Clara Peeters, *Still Life with Shellfish, Salt Cellar, Artichoke and Cherries*, signed, *c*.1612–21, oil on panel, 33 × 46 cm (13 × 18⅛ in), private collection

Peeters apparently did not produce exact copies of her paintings, but in at least one case she came extremely close. The painting *Still Life with Cheeses, Almonds and Pretzels* (fig.33) is nearly identical to another picture that is reproduced in an important publication on the artist, but is otherwise unknown.[10] The differences between the two works amount to a few small details: the porcelain plate has been moved on its axis, and three almonds that are placed on the ledge or table are in the exact same place and grouped identically in both paintings, but their narrow end now points in the opposite direction. Why did the artist make such minute changes in two paintings that are otherwise identical? Whatever the reason, it is a manifestation of her scrupulous attention to detail and variation among her works.

ARTISTIC QUALITY AND ICONOGRAPHIC INNOVATION

Explaining the many repetitions in the still lifes of Clara Peeters can be confusing because they are so varied. What is important is that they show Peeters using methods that had been standard practice for well over a century, and that she repeated motifs extensively but also carefully, creating many different combinations to avoid the impression of excessive repetition. Using stencils and repeating motifs was a consequence of the economy of art in early modern Europe, where an increasing demand for paintings existed since the fifteenth century. Another response to this situation was the workshop system. This explains one of the more puzzling aspects of Peeters's art when it is considered as a whole: the striking differences of quality that exist between some of her paintings. Master painters worked with collaborators who assisted them in the preparatory stages of their works, or even in completing paintings that they had only designed. We know of this type of workshop system in the case of established painters from the Renaissance onwards, including Raphael and Titian, the Brueghel family, Rubens and a host of others.

The market for paintings was so varied in terms of demand that products of different quality and cost coexisted. A collector may have wished to purchase a high-end painting (one very carefully executed) as an example of a master's brand (a famous artist). Another may have wanted the same brand (artist), but a less expensive picture (one made by an assistant, for example). And some buyers went after works by lesser-known artists. In 1618, Rubens, who based his practice in Antwerp as Peeters did, and who was close to her in age, explained in a letter written to a collector that he could offer him paintings made by himself, others made in collaboration with specialists who painted animals and landscape backgrounds, and others made by his assistants but retouched and thus finished by him.[11] Of the entirely autograph paintings, he wrote that one was considered the best he had ever painted. The prices for all these paintings were different, determined by the degree of participation by the master painter: the greater the participation, the higher the price. This kind of production and marketing system was common.

Clara Peeters produced several tiers of paintings defined by the effort that she put into them – what can be described as their quality, in comparative terms. One group is made of works which were very carefully and skilfully executed, with a strong sense of form, a great variety of texture, conspicuous relational richness and a painstaking attention to detail. Approximately a dozen known paintings fit into this category: the four paintings in the Prado (figs 9, 14, 29, 30) and single examples in the Kunsthalle Karlsruhe (fig.10), the Mauritshuis (fig 33), the Los Angeles County Museum of Art (fig.34), The Metropolitan Museum of Art (fig.36), the flower piece in the National Museum of Women in the Arts (fig.53) and a few of the paintings that belong to private collections. To some extent this judgement of quality is subjective, for some viewers may be more sensitive to some features in paintings than others. But in most cases the effort Peeters put into a painting shows on its surface.

An example of the highest level among the paintings of Peeters is *Still Life with a Sparrow Hawk, Fowl, Porcelain and Shells* (fig.29), signed and dated in 1611, and one of the paintings that was in the Spanish royal collection by 1666. Perched on the rim of a wicker basket is a female Eurasian sparrowhawk painted approximately life size. Peeters could have sketched this bird from life as it rested on the hand of a falconer, used a bird prepared by a taxidermist, or relied on drawings or prints kept in her studio. The absence of jesses may indicate that indeed she did not use a live animal as a model. In any event, the glimmer in its eye makes it seem alert, animated with life. The larger birds in the painting are a male mallard (in the basket), a woodcock, a hen (to the left, its head hanging from the table or ledge) and a rooster, with only its tail barely visible in the background. The green colour of the tail has aged and become a dark tone, a transformation typical of green glaze copper pigments. In its original state it must have added a powerful colour accent that rhymed with the head of the mallard and contrasted with its red feet.

Two young pigeons displayed on a clay plate have been plucked in preparation for cooking; the same would presumably soon happen to the rest of the birds. Next to the pigeons is a thrush and hanging over the rim of the basket is the head of another bird of the same species. The small red bird to the right is a male common bullfinch. Peeters must have chosen this bird for its striking red colour, which is beautifully combined with the green head of the mallard. The smaller birds that hang by their neck were used for cooking by simmering in a pot or adding to a broth. They are finches, with their winter plumage, which is less colourful than during their mating season in the summer. The soft bodies and feathers of the birds are contrasted in the right

section of the painting with the hard, fine surface of porcelain and shells.

The painting *Still Life with Flowers, Gilt Goblets, Coins and Shells* (fig.10) which Peeters signed and dated in 1612, demonstrates the painter's adaptability in terms of an unusual composition among her works: vertical instead of horizontal. The placement of the objects is skilfully adapted to this format. A table is laid with two gilt cups, both with a finial topped by soldiers. One of the cups has a lobed body. Discussed in Chapter 1 regarding the reflected self-portraits of the artist, this example is unique among her known self-portraits insofar as she holds a palette and brushes. The two gilt goblets belong to a type that was made from the second half of the sixteenth century in Germany, mainly in Nuremberg, but also in Strasbourg and other cities. A number of these exquisite cups survive. To the left is a ceramic vase with an assortment of flowers that is sparser but equally exquisite as others that we see in paintings by Peeters, and between the two gilt cups is a plate of *kraak* porcelain, an export of Ming China, with a chain inside. As she also did in *Still Life with a Sparrow Hawk, Fowl, Porcelain and Shells*, Peeters painted four shells next to the porcelain plate, calling attention to the exotic origin of both, and to the similarity of the materials. All these objects overlap thoughtfully, and their proportions and colour scheme stress the concept of elegance.

The painting *Still Life with Cheeses, Almonds and Pretzels* (fig.33), which is inscribed with the artist's name but undated, demonstrates Peeters's passion for the precise rendering of detail, and her inclination and talent for contrasting and harmonising different shapes, textures and colours. On a stone ledge are displayed a tin plate with a stack of cheeses and a plate with butter. In the foreground are two pretzels, a silver knife and a blue and white porcelain plate with almonds, dried figs and raisins. To the right are a *façon de Venise* covered glass and a roll of white bread. A stoneware jug from Raeren is at the back. On its metal

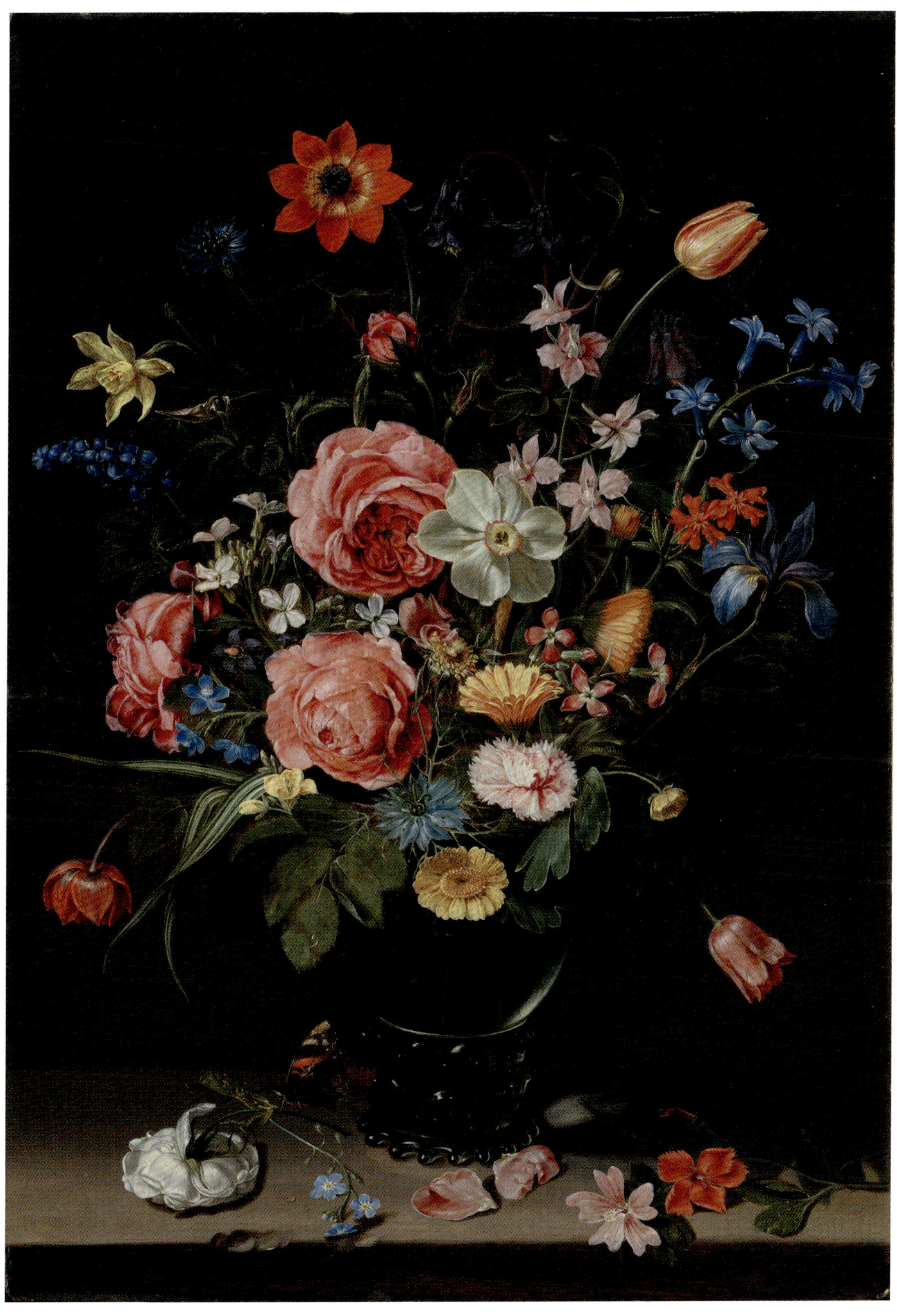

36 Clara Peeters, *A Bouquet of Flowers*, c.1612, oil on panel, 46 × 32 cm (18 ⅛ × 12 ⅝ in), The Metropolitan Museum of Art, New York

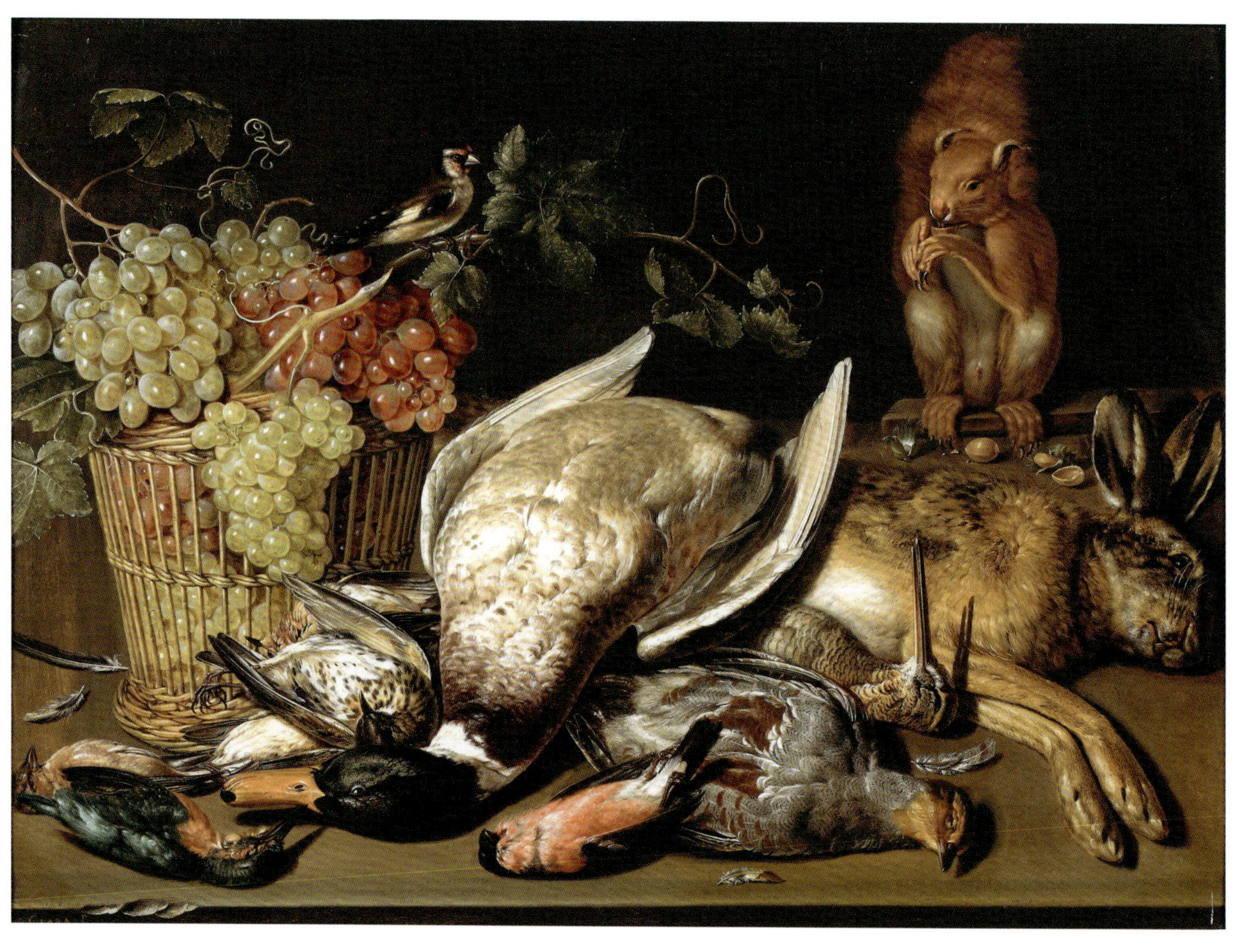

37 Clara Peeters, *A Basket of Grapes, a Goldfinch, Game and a Squirrel*, signed, *c.*1612–21, oil on panel, 51 × 75 cm (20 ⅛ × 29 ½ in), private collection

lid we can see another reflected self-portrait of the artist. The textures of the different surfaces are rendered with extreme care. There is an aesthetic tension between the different but similar shapes and tones of the objects that contemporaries must have found satisfying, perhaps even remarkable. The painting has been cut down by a few millimetres on all four sides (as indicated by a report from the museum). This alters the composition just slightly, making it more compressed than Peeters intended; such a tight cropping of a composition is not characteristic of the artist. Changes such as this, or alterations in tone mentioned above for other paintings, are common in paintings that are over 400 years old.

Several flower paintings by Peeters are equally of striking quality. A *Bouquet of Flowers* (fig.36) shows a variety of plants in a *roemer* glass set dramatically against a dark background. Among them are tulips, roses, narcissi, daisies, carnations, irises, dropping anemones and others. Paintings such as these were meant to be closely and carefully observed. Attentive looking reveals additional features such as dew drops and a red admiral butterfly. Like the nick in the edge of the ledge in the left foreground, these elements underscore the ability of the artist to create pictorial illusionism. Her skill with these effects is apparent as well in the carefully executed *Still Life with Fish, Candle, Artichokes, Crabs and Shrimp* (fig.30), signed and dated 1611. In the painting we see several objects: a dark glass goblet, a brass candlestick with a partially burnt but flameless candle, a copper strainer with a brass skimmer and two artichokes, and a Rhenish stoneware jug with a self-portrait reflected on its lid. The burnt candle adds a temporal quality to the image. Laid before these objects on a wooden table or ledge are boiled crabs and shrimp and several freshwater fish (two carp, a roach, possibly several ides and a northern pike).

Still Life with Fish, Candle, Artichokes, Crabs and Shrimp points to an important virtue of Clara Peeters that must have added value to her work: her iconographical innovation. This is the earliest known fish still life painted in Europe (albeit this kind of 'first' status can easily change as new paintings come to light). A similar virtue illuminates her paintings with references to falconry (fig.29), which apparently are the first still lifes devoted to the activity in Europe, where innovation of this kind was valued. Antwerp was no different. Clearly Peeters was sensitive to the penchant for new approaches and features and produced paintings accordingly. Her reflected self-portraits, discussed in Chapter 1, are one indication of this, and the decision to make fish the central elements of a still life, or to incorporate falconry, are others. These new approaches to painting are indicative of someone who skilfully tapped into contemporary interests and who was sensitive to the desires of discerning buyers.

WORKSHOP PRODUCTS AND DISSEMINATION

Beyond the paintings that were made with the greatest care is another category of pictures also signed by the artist in which the forms are more generalised and are painted with less effort, adjustments to repeated objects are less carefully concealed and the backgrounds are painted more succinctly. These works' quality suggests they were made by assistants who must have worked for Peeters. An example of this kind of painting is *A Basket of Grapes, a Goldfinch, Game and a Squirrel* (fig.37),[12] which is signed by Peeters. In this work, some parts are beautifully painted, such as the texture of the feathers of the mallard or the fur of the hare. Others, such as the bird perched on the stem of a grapevine, are too schematic. The overall impression is additive, as if more than one hand was at work. This impression probably stems from the participation of collaborators.

More revealing of the collaboration of workshop assistants is an analysis of three extant versions of a painting showing a peregrine falcon perched on

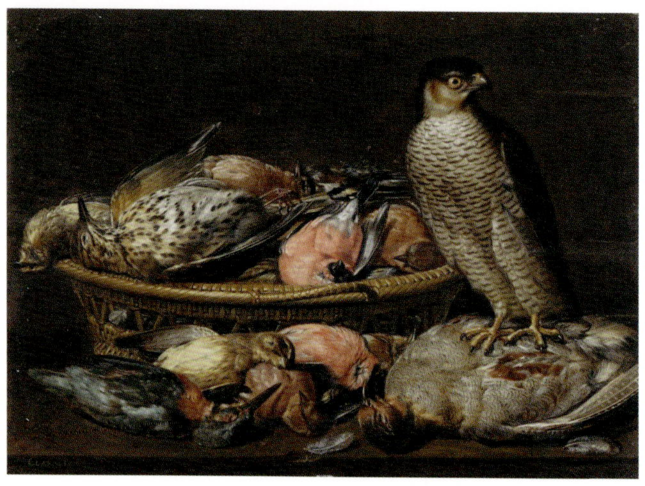

38 Clara Peeters, *Still Life with Game*, c.1612–21, oil on panel, 33 × 46 cm (13 × 18⅛ in), Art Museum of Estonia, Tallinn

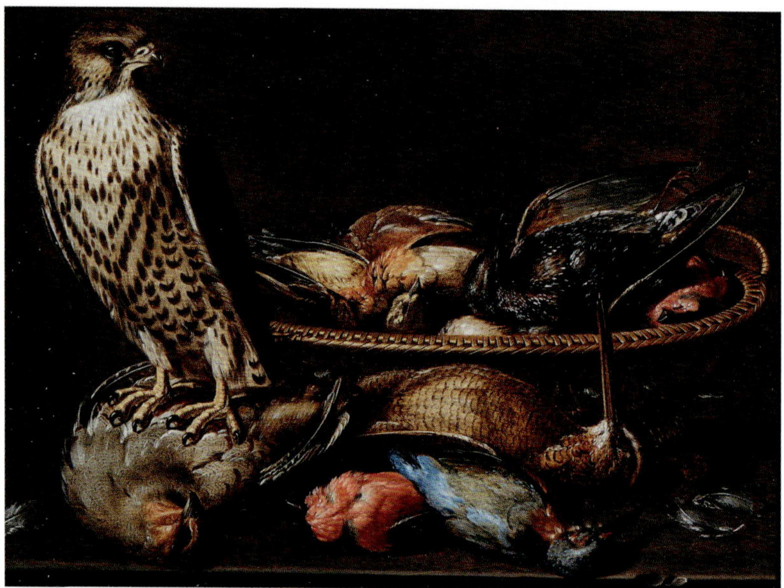

39 Clara Peeters, *Still Life with a Peregrine Falcon and its Prey*, c.1612–21, oil on panel, 33 × 46 cm (13 × 18⅛ in), private collection, Antwerp

40 (below) Nicolaes Cave, *Still Life with a Peregrine Falcon and its Prey*, c.1625, oil on panel, 35 × 54 cm (13¾ × 21¼ in), location unknown

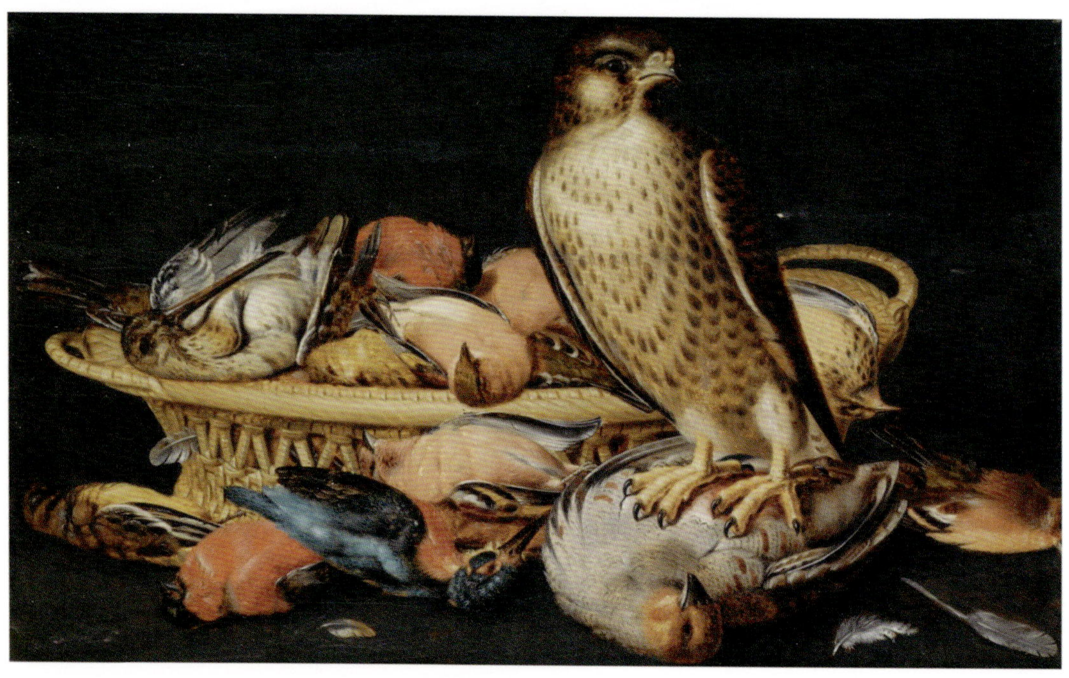

top of a partridge. A version in the Art Museum of Estonia appears to be the most carefully painted (fig.38). In another version (fig.39) some parts are equally skilful and suggest that Peeters was personally involved in its making: many of the birds are true to life and painted with characteristic care. The feet of the raptor appear too thick, however, and the toes too short for an animal that is primarily a bird hunter (they are more appropriate for a hunter of small mammals, such as a kestrel). Also noticeable is the schematic rendering of the feather pattern on the breast and belly of the falcon and of the body of the partridge. The neck of the partridge that lies under the falcon is rendered as a long curve that appears unnatural and summary, and thus at odds with the pictorial language of the diligent Peeters. These same traits are visible in a third picture (fig.40).[13] Interestingly, this is signed by an unknown painter: Nicolaes Cave. The painting is a partial repetition of Peeters's compositions (the similarities with the two paintings of falcons just described are evident). These similarities suggest the possibility that Cave worked as an assistant of Peeters, and that he later went on to make versions of her still lifes.[14] As a workshop collaborator, he could be the painter responsible for some parts of paintings by Peeters that are not produced to her best standards.

Drawing conclusions regarding authorship from this kind of information is not an exact science. The best explanation for the discrepancy in quality between the different paintings by Peeters is that she worked to streamline her studio production.[15] Perhaps she painted parts of these works (figs 38, 39), and other similar paintings herself, leaving the rest unfinished. Clients could then choose the details – the type of bird they wanted, for example – or propose another way to fill the composition. An assistant would complete the scene using models. We know this method of making paintings from the fifteenth century onwards, when some compositions were repeated by artists who introduced variations at the will of a client, such as changing the image of one saint for another. However, in the case of Peeters, pertinent documentation such as correspondence with collectors or others has not emerged. Also, we do not have a very clear idea of the different events that affected her life. We do not even know the dates of many of her still lifes. With the high level of accomplishment in some of her paintings, it is surprising that there are so few of them. More must have existed. The frequent repetitions and the lower quality of some works are signs of at least a relatively high volume of production and presumably a sufficient income (although it is possible that another source was available to her, presumably from her family or husband, as was the case with other artists such as Hieronymus Bosch and Johannes Vermeer (1632–75)). We do not know if these pictures were painted simultaneously with her higher-end products, as seems most logical and as was usually the case with artists, or if they were the consequence of events in her life that shaped how she went about her profession at a given point in time. If, as assumed in this study, she is the same person as Clara Lamberts, the house that her husband purchased in 1609 had to be mortgaged a year later, and in 1621 it was transferred to a creditor. In 1630 she still lived in Antwerp but in 1636 she and her husband had moved to Ghent where she received money from her siblings in exchange for her part of their parents' will. Perhaps financial pressure forced Clara to increase her production and lower its quality in order to sell more paintings and raise the family income.

There is no direct evidence for the way in which the paintings by Clara Peeters reached their owners. None are of the type of subjects that most often involved direct commissions, such as altarpieces. Formal portraits were also contracted by or for a sitter, but we have no information on the single known portrait by Peeters (fig.16), which could have represented her or someone else. Some of the most important collectors of the early seventeenth century have been shown to have commissioned varieties of still-life paintings directly from leading artists such as Jan Brueghel or Frans Snyders. Among them were Cardinal Borromeo of Milan and Philip IV of Spain (the courts of London, Paris, The Hague and Prague also collected still lifes). The two still lifes by Peeters that were owned by the Spanish King do not necessarily prove that he sought works by her; the fact that they are first documented in the seventeenth century as anonymous suggests that they were not. Despite some examples of very high patronage, most still-life paintings were made to be sold in the open market.[16]

Peeters may have exported her art through dealers, which would explain the wide distribution of her paintings beyond her homeland, in collections from the United Provinces of the Netherlands to Spain. The case of Jacob van Hulsdonck, the Antwerp still-life painter who was a contemporary of Peeters and who worked in a similar style, provides an example of this practice. In the late 1630s, some of his paintings were offered to Philippe-Charles d'Arenberg, Duke of Aarschot (1587–1640), a leading aristocrat from the Southern Netherlands (at the time he was being held in home internment in Madrid). We know from his correspondence that the Duke gathered an important collection of paintings in Madrid by using agents: the painter Salomon Noveliers, the unknown Felipe d'Ursel from Brussels and Antonio Lasser from Antwerp. In April 1639, Aarschot asked his dealers for 'paintings of flowers and other things' and received a response stating that Van Hulsdonck offered to paint them for a reasonable price, although in the end the Duke did not buy the paintings.[17] Peeters must have considered Antwerp's export economy to be of great benefit for artists like her who wished to market their works widely: it contributed to spreading her reputation as a leading still-life painter beyond the Southern Netherlands to other parts of Europe.

4

Social Practice and Material Culture

Clara Peeters's life as an artist coincided with a time of dramatic transformation in all areas of life in Europe. Changes in the economic and social order, the enlarging of the known world as the result of exploration and conquest, and the growth of scientific explanations for natural phenomena all threatened established truths and created a sense of crisis. Elite sectors of society – encompassing the kind of people who collected quality paintings – responded with curiosity towards the new, and at the same time reaffirmed traditional privileges and customs from which they benefitted. The objects that appear in Peeters's paintings reflect the social practices and material realities of early modernity, and they provide an opportunity to learn about them. Although she was an occasional iconographic innovator, most often her paintings suggest a desire to tap into both established and novel cultural interests to enhance her reputation as a painter.

COLLECTING

In choosing subjects for her paintings, Clara Peeters responded to the interests of contemporary collectors to increase the marketability of her art. The objects represented in her still lifes can in many ways be considered painted versions of collections formed in

Europe during her lifetime, including in Antwerp. The practice of dedicated collecting arose in the fourteenth century and was significant enough to become the subject of books by the sixteenth. One such volume is *Inscriptiones* (Munich, 1565) by Samuel Quiccheberg, a Fleming by birth who moved to Nuremberg as a child and later worked for Albert V of Bavaria. The book is a practical guide for princes and other elite collectors who wanted to assemble 'exemplary objects and exceptional images of the entire world'. These included objects from nature (*naturalia*) and works of art, religious objects, coins, precious objects, examples of cartography, weapons, armour and other fabricated items (*artefacta*). He wrote that these items served 'to enhance the refinement of the entire world and to illuminate all disciplines of study', adding that they were 'objects that are pleasant to observe'.[1] Collections and collecting were therefore signs of elevated social standing as well as sources of pleasure.

Paintings were an important part of the collector's vision. Clara Peeters and other artists of the early seventeenth century benefitted from this aspect of the practice, for it enlarged the market for their works. It also led to new iconographies, including images of collectors' cabinets or *constkamers*. As discussed in Chapter 2 in relation to artistic innovations in Antwerp in Peeters's era, these images of multidisciplinary collecting variously included paintings hanging on the wall, coins, Chinese porcelain, silver and gilt cups, jewellery, shells and other objects of interest, usually shown with elegant observers looking on (fig.19). Commissioned portraits sometimes featured objects that a collector presumably had amassed, thereby implying elevated economic and social status and a refined intellect: a likeness of the Dutch merchant Jan Govertsz. van der Aar by Hendrick Goltzius (1558–1617) of 1603 shows the subject proudly studying his collection of marine shells (Museum Boijmans Van Beuningen, Rotterdam).

Among the abundant testimonies of the taste for the type of interdisciplinary collecting made evident in the *constkamer* paintings is the correspondence of 1590 between the Flemish garden designer and naturalist Jodocus de Goethuysen (known in Italy as Giuseppe Casabona; d.1595) and Vincenzo Gonzaga, Duke of Mantua. Goethuysen wrote to the Duke describing the interesting plants that he had seen in Candia, Crete, which he had asked a German artist to illustrate. In the same letter he added: 'Here in Candia beautiful peregrine falcons are to be found. If you need some, I can take care of it for you.'[2] In this case, one collector offered to assist another in expanding the number and type of objects he owned. Rulers such as Philip II of Spain and his nephew Rudolf II are models of this type of elite collector. They gathered in their palaces in Madrid and Prague works of art and books documenting the wonders of the world; exotic attire and other objects from America, China and elsewhere; exotic animals and remains of rare animals; stones and shells of different types.[3]

SHELLS

The marine shells in Clara Peeters's paintings capitalised on the contemporary fascination with *naturalia* of this kind. Several of her works include shells of non-European origin. Their perceived exoticism made them valued in Europe, along with their peculiar beauty, intriguing shapes, and surface glosses and textures.[4] In *The Beach* of 1611, the Dutch poet Philibert van Borsselen praised shells for how they shined and compared them to works of art. Collectors stored shells in cabinets and boxes and brought them out to hold: touching, not only seeing, was a way of appreciating these objects. Some shells were considered so singular that they were mounted in precious metal.

Shells had interested people throughout the world as objects for personal adornment and as currency for millennia. In Europe, the ancient Greeks studied shells and referred to their wondrous shapes and beauty, while also considering their origin and function, as Aristotle did in his book on biology titled *Parts of Animals*. Pliny the Elder discussed shells extensively in his *Natural History*, stating, for example, that 'the shell of murex or other shell-fish reduced to ash clears spots from the faces of women, remove wrinkles, and fill out the skin, if applied with honey for seven days'.[5] Cicero famously wrote in *De Oratore* of men who collected shells as a form of mental rejuvenation necessary because '[. . .] our human minds, when worn out by the business of the Courts and the work of the City, grow restless and yearn to go a-roving, in freedom from worry [. . .]'.[6]

The fascination with marine shells exhibited in the paintings of Peeters therefore had a long history. They became a focus again in the early modern period, as part of a renewed interest in exotic objects and the natural world. The first books on shells were published in the 1550s. Works of art by Jacopo Zucchi (*The Treasures of the Sea*, painted for Francesco I Medici *c.*1560) and Joris Hoefnagel (*Mira calligraphiae monumenta*, which Hoefnagel illustrated in the 1590s) contribute to demonstrating this revival. Shells were imported to Europe via different commercial and colonial routes, likely Dutch, Portuguese and Spanish. They were used as currency, to pay for the enslaved

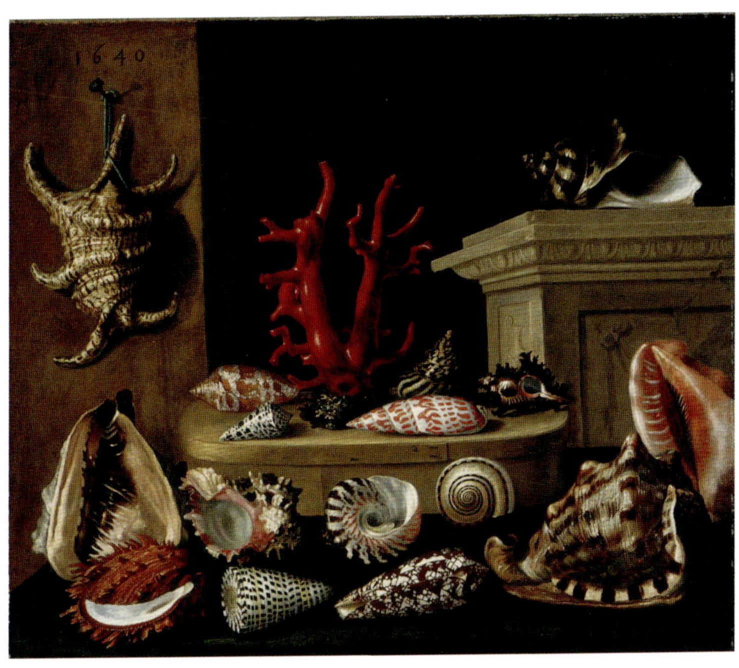

41 Jacques Linard, *Still Life with Shells and Coral*, 1640, oil on canvas, 53.3 × 62.2 cm (21 × 24 ½ in),
The Montreal Museum of Fine Arts

people who gathered them, among other things. They also were increasingly incorporated into collections, such as that of Jan Govertsz. van der Aar. Some shells could reach very high prices, which occasionally brought criticism to the practice of collecting. In the emblem book *Sinne-Poppen* by Roemer Visscher, published in Amsterdam in 1614, an image of several shells is accompanied by the statement 'It is annoying what people spend their money on.'[7] Like every object in the paintings by Peeters, their cost and luxurious associations could have an admonitory meaning. Yet they continued to be the subjects of paintings, whether as primary or secondary elements, as seen to an unusual degree in *Still Life with Shells and Coral* (fig.41) by Jacques Linard (1597–1645), a leading still-life painter from France. Artists also found ways to incorporate them into mythological paintings, as did Jacques de Gheyn II, who painted

Amphitrite and Cupid with a Nautilus Shell (Wallraf-Richartz Museum, Cologne, fig.55) in which shells, large and small, figure prominently.

The presence of shells in still-life paintings by Clara Peeters and others is further evidence of their interest to collectors. In the painting *Still Life with a Sparrow Hawk, Fowl, Porcelain and Shells* (fig.29) is a reddish *Harpa harpa* from the Indo-Pacific region; next to it a *Harpa doris* from the West African coast; and below them a *Hexaplex rosarium* from the same region, and a black and white Caribbean *Cittarium pica*. In *Still Life with Flowers, Gilt Goblets, Coins and Shells* (fig.10) Peeters painted the same four shells, and again, she placed them next to a porcelain dish, calling attention to the exotic origin of both, and to the similarity of the materials. In *Still Life with Tart, Silver Tazza, Porcelain and Oysters* (fig.42) foodstuffs and collectibles share a tabletop with three exotic shells. Peeters repeats here a *Harpa doris* and adds a *Conus genuanus* from the western coast of Africa and the Indian Ocean, and a *Conus marmoreus* from the Indian and the Pacific Ocean.

Peeters easily could have observed and even acquired shells, for they were as prized, and as present, in Antwerp as they were elsewhere. She represented the same shells in several paintings, which suggests that she owned them or had made studies of some she had observed to store in her studio for reference. Other artists possessed them as well, and some exported them. Frans Francken the Elder (1542–1616), father of Hieronymus and of the more famous Frans Francken the Younger mentioned in Chapter 2, owned 'a big box with three drawers of shells', 'two mother of pearls shells' and 'two large *kieckhorens*'.[8] In 1606, Jan Brueghel wrote to his patron Federico Borromeo in Milan that he was sending him a small box with 12 rare and beautiful shells of the type that were arriving from India on Dutch ships. He added that he was making a painting of flowers which would also include a piece of jewellery, medals and '*rarita del maro*' ('rarities from the sea').[9] One of the five paintings in the *Five Senses* series in the Prado by Jan Brueghel, *Sight*, which the author signed and dated in 1617, includes a group of shells on the lower right corner gathered in a lacquer box, another exotic import. In the painting by Frans Francken the Younger, *Ulysses Recognising Achilles among the Daughters of Lycomedes*, painted after 1620 (Musée du Louvre, Paris), numerous exotic shells are shown on a table. In this context, in addition to standing for the exotic commodity that they were, the shells can also be considered symbolically, based on their shapes, which invoke female and male sexual organs. They encourage viewers to see this as a painting about a young man disguised as a woman.

The prestige of shell collecting in Antwerp is demonstrated by the frequent presence of exotic shells in paintings of collectors' cabinets made by artists in the city. They are conspicuous in *constkamer* paintings by Frans Francken the Younger and are present in works by many others, sometimes with politicised associations. In the picture known as *The Sciences and the Arts* (fig.19) by Adriaen van Stalbent (1580–1662), a group of distinguished connoisseurs, elegantly dressed and wearing swords that are a sign of their high status, study maps, paintings and shells gathered on a table, among other goods – one of the men holds a shell. Two more seashells sit on the mantle shelf of a fireplace in the background. On the floor is a painting that shows animals dressed as men destroying works of art. They are a clear reference to the Protestant iconoclasts who had destroyed religious paintings in Catholic churches in Antwerp and other cities in the Southern Netherlands in the sixteenth century. The message is clear: gentlemen from the Catholic South are more civilised than their Protestant counterparts in the United Provinces of the Netherlands to the North. Collecting and studying exotic marine shells was part of what these sophisticated southerners did (notwithstanding the fact that all over Europe men of high class shared the same interests and collecting habits). When Clara Peeters included similar shells in her still-life pictures, she was offering viewers images of that which was highly prized.

IMPORTED TABLEWARE

Imported Chinese porcelain plates are present in several paintings by Peeters. These objects reflect a growing interest in Asian cultures as well as Peeters's choice to include them to elevate interest in her paintings. Chinese ceramicists developed and specialised in the technique of making porcelain. The name derives from the Italian term *porcellana*, used for a type of white shell. This is what came to mind for the first Europeans who saw the fine, translucent surface of this chinaware. The 1298 account of Marco Polo's voyage to China is the earliest known surviving text to use the term for both shells and porcelain objects.[10] These Chinese ceramics began to trickle

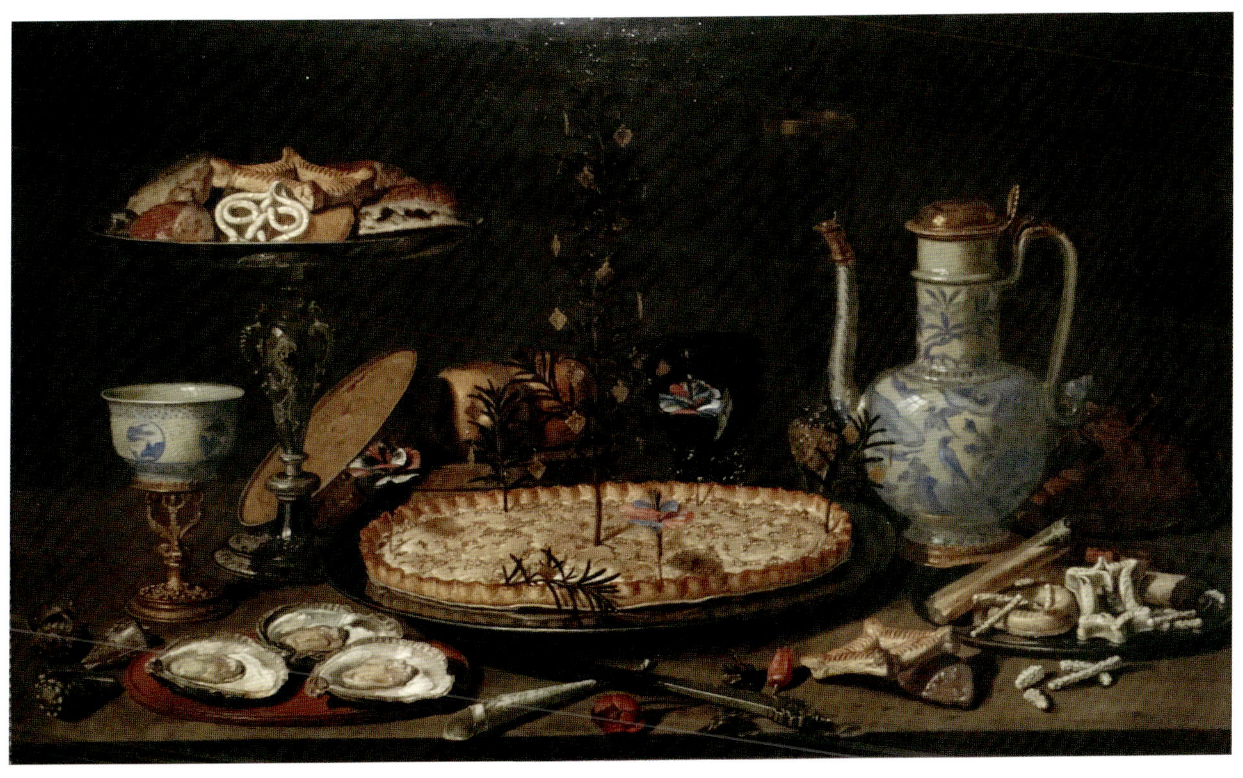

42 Clara Peeters, *Still Life with Tart, Silver Tazza, Porcelain and Oysters*, inscribed with the artist's name on the knife, *c.*1612–13, oil on panel, 52 × 84 cm (20 ½ × 33 ⅛ in), private collection, Russia

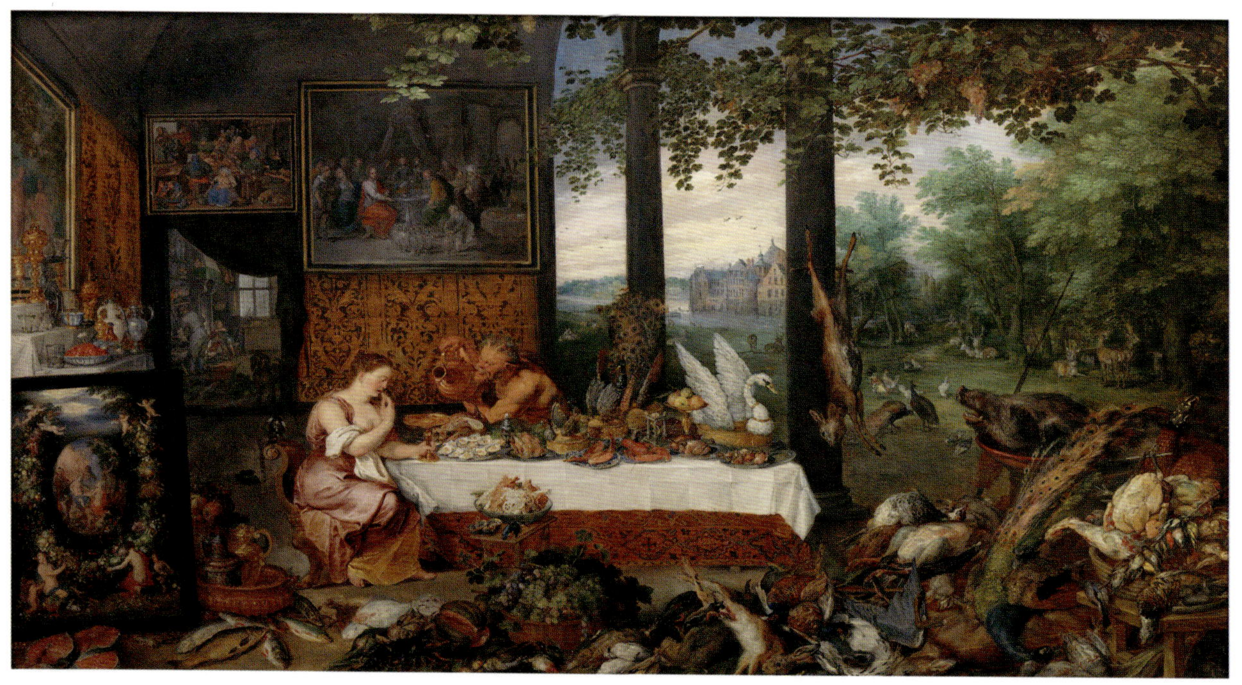

43 Jan Brueghel the Elder and Peter Paul Rubens, *The Sense of Taste*, from the series *The Five Senses*, 1618, oil on panel, 64 × 109 cm (25 ¼ × 42 ⅞ in), Museo Nacional del Prado, Madrid

into Europe during the Renaissance, much of them via Portugal. They were seen by the European elite as exotic goods, and as such were painted by Andrea Mantegna in an *Adoration of the Magi* of *c*.1500 (The J. Paul Getty Museum, Los Angeles, CA) and Giovanni Bellini in *The Feast of the Gods* of 1514 (National Gallery of Art, Washington, DC), among other rare examples. Works by Peeters and other still-life painters such as Frans Snyders show how these objects were sometimes mounted on gilt stands (figs 21, 42), a sign of their high valuation by collectors.

Indeed, by the early sixteenth century collecting porcelain was a sign of rare distinction among the European elite. In the Southern Netherlands, the governor Margaret of Austria owned approximately 15 pieces of porcelain that she kept in her palace in Mechelen in 1524, many adorned with silver-gilt handles and lids. Her nephew, the Emperor Charles V, also kept a few rare porcelain pieces adorned with silver chains and lids in his Brussels palace.[11] When visiting Antwerp in 1520, Dürer received three pieces of porcelain as gifts from a Portuguese host.[12] In the last quarter of the century small amounts of porcelain were recorded in ten private collections in the city, coinciding with the growth of the collection of Philip II of Spain, who was also King of Portugal after 1580, who assembled over 3000 pieces before his death in 1598. This was the largest collection in Europe at the time, which he housed in a special section of his palace in Madrid. These objects were probably a combination of purchases in Lisbon and Seville and gifts. And it was also through gifts, in this case by the King, that porcelain spread throughout the Habsburg network and reached several courts in Europe. The King's daughter Isabel Clara Eugenia already collected porcelain before leaving Spain to govern the Southern Netherlands, and once in Brussels gathered additional pieces. In 1602 she received a shipment of approximately 300 pieces that had belonged to her father, and in 1603 her brother, King Philip III, sent her 1500 items of porcelain. A

room in the Coudenberg, the Archduke's palace in Brussels, was referred to as '*caemer vande porceleynen*' ('the porcelain room') in 1609–11.[13] (This collection inspired Jan Brueghel to include porcelain in three of the paintings in the series of the five senses that he painted in 1617–18 (fig.43), which is an ideal representation of goods owned by the Archdukes, and also the inclusion of porcelain in paintings by Snyders (fig.21) and other Flemish artists close to the court.) In Antwerp in 1606 a man named Servaas Wouters dealt in porcelain and other types of objects. In 1617, Isabel da Vega, the widow of the important Antwerp banker and merchant Emmanuel Ximenes (1564–1632), listed several dozen pieces in her possession which were kept in a 'small porcelain room'.[14]

The porcelain illustrated in Peeters's paintings was made during a period in which Chinese artists developed new types, partly in response to European interests. By the last quarter of the sixteenth century, during the reigns of Wanli (1572–1620) and his successors, the Jingdezhen kilns in Jiangxi province started to produce blue and white porcelain vessels and also light grey monochrome dishes that became known as *kraak* porcelain (possibly because of the ships known as *carracas*, with which their import was associated).[15] It was made primarily for export to Japan, Southeast Asia and Europe, and exported through Portuguese and Spanish commercial routes, from Macao to Manila, both part of the Habsburg Empire, and from there to Acapulco, in Mexico. It then travelled overland to Veracruz, where it joined other goods from the Americas being shipped to Lisbon and Seville. Large quantities of *kraak* porcelain arrived in the Northern Netherlands for the first time with the capture by the Dutch of two Portuguese ships, the *São Tiago* and the *Santa Catarina*, in 1601 and 1603 in Southeast Asia, with the porcelain they carried auctioned in Middelburg and Amsterdam.[16] The Dutch traded in these objects enthusiastically. In 1607 the director of the Dutch East India Company wrote that 'one cannot bring enough [porcelain] [...] Even if one should

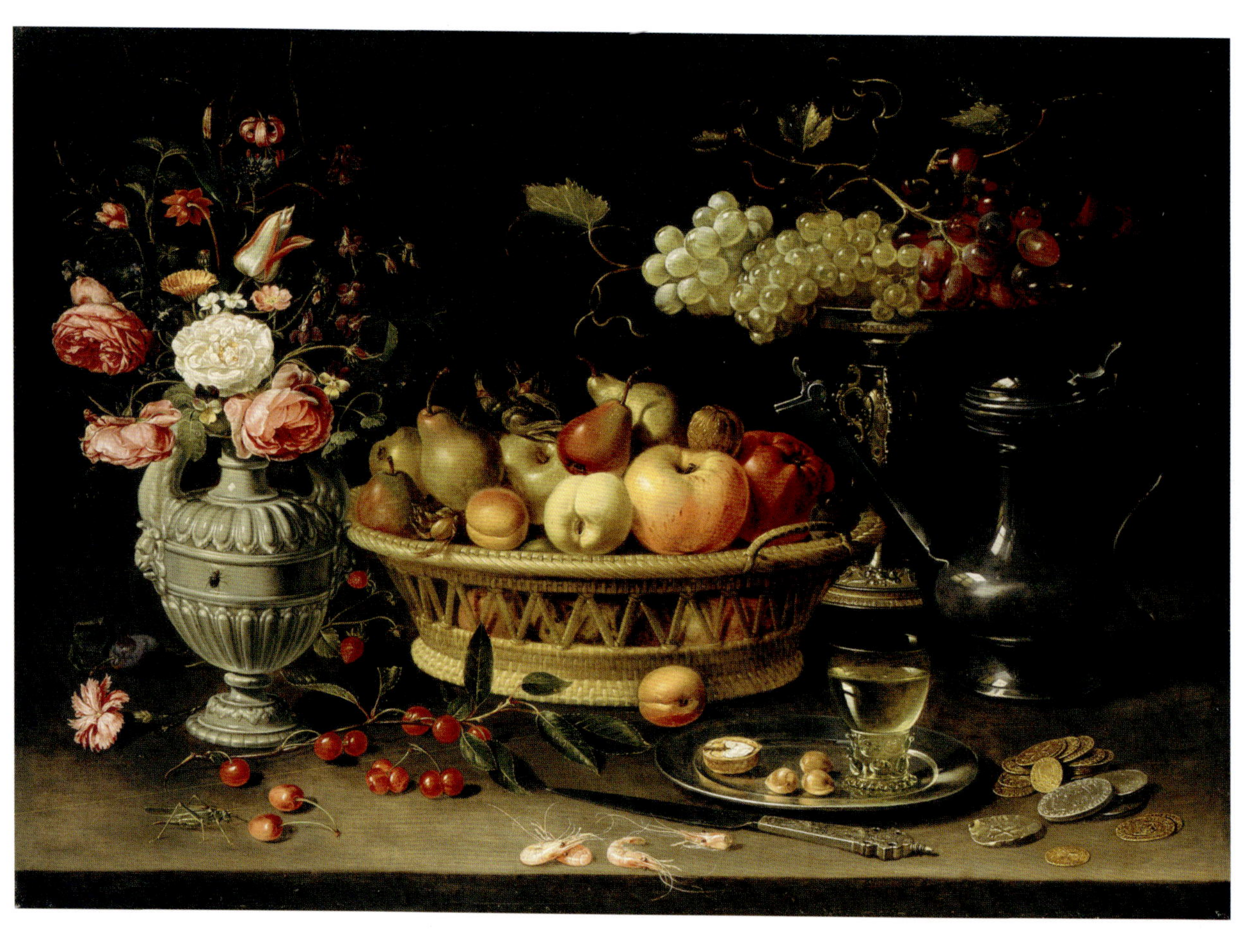

44 Clara Peeters, *Still Life with Fruits and Flowers*, inscribed with the artist's name on the knife, 1612–13, oil on copper, 64 × 89 cm (25 ¼ × 35 in), The Ashmolean, Oxford

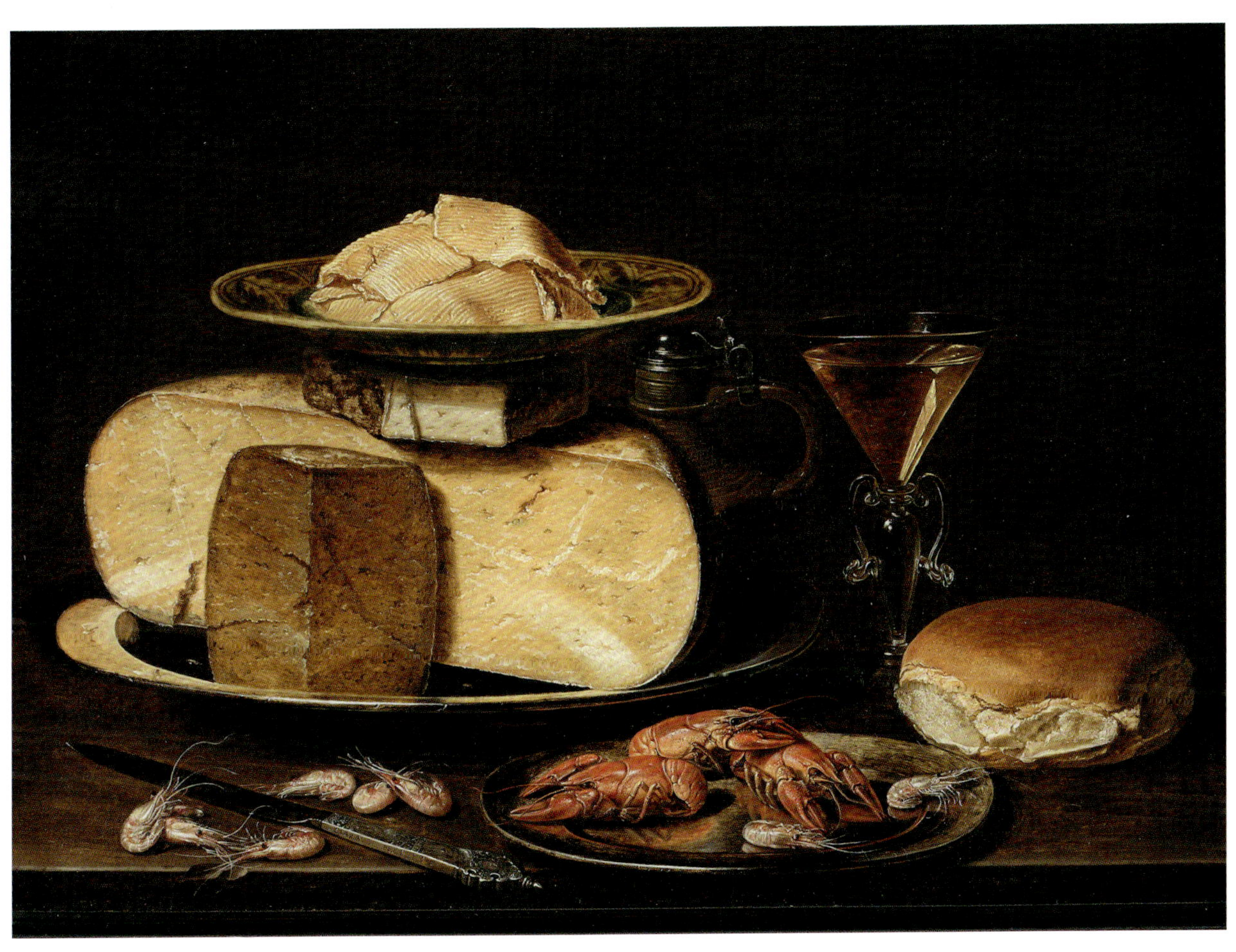

45 Clara Peeters, *Still Life with Cheeses, Shrimp and Crayfish*, inscribed with the artist's name on the knife, *c.*1612–21, oil on panel, 41 × 58 cm (16 ⅛ × 22 ⅞ in), private collection, Antwerp

bring 50,000 [pieces] they can be sold.'[17] This is the
type of porcelain evident in Peeters's *Still Life with
Cheeses, Almonds and Pretzels* (fig.33). In *Still Life with
a Sparrow Hawk, Fowl, Porcelain and Shells* (fig.29),
several plates and bowls of white *kraak* porcelain are
stacked on top of a blue and white *kraak* plate (now
partially discoloured).

Certain paintings by Peeters demonstrate her
exposure to other types of tableware from abroad,
or to images or reproductions of them. The Italian
earthenware maiolica appears as a plate with butter
above a stack of cheeses in *Still Life with Cheeses,
Almonds and Pretzels* (fig.33), which also includes an
earthenware pitcher of a type that was made in Raeren,
a German-speaking town on the current Belgian–
German border. Pitchers of this type were used to serve
drinks, mainly beer. They were more expensive than
the earthenware produced in Antwerp because they
were more resistant. Water or beer was poured into this
type of vessel from larger containers, and then taken to
the table. Wine would have been served from flagons
made of more expensive materials. A frequent presence
in Peeters's paintings are silver standing cups or *tazze*
inspired by Italian prototypes, some of them holding
an assortment of candied fruit and confections (fig.42)
or of fresh fruits (fig.44).

Other tableware of international origin or
inspiration that appears in Peeters's still lifes also
invokes wealth, good taste and worldliness. *Façon
de Venise* blown glass is visible in several of her
paintings, as it is in still lifes by Osias Beert and
other contemporaries working in Antwerp. In *Still
Life with Cheeses, Shrimp and Crayfish* (fig.45), the
winged Venetian-style glass adds a note of distinction
to the scene. In *Still Life with Flowers, Gilt Goblet,
Eatables and a Pewter Flagon* (fig.9) there is a fluted
glass in the background that contains red wine. In
this same picture, dried fruits and sugar candy fill
a large *bianchi di Faenza* vessel, a type of Italian
earthenware made in Faenza in the late sixteenth and
early seventeenth centuries. Very similar bowls are

included in a still life by Juan van der Hamen painted
in Spain, and in another by Roelof Koets probably
painted in Haarlem.[18] Regarding the Venetian-style
glass, Ludovico Guicciardini wrote in 1567 that there
was a glasshouse in Antwerp 'where all kind of crystal
glasses in the Venetian manner are made by Jacomo
Pasquetti of Brescia at great cost and with various
privileges of the king and the city'.[19] In the early
seventeenth century this business was flourishing,
with eight Italian master blowers working in the
glasshouse.[20] Documents confirm that, at least up
to the political and religious conflicts of the 1570s,
living rooms in the better houses in Antwerp were
furnished to display glass cases and glasses, including
façon de Venise, in addition to dishes of different
types, textiles, shining pewter mirrors and other
items.[21] Locally produced objects were also present in
these households. In several paintings by Peeters we
also see *roemers* (figs 1, 35) with their raspberry-like
doornnoppen on the stems for a better grip, useful,
probably, because of the custom of eating with the
hands instead of with forks.

CULINARY RITUALS AND THEIR STAGINGS

The still lifes of Clara Peeters sometimes reflect aspects
of contemporary social events and gatherings for
which people attached a special significance to the
culinary arts, such as weddings and different kinds of
anniversaries, a goal of which was to display status.
Numerous written descriptions from the early modern
period, as well as paintings of celebrations and feasts,
testify to displays and performances that were central
to these enactments, which were visually and materially
elaborate. Peeters's scenes underscore the significance
of ritualised objects as markers of refinement and,
as well, her understanding of the importance of
translating them into the language of painting.

During the Renaissance, courts across Europe
expanded and codified the use of the kinds of luxury
objects to which the paintings of Peeters refer. A

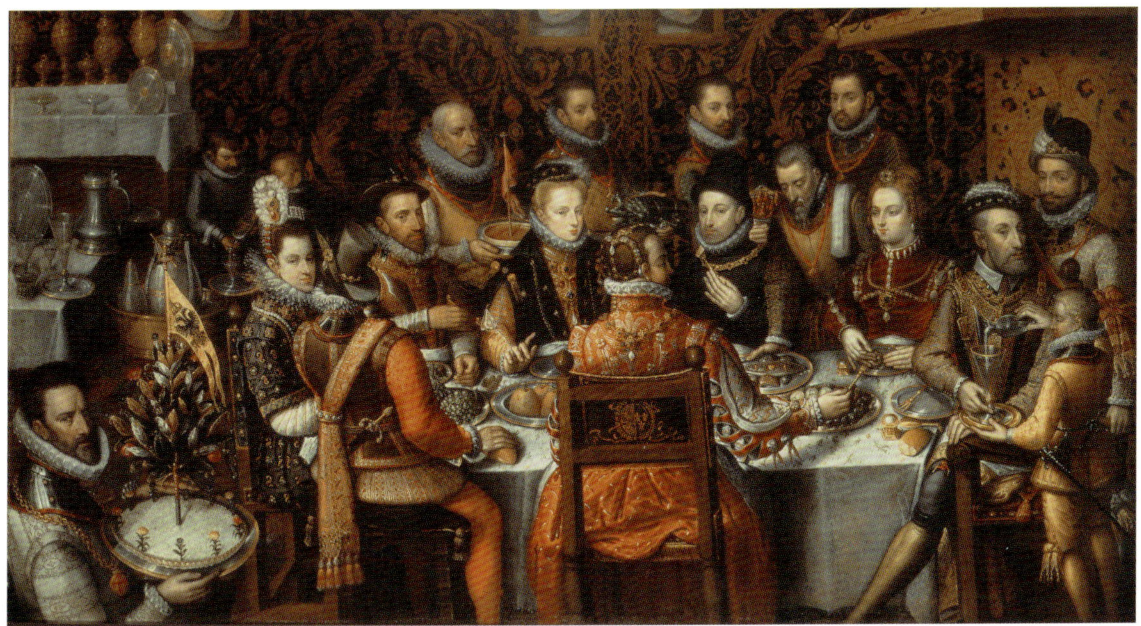

46 Anonymous, *Allegorical Banquet of Habsburg Rulers*, 1596, oil on canvas, 110 × 202 cm (43 ¼ × 79 ½ in), Muzeum Naradowe, Warsaw

cookbook titled *L'arte et prudenza d'un maestro cuoco* (Venice, 1570) by Bartolomeo Scappi, who worked for several popes, contributed to this codification.[22] Scappi declared that, for formal meals, '[…] it is necessary that the sideboard [be furnished with] fine and coarse cloths and towels, salt dishes, gold and silver knives, forks and spoons, several sorts of candlesticks, gold and silver dishes […], bowls and cups of porcelain, majolica […]'.[23] Scappi's text, which circulated across Europe, reflected an already elaborate approach to the staging of meals in the courts in the later sixteenth century. A chronicle by Juan Cristóbal Calvete de Estrella of the travels of Prince Philip of Spain through northern Italy, Germany and the Netherlands from October 1548 until the summer of 1551 describes that in Milan, on New Year's Day 1549, Ferrante Gonzaga offered a banquet to the Prince in a room containing a large cupboard consisting of nine levels that displayed 'many and very rich pieces of gold and silver, displayed to honor the visitor, and for grandeur and ornament'. Dinner included elaborate and large sculpted dishes in the shape of towers, castles and cities, all 'of excellent taste and very pleasing to see', and sweets, fruits and preserves, 'full of small coloured flags and golden windmills'.[24]

A high point of Prince Philip's trip was the festivities planned by Mary of Hungary in 1549 at the palace at Binche in the Southern Netherlands, which likewise demonstrated the lavishness of this culinary display culture. One of the palace rooms visited by the royal retinue displayed an elaborate simulation of a storm. Tables came down from the ceiling adorned with 'many and diverse porcelain plates', with all sorts of 'preserves', 'excellent and beautiful'. Soon a new table descended from the ceiling full of plates and glasses, with 'pastries of various colours and a thousand other confections, all white'. A third table once again lowered from the ceiling featured many plates made of sugar, salt cellars and abundant game and fish. On a mountain made of sugar were five laurel trees, with gilt and silver

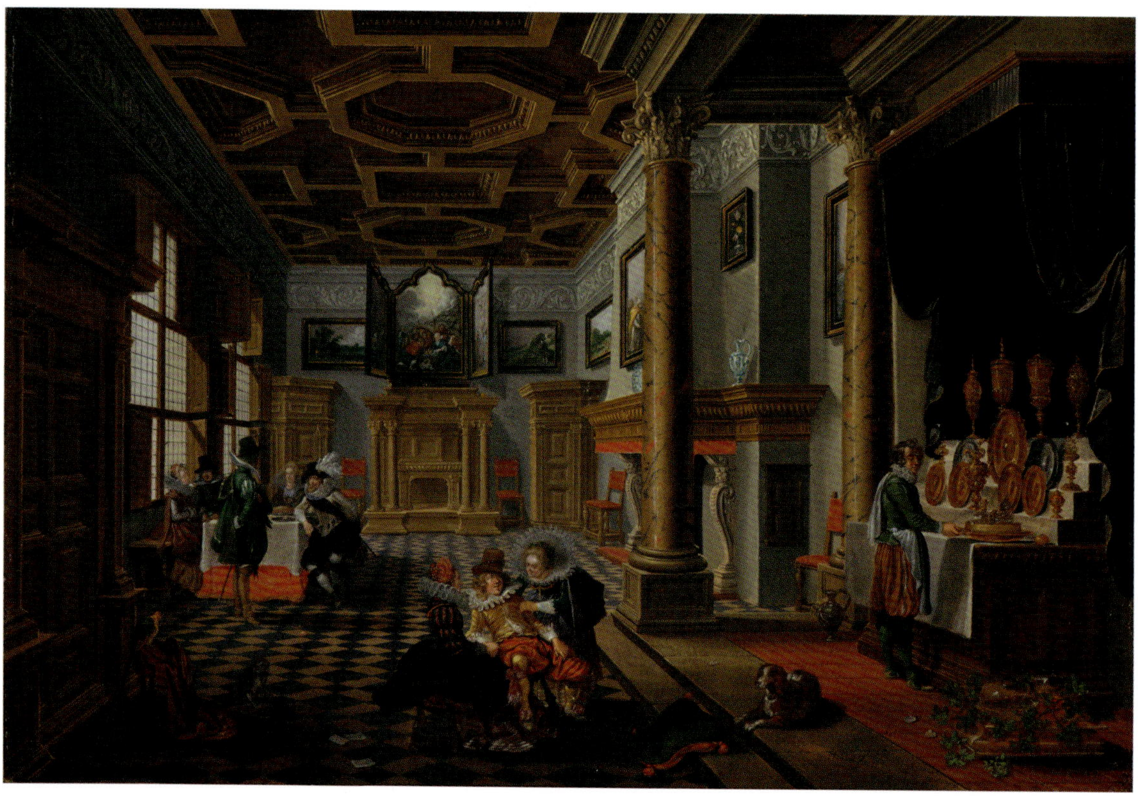

47 Bartholomeus van Bassen, *Renaissance Interior with Banquet*, c.1620, oil on panel, 57 × 87 cm (22 ½ × 34 ¼ in), North Carolina Museum of Art, Raleigh, NC

leaves, full of silk flags and a live squirrel, tied to a chain (an animal that Clara Peeters, as well as other painters of food still lifes such as Snyders, included in some of their paintings; figs 21, 37).[25] These courtly ideals were prolonged into the seventeenth century. The government of the Archdukes employed silver- and goldsmiths and other craftsmen devoted to the making and care of luxury items. Their court also included a large number of specialised servants devoted to buying food, salting meat and fish, supplying and caring for bread, cheese, fruit and sweets; a cellar master who was responsible for the wine; and a cook who in 1605 had a staff of 29

assistants.[26] The banquets that occupied this staff were transformed into art in the paintings by Jan Brueghel, painter for the Brussels court (fig.43).

The practice of asserting wealth and position through banquets became an ideal that artists expressed in paintings in the period prior to Peeters's career. A culinary ritual from the highest social echelon is represented in a painting that shows an imaginary banquet attended by three generations of Habsburg rulers (fig.46).[27] Seated around a table are the Emperor Charles V and his wife Isabella of Portugal, their son Philip II and his fourth wife Anne of Austria, and Archdukes Albert and Isabel Clara Eugenia (Philip's

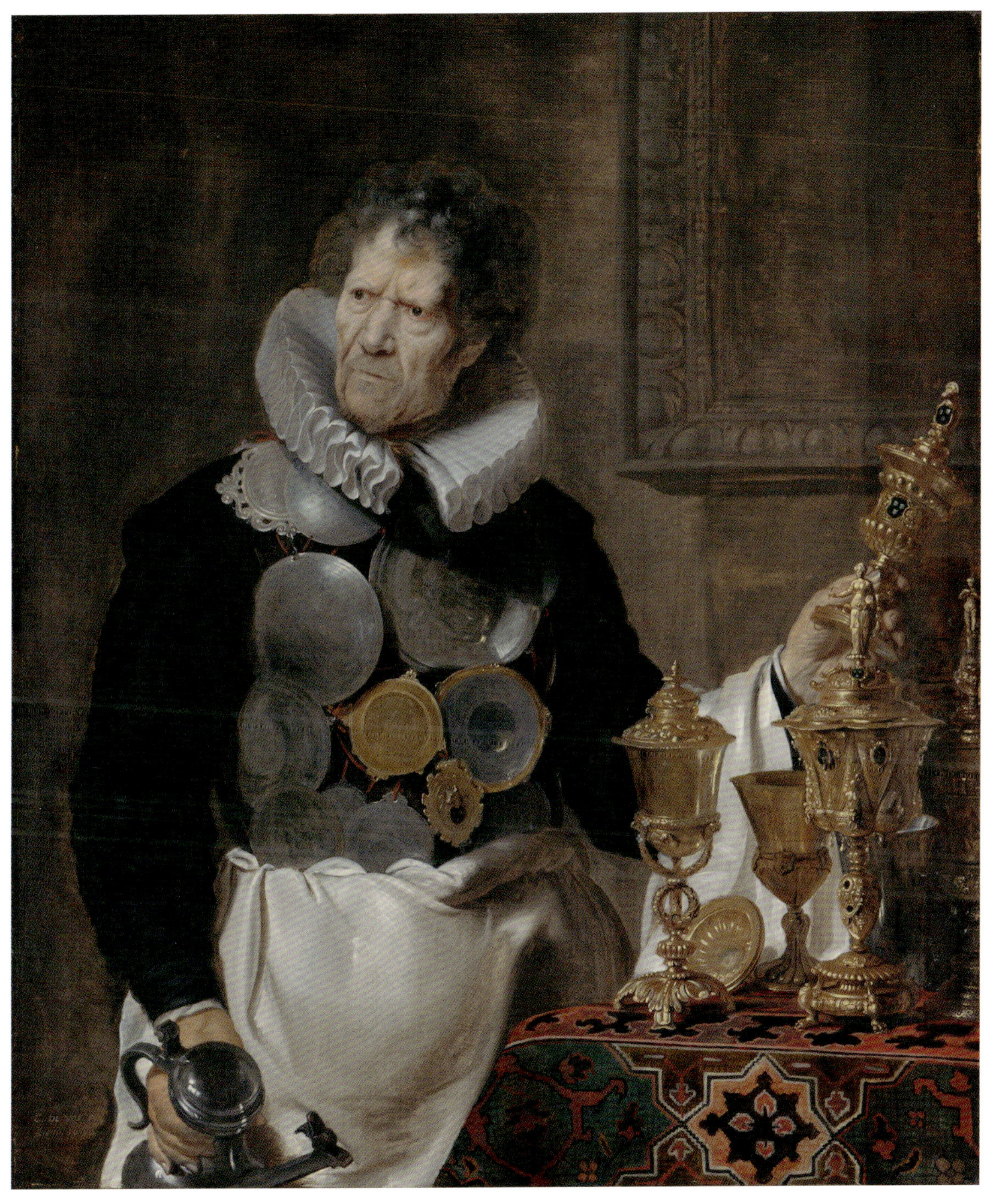

48 Cornelis de Vos, *Portrait of Abraham Grapheus*, 1620, oil on panel, 120 × 102 cm (47 ¼ × 40 ⅛ in), Royal Museum of Fine Arts, Antwerp

daughter by his third wife Elisabeth of Valois), among others. They are surrounded by other members of the royal family and by aristocrat-servants of the highest rank (including Alessandro Farnese, to the left, and Fernando Álvarez de Toledo, third Duke of Alba, next to Philip). The table is covered with a white cloth and sprinkled with what appears to be rosemary and flower petals. Two pies are carried to the table, both highly adorned, and sweets and fruits seem abundant. On the far left is a display of gold and silver standing cups and dishes in several levels, and next to this is a more functional table with plates, glasses and a jug. On the table, next to Charles V, is a salt cellar (a container for salt), a subject to which we will return. A painting made by the Antwerp artist Bartholomeus van Bassen (*c*.1590–1652) around 1620 (fig.47) shows a large room with diners sitting at a table. Opposite them is a luxurious tiered buffet with an ordered display of expensive goblets and plates, as well as a tart that a servant prepares to pick up or place on the shelf. Paintings hang on the walls and, on a mantle above a hearth, are objects of blue and white porcelain. Like the festivities organised in 1549 by Ferrante Gonzaga for Philip II, still-life paintings of this type were created 'for grandeur and ornament' and to honour their owners.

The still lifes of Clara Peeters and similar works of the seventeenth century invoke these traditional courtly displays, if in downscaled form appropriate for the lower aristocracy and members of the emerging burgher and merchant classes. Her paintings include the types of 'candlesticks, gold and silver dishes [...], bowls and cups of porcelain, majolica [...]' described by Scappi, in a comparatively modest presentation in terms of quantity. Gilt goblets are the stars of several paintings (figs 10, 31). They are of a type that was made in Nuremberg and other German cities. Because of the soldier at the top of the lids, which has been interpreted as a Christian soldier, these paintings have been said to have a moralistic, Christian meaning.[28] Importantly, the gilt cups were meant to demonstrate

refinement and wealth, a reflection of ritualised practices in contemporary culture. Two important Flemish artists, Sebastian Vrancx (1573–1647) and Wenzel Cobergher (1560–1634), owned expensive goblets of this type, which they presented as gifts to a civic association of Antwerp known as De Violeren.[29] In a painting by Cornelis de Vos (*c*.1584–1651) of 1620, Abraham Grapheus, who was a servant of De Violeren, prepares to fill a similar goblet from a pewter flagon, while others are displayed at a table (fig.48).

Linens, too, could play a part in these stagings. Peeters's painting *Table with Cloth, Foodstuffs and Other Objects* (fig.14) includes a meticulously painted fine square-creased linen damask cloth, with a design pattern visible in dark and light shades. This type of expensive table linen was exported from the Southern Netherlands to the rest of Europe. Its presence in the painting, and the precision of the creases that suggest careful folding, implies a wealthy and neat household, where goods were properly kept.

Salt cellars, mentioned by Scappi, are also conspicuous in paintings by Peeters, represented as silver containers decorated with patterns. The importance of these vessels resulted from the high cost of salt at the time, which was a consequence of pre-industrial extraction methods from mines and salt water. We can still find traces of the past importance of salt in our language. The word 'salary' derives from the Latin '*salarium*', which described payment with salt in ancient Rome. Place names such as Salzburg also derive from the word salt. Important centres of salt production existed in Cyprus, Ibiza, Setúbal and southern France, and in the Caribbean. Among the many crucial uses of salt are a few that apply to objects in the still lifes of Clara Peeters: it was used to preserve meat and fish such as herring, and to make cheese and prepare olives. Salt cellars had been among the most prized objects at dining tables for centuries. In the painting of a Habsburg banquet mentioned above (fig.46), the salt cellar is placed near the most prominent figure present, the Emperor Charles V.

These objects were sometimes true works of art. The famous piece made by Benvenuto Cellini for Francis I of France in 1543 (Kunsthistorisches Museum, Vienna) is but one example. The refined salt from a salt cellar placed at a dining table was taken by each guest with the tip of knives like the ones we see in the still lifes of Peeters and put on individual trenchers.[30] Until the middle of the twentieth century it was still customary in homes to demonstrate status by serving salt from silver cellars.

Paintings by Peeters often include the two most important pieces of cutlery of the early seventeenth century: knives and spoons. Knives were used for carving food, which could be an honour depending on the occasion, and to move food from a tray to a plate.[31] They were not yet provided by hosts, and thus guests carried their own when attending a dinner. Common knives were made of iron and steel, but the more expensive ones that were worthy of being painted had silver handles and were carried in elaborate cases. A knife that Peeters repeated in several paintings (figs 14, 33, 42, 44, 45) features designs on the handle that were based on engravings of late Mannerist patterns by the Flemish artists Theodor de Bry (1528–98) and his son Johann Theodor de Bry. Like other features that she repeated in her paintings, Peeters must have either owned or had drawings of it. Silver knives were used at the time as wedding gifts. If the knives that Peeters painted were her own, she may have received them as a wedding present. Forks, on the other hand, are not present in works by Peeters, albeit Scappi mentioned them; they were only then beginning to be used by the more elite members of society, especially in Italy.[32] In the group portrait of Habsburg rulers at a banquet (fig.46) we can see small gold forks, but artists rarely depicted them.

FOODSTUFFS

The cookbook by Bartolomeo Scappi, *L'arte et prudenza d'un maestro cuoco*, that has guided this

discussion of culinary objects and rituals, is but one example of the importance of the culture of food to Europeans in the early modern period. Additional evidence is seen in the approximately one hundred books on cooking and diets that were written in Europe from the 1470s to the 1650s. This is a large number on a single subject for the time, and many of them went through numerous editions and were widely translated.[33] These publications illuminate some of the social prejudices involved in eating; certain foods were considered unworthy of the wealthy and powerful, and others were exclusively for them. Rye bread, for example, was called bread for 'laborers, servants and workmen',[34] while processed white bread was considered more appropriate for the upper class. Beans and sausages, organ meats and pancakes were considered lower-class foods, and as with vegetables are not mentioned as often as fruits and other eatables, probably reflecting their lower symbolic rank. Beyond this, cookbooks and dietaries provide confusing, often contradictory information reflecting passing vogues and disagreements among experts. Also, they often aim at promoting certain types of foods or diets. The Spanish doctor Francisco Núñez de Oria wrote in his *Regimiento y aviso de sanidad . . .*, which was published in several editions from 1569, that meat should not be fried, that fatty meat should be roasted and drier meats boiled, but added that these rules were not generally followed.[35]

Concerns such as those expressed by Núñez de Oria were important to the consumption of food in the early modern period. Views on health were based in humoral theory, which was inspired by the writings of the Greek Hippocrates (fifth/fourth centuries BCE) and the Roman Galen (second century CE). Accordingly, good health resulted from balancing the humours that existed in the body as liquids. Foods should be selected for their contributions to this goal.[36] Certain kinds of foods (a given type of fish, for example) should be complemented by another food (a certain sauce) to achieve balance. But the identification of corrective foods could be haphazard and disagreements among contemporary nutritionists abounded. The application of this system could be so complex, and involved so many combinations, that finding traces of it in paintings of food is nearly impossible. According to one recent author, assessing the effect of the possible combinations of foods on an actual meal 'would tax the powers of a computer'.[37] Most contemporaries may not have had a clear idea of this system, and they may not have been any more prone than we are today to select favourite dishes because of their health benefits. Be this as it may, the literature from the sixteenth and seventeenth centuries proves that the subject of food received a good deal of attention.

It was only natural, then, that paintings of eatables would interest the public, as Clara Peeters was certainly aware in choosing to represent them. Nearly all the foodstuffs identified by Scappi as part of an ideal meal are present in her still lifes. Among them are cherries, several shapes of marzipan creations, sugar confections, biscuits, 'always rolled wafers', olives, raisins, pomegranates, quince, sweet, semi-sweet and bitter oranges, and cheeses of many different types. Scappi also commented on meat days, for which, he added, the sideboard should include 'big cold pies' of game and fowl, and for lean days smoked herring and many other types of fish, or fish pies. The sideboard also should have 'fruit according to the season'.[38] The presence of these foods in Peeters's works helps us to understand her access to these items, whether directly or through representations available to her. Assessing perceptions about them in early modern culture reveals why they became an important focus for artists like her, for collectors and for paintings.

FISH AND GAME

We saw in Chapter 3 that Clara Peeters's painting *Still Life with Fish, Candle, Artichokes, Crabs and Shrimp* (fig.30), signed and dated in 1611, was the first known still-life painting of fish produced in Europe.

Peeters would become somewhat of a specialist in this subject, for approximately ten of her paintings, or nearly a quarter of her known works, depict them.[39] The interest in the representation of animals as part of early scientific inquiry contributed to the emergence of representations of fish in the sixteenth century. Books such as Pierre Belon's *L'histoire naturelle des estranges poissons* of 1551, Guillaume Rondelet's *Libri de piscibus marinis* of 1554 and book four of Conrad Gessner's *Historia animalium* of 1558 advanced the study of fish and included images aimed to offer comprehensive views of the animals. Illustrations of this type had become a speciality of Antwerp by the end of the sixteenth century. An example is the collection of engraved images by Adriaen Collaert of fish, *Piscium vivae icones*, published in Antwerp around 1610. Also influential were the paintings of markets and kitchens by Pieter Aertsen and Joachim Beuckelaer that often included splendid-looking, succulent fish. These were not yet still-life paintings, but they point to the importance of this staple food and provide an artistic precedent for the paintings by Peeters.

Still Life with Fish, Candle, Artichokes, Crabs and Shrimp displays boiled crabs and shrimp and several freshwater fish (two carp, a roach, possibly several ides and a northern pike). Crabs and shrimp were common and could be caught next to the shore, at low tide. Their reddish colour in the painting indicates that they are already cooked. In this, Peeters probably meant to suggest custom: raw seafood goes bad and develops a strong odour in a short period of time, and therefore demands quick preparation. Adjacent to these foodstuffs are other objects familiar in Peeters's paintings, including a glass goblet, a brass candlestick with a partially burnt candle, a copper strainer with a brass skimmer, a Rhenish stoneware jug with the self-portrait of the artist reflected on its lid, and two artichokes. In *Still Life with Fish* (fig.49), a large carp lies over a northern pike and presumably other fish in a redware strainer. Lying directly on what appears to be a stone ledge are two

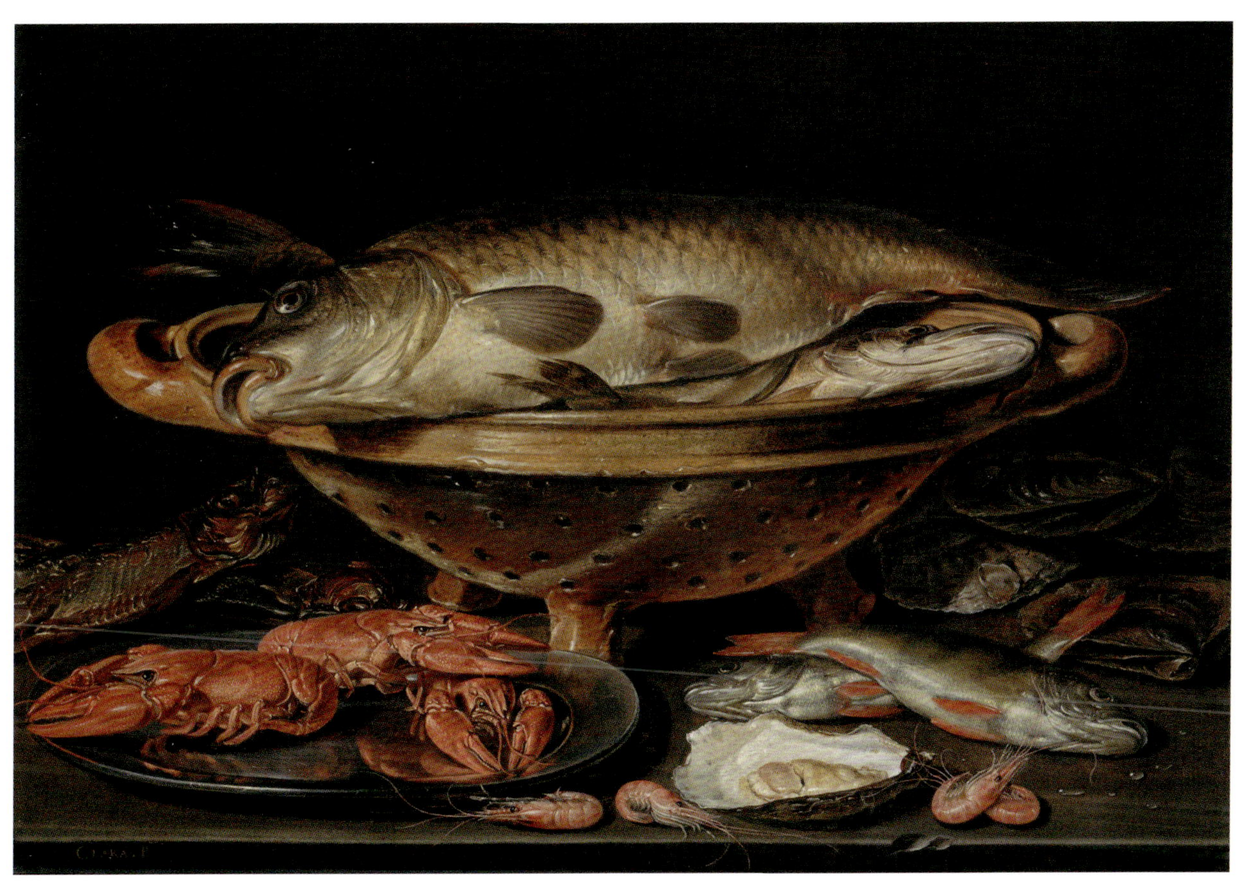

49 Clara Peeters, *Still Life with Fish*, inscribed with the artist's name on the knife, *c.*1612–21, oil on panel, 35 × 48 cm (13 ¾ × 18 ⅞ in), Koninklijk Museum voor Schone Kunsten, Antwerp

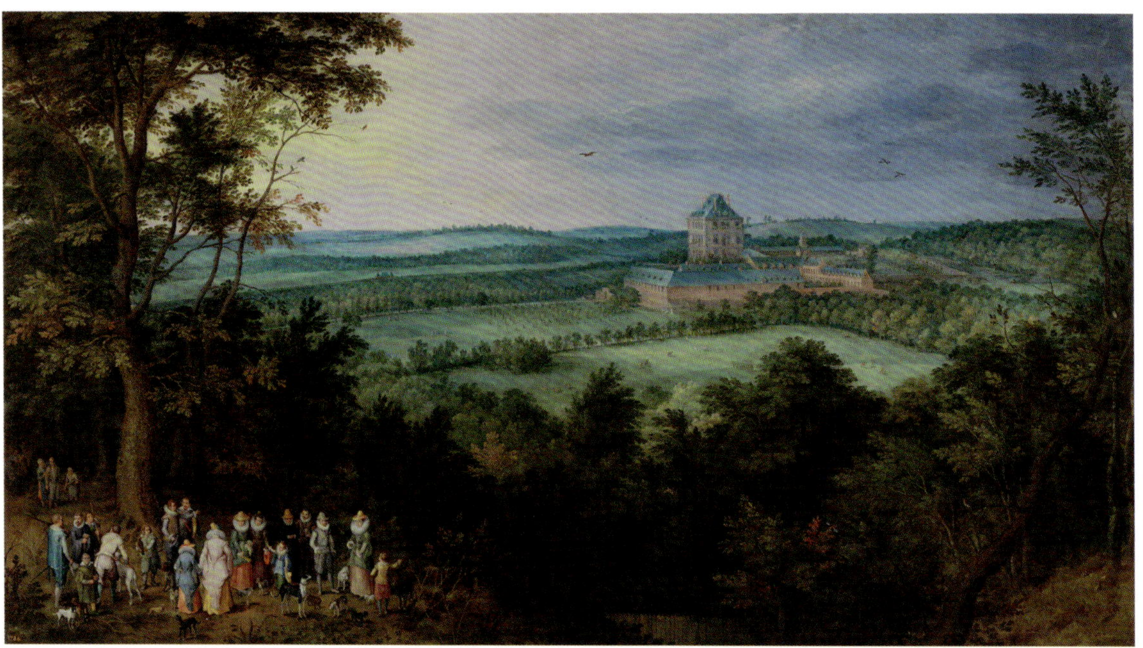

50 Jan Brueghel the Elder, *Hunting Party with the Archdukes*, c.1611, oil on canvas, 135 × 246 cm (53 ⅛ × 96 ⅞ in), Museo Nacional del Prado, Madrid

salted herring (the only saltwater fish in the painting), boiled crayfish and shrimp, oysters and two ides. The carp appears again, in the same size and shape, in another painting by Peeters (fig.17), an example of her use of stencils or some type of tracing paper to repeat motifs. Also in this painting are a northern pike and an eel, stacked on a red clay strainer. Eels migrate from the sea to freshwater and back. The rest of the fish in this painting are freshwater creatures. Nearby are oysters and boiled shrimp, and a cat that holds a small fish (perhaps an ide) in its paws.

The products of the sea that Peeters included in her still lifes were easily available in the rivers and coastal waters of the Southern Netherlands near Antwerp. An important fishing industry existed there in the early seventeenth century. Ludovicus Nonnius, in his treatise *Diaeteticon*, mentions herring among fish that were caught and exported from the Southern Netherlands, although other sources demonstrate that it could also be imported.[40] A painting by Denis

van Alsloot and Antoon Sallaert of 1616 (fig.6), recreating a procession that took place in Brussels a year earlier, shows the members of many different professions, all identified by inscriptions. One of them, with 128 members, is identified as '*Poissoniers de poisons sale*' ('makers of salted fish'). Another group of 15 is identified simply as '*Poissoniers*' ('fishmongers'). Among others present in the parade are 120 butchers, 60 goldsmiths, 70 fruit vendors and 340 bakers, all associated with goods that we find in the paintings of Clara Peeters. This parade was staged as a show of economic strength and was part of a series of events that celebrated the prosperity of the land under the rule of the Archdukes Isabel Clara Eugenia and Albert of Austria. Even though the event in the painting reflects the economic life of Brussels rather than Antwerp, it provides a measure of the economic activities of the Southern Netherlands that we see reflected in the paintings of Peeters, including the importance of the fishing industry.

Peeters portrayed herrings in several works, including in *Still Life with Herring, a Porcelain Dish with Butter and Other Eatables* (fig.27) where it takes centre stage on a red clay plate. Its status as a saltwater fish could make it less favoured than its freshwater counterparts. Saltwater fish were more prone to rot and therefore required salting soon after the catch for preservation; legislation enforced this practice, to ensure the consumer was protected. Freshwater fish, by contrast, were sold alive at fish markets and eaten fresh. This practice pleased the Spaniard Vicente Alvarez, a steward who accompanied the future Philip II on his tour of the Netherlands in 1549 and wrote about his experiences. He was impressed that freshwater fish could be bought and carried home alive: 'it is a thing of beauty to bring to the kitchen the fish still jumping' (less appealing were the fish kept in enclosed waters, which were not as flavourful as those that one could eat just after a catch).[41] Freshwater fish were therefore more desirable, and more expensive, than saltwater types. It follows that Clara Peeters surmised that her paintings of freshwater fish would be more appealing among those whom she hoped to attract as buyers; they presumably understood these distinctions and appreciated images that appealed to quality. It also explains why she favoured them for her works.

Other still-life paintings by Peeters are among the first to be devoted to hunting. Her *Still Life with a Sparrow Hawk, Fowl, Porcelain and Shells* (fig.29) is, in fact, the first known still life that pertains to the subject of falconry. In this work, a sparrowhawk that seems aware of its preeminent place in a hierarchy presides over other birds. It shares the stage with other elite objects discussed above, including porcelain plates and exotic shells. In this painting, several cultural associations coexist: the taste for exotica, as witnessed by the porcelain plate, and the idea of abundance and upper-class pursuits associated with fowl and the hunt. Other paintings of this period invoked the hunt indirectly, including *Table with Cloth, Foodstuffs*

and Other Objects by Peeters (fig.14). On a pewter plate are two roasted pheasants, an animal which was maintained for hunting as well as serving as an important luxury food (they may alternatively be francolin, a bird related to the partridge, sometimes known as a black partridge). It was probably for the purpose of hunting that pheasants were sent from Brussels by the Infanta Isabel Clara Eugenia to her brother King Philip III of Spain with descriptions of their behaviour and instructions for keeping them.[42] The game birds Peeters included on these tables were assigned an elevated status because of their association with the hunt. The combination of high-value or unusual natural and fabricated curiosities with ancient customs such as falconry was characteristic of the ideals of aristocratic culture and indicative of the status of hunting as the favourite sport of the elite throughout Europe.[43]

Artists took advantage of this interest to produce paintings with hunting themes for princely and aristocratic patrons and collectors, and for other high-end clientele. Several paintings by Jan Brueghel reflect the taste for hunting with birds in the context of the Brussels court in the early seventeenth century. In *Hunting Party with the Archdukes* (fig.50), the rulers of the Southern Netherlands, Isabel Clara Eugenia and Albert of Austria, take part in a hunting excursion with the palace of Mariemont in the distance. They are accompanied by gentlemen and ladies of their court; among them is a youth with a hooded sparrowhawk perched on his hawking glove. In the first two decades of the seventeenth century the Spanish King often sent his falconers to the Spanish Netherlands to acquire new birds.[44] They may have come from the town of Valkenswaard, which was known at the time for exporting falcons caught during their annual migration. The painter and writer Gerard de Lairesse (1640–1711) wrote in the late seventeenth century of paintings of 'boars, deer, hares, as well as pheasants, partridges and other dead birds, which generally Princes and Aristocrats like to hang'.[45] Sparrowhawks like the one in Peeters's *Still Life with a Sparrow Hawk, Fowl, Porcelain and Shells* were used in the early seventeenth century in much of Europe for a type of hunt that was a lighter form of entertainment than a proper hawking party, which would have involved travelling longer distances with a cortege of horses and a retinue of huntsmen. Sparrowhawks would typically be used in the gardens surrounding a palace or a city, not only by men but also by women and children learning the art of falconry.

The references to falconry in the paintings by Peeters are roughly contemporary with legislation about hunting passed by the ruling Archdukes. In the early seventeenth century in the Southern Netherlands, aristocratic hunting privileges were questioned in practice and laws were subsequently passed to uphold traditional rights. In 1613 legislation was introduced on the subject stating that previous rules 'have not been maintained and observed'.[46] The new law proclaimed the exclusive right of the nobility to hunt *de poil avec poil et de plume avec plume* ('fur with fur and feather with feather'). This meant that hunting should be done only with dogs and birds. Peter Paul Rubens and artists associated with him painted numerous hunting scenes in this same context. Like the painting of the Archdukes at the hunt but on a more modest scale, some of the still lifes of Clara Peeters allude to the noble preference for hunting 'feather with feather'. The need to legislate the hunt suggests that the traditions that attracted those of elite status to it were under threat of erosion. Paintings like those of Peeters and her contemporaries may have been desired by collectors because they celebrated and upheld these traditions.

CHEESE AND BUTTER; FRUITS AND VEGETABLES

Some of the foods represented by Peeters had a long history of production in northern Europe. Among them are cheese and butter, items that Peeters chose to include in several paintings. On the stone ledge of *Still Life with Cheeses, Almonds and Pretzels* (fig.33) is a dark, Edam-type cheese, a larger cheese probably from Gouda, and a smaller, triangular sheep's cheese. Some of them are probably Dutch imports, and it is possible that Peeters painted them to appeal to a market where there was demand for this product. In support of this possibility is the fact that several of her contemporaries from Haarlem, in the Northern Netherlands (the present-day Kingdom of the Netherlands), specialised in painting cheeses, among them Floris Claesz. van Dijck, Floris van Schooten (1585/8–1656) and Nicolaes Gillis.[47] However, cheese was also exported from the Southern Netherlands, as attested by Calvete de Estrella in his *Felicíssimo viaje* mentioned earlier, and therefore eaten there, too.[48] Milk, cheese and butter were in fact singled out as the main staples of Flanders, Brabant and other provinces of the Netherlands by commentators such as Captain Alonso Vázquez, who wrote of his experience in the Netherlands from 1577 to 1592.[49] Provisions for a banquet in honour of King Philip IV of Spain during a visit to Andalusia in 1624 included nearly 600 kg of 'butter from Flanders' and 300 'cheeses from Flanders'.[50] Miguel de Cervantes, in his short novel *Rinconete y Cortadillo*, of 1612, mentions Flemish cheese among the food supplies of the two Sevillian characters (the term 'Flanders' and 'Flemish', or *'Flandes'* and *'flamenco'*, were used in Spain at the time to refer to the entire Netherlands).[51]

Certain fruits represented by Peeters were local, however, having been cultivated and harvested in the Southern Netherlands. Cherries such as we see in several paintings (figs 34, 35, 44) had been grown there from at least Roman times: Pliny the Elder wrote that cherries were cultivated in Belgium and other regions in the north.[52] Sour cherries were used for cooking, and sweet cherries were eaten raw. Even fruits that traditionally came from different Southern ports were increasingly grown locally, as suggested in correspondence about the trip of the Infanta Isabel

Clara Eugenia from Milan to Brussels in 1599. She wrote that upon approaching her destination villagers presented her with large amounts of fruits: 'I don't know who said there weren't all kinds of fruits here, because there are none that I have not found; there are so many grapes and melons and quince [. . .]'.[53] In the 1617–18 painting by Jan Brueghel, *The Sense of Smell* (Museo del Prado, Madrid), a fig tree in a garden very probably evokes the gardens of the Archduke's palace in Brussels. It is a small tree and is planted in a pot, so that it could be moved indoors in cold weather. In elite gardens such as this, exotic plants and fruits were cultivated.

Many of the eatable provisions in Peeters's paintings could be grown only in warmer, dryer climates, however, and early modern writings about commerce describe the importation of these and other foods to the Southern Netherlands.[54] Oranges, for example, as seen in Peeters's *Table with Cloth, Foodstuffs, and Other Objects* (fig.14), had traditionally come from Italy, Portugal and Spain, and were used to make preserves and for sauces; sweet oranges were used for their juice.[55] They were also used in various recipes: an English recipe for roasting pheasants included orange mixed with egg yolk.[56] Perhaps this was also common in the Southern Netherlands and explains the presence of an orange on this table. Grapes, too, were imported. They were attractive to painters not only for their visual interest and social messaging but also for their artistic associations. Some of the stories about art that all painters knew at the time favoured the representation of grapes in paintings. Pliny the Elder wrote in the *Natural History* that Zeuxis (late fifth–early fourth century BCE) painted a bunch of grapes so skilfully that birds flew up to them and tried to eat them.[57] On another occasion, the same painter was disappointed with himself after painting a child holding grapes that some birds tried to eat – if the boy had been well painted, he thought, the birds would not have dared approach the grapes.[58] This fruit was also popular

in art because of its association with pagan and Christian religions, for example through Bacchus, the Roman god of wine, and the wine in the Eucharistic rite of Catholicism. In the paintings of Clara Peeters, grapes, like all else, are drawn with painstaking attention to detail: the dusty looking residue that sits on their surface often received emphasis (figs 37, 44, 56).

Many other foods imported to Antwerp and the surrounding regions are evident in the paintings of Peeters. White wine came from the Rhine region of Germany and from France along with red wine and prunes. The red wine represented in some paintings was probably from France, Italy or Spain. The Danish historian Johannes Pontanus, writing in 1614 about many of the products that existed in Amsterdam, identified wine, oil, salt, raisins and figs as having a Spanish origin.[59] The same was probably true for nearby Antwerp, which had closer ties to Spain. Raisins from Málaga are also mentioned among the cargo of a ship arriving in Dunkirk in February 1589.[60] From Spain also came vegetables 'of many types', dried and fresh fruits (including pomegranates, olives, figs, grapes) and almonds. Almonds were used to make tarts, puddings and many sweets. Together with dry figs, almonds were also used as snacks.[61] The olives in a painting by Peeters (fig.14) are probably of the abundant *manzanilla* variety from southern and south-western Spain. In the north of Europe, olives were a luxury and they were considered healthy. The Antwerp doctor and antiquarian of Jewish origin Ludovicus Nonnius (or Luis Nunes), who is well known to art history because he was portrayed by Rubens (in a painting now in the National Gallery, London), wrote in his book *Diaeteticon sive de re cibaria* (Antwerp, 1627) that olives were nourishing and also that they were useful for stimulating the appetite.[62] In exchange for this and other products coming from Spain, Antwerp merchants sent their own products, including textiles, metal wear, salted meat, fish, cheese and butter, to Spain.

Other fruits and vegetables that were familiar in Antwerp appear in Peeters's paintings. In *Still Life with Gilt Goblet, Porcelain and Eatables* (fig.31), an imported Mediterranean pomegranate accompanies three porcelain plates and a gilt cup in a display meant to demonstrate refinement and wealth. Pomegranates appear in recipes from the time, and its seeds and juice were used as embellishments and for cooking, as shown in the *Livre fort excellent de cuysine* of 1555 as well as in Scappi's book of 1570.[63] Apples, pears, apricots and plums are also present in some paintings by Peeters (figs 44, 56). They could be preserved with sugar or cooked, individually or with other foods, or in tarts and pies: the literature on nutrition did not favour eating them raw.[64] Apples and pears were also used to make cider.

Peeters included artichokes several times in her paintings (figs 30, 34, 35), following from Giuseppe Arcimboldo (1526–93) and Beuckelaer, who first painted them in the 1560s. They are an unusual-looking food, with spiked leaves and colourful flowers. Not long before Peeters's time they were a rare presence in the diet of northern Europeans. Artichokes are an offspring of the wild cardoon, which seems to have been cultivated in Arab North Africa and brought into Europe through Spain and Italy before spreading slowly throughout the continent from the fifteenth century onwards. By the early seventeenth century they had become relatively common. In 1604 they could be found in restaurants in Rome. Police records from April of that year explain that the painter Caravaggio was served 'eight cooked artichokes, four cooked in butter and four fried in oil' at a restaurant in Rome – he was apparently offended by a waiter and a fight ensued.[65] Similarly, restaurants in Antwerp may also have served artichokes by the time Peeters was active there. According to the cookbook *Ouverture de cuisine*, by Lancelot de Casteau, published in Liège in 1604, artichokes were among the 'herbs and greens that are needed for the kitchen'.[66] The book includes recipes to make artichoke pies. Lancelot worked for

the Prince-Bishop of Liège and had knowledge of developments in food and cooking culture in Italy. His recommendations are elite or upscale.

Peeters approached the representation of artichokes aware of their visual appeal. The edible part of the artichoke is the unopened flower head of the plant, which if left to grow will turn into a striking, bright red, pink or purple flower. Peeters instead emphasised the culinary aspect of this vegetable by showing it cut apart or sliced for eating, exposing the patterns and hues of the inner leaves. In one case she showed an artichoke inside a copper colander and next to a skimmer, ready for cooking, or perhaps just cooked. Certainly, Peeters was aware that this dimensional, colourful vegetable, and its associations with the pleasurable experiences of consumption, would capture interest and thereby enhance the allure of her paintings.

SWEETS

Clara Peeters was one of the first still-life painters of the seventeenth century to represent many types of luxury sweets, together with Osias Beert and Georg Flegel. Scappi had written that high-end meals should include several shapes of marzipan creations, sugar confections, biscuits and rolled wafers.[67] Sugar was used for luxurious, extravagant sculptures and constructions designed by renowned artists and was the main ingredient in desserts and cookies of different kinds. Sweets were a very important part of celebrations, so much so that they caused tooth decay among those who could afford to eat them in large amounts.[68] A representative example of Peeters's inclusion of sweets in her compositions is the painting *Still Life with Gilt Goblet, Porcelain and Eatables* (fig.31). Among them is a rolled wafer (or wafer cornet). These were difficult to make – some cooks specialised in making them – and were reserved for special occasions. Originally, they may have been intended solely as Communion bread but from the Middle Ages onward

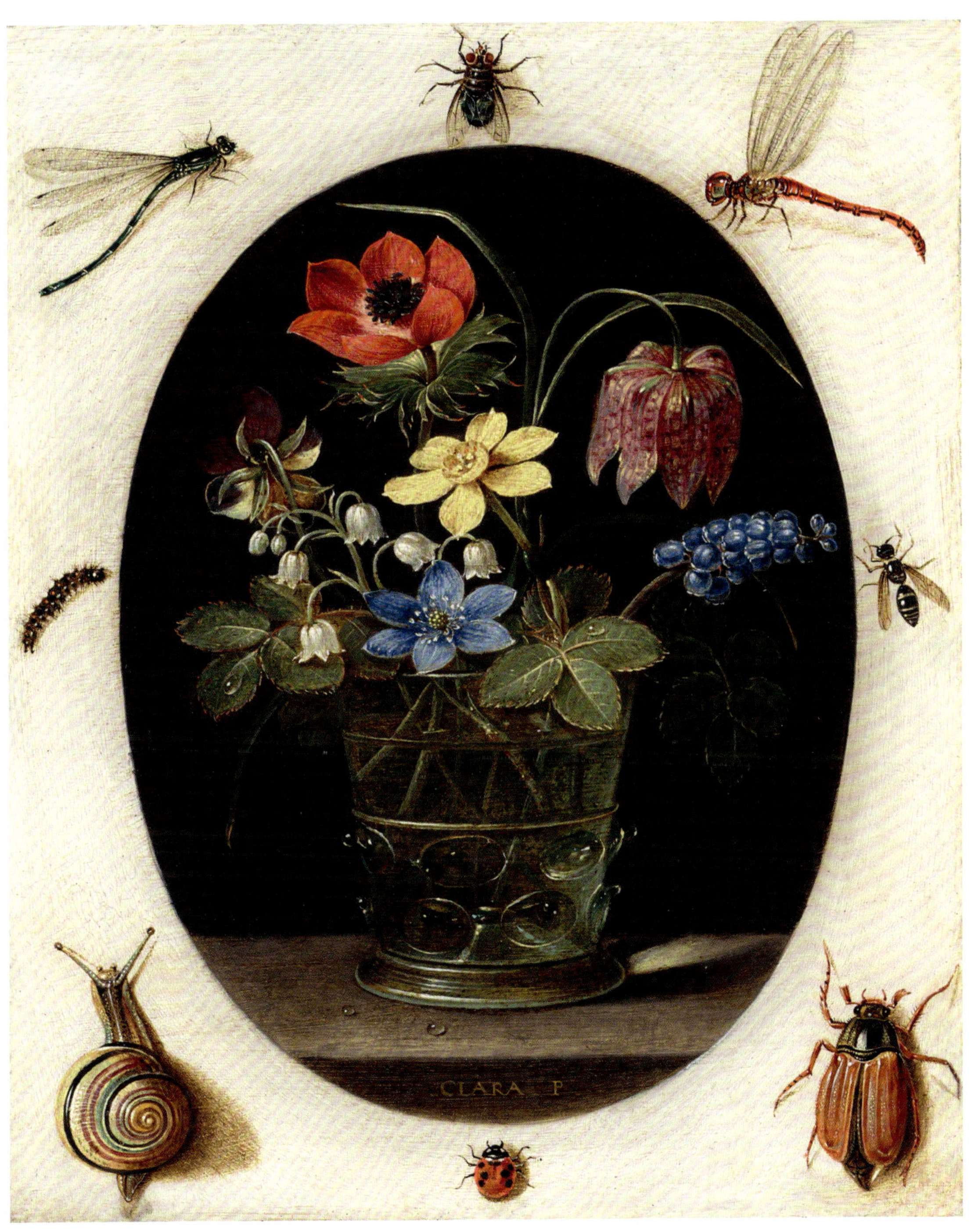

51 Clara Peeters, *Still Life with Flowers Surrounded by Insects and a Snail*, signed, *c.*1610, oil on copper 16.6 × 13.5 cm (6 ½ × 5 ⅜ in), National Gallery of Art, Washington, DC

they were enjoyed in other settings. To achieve the shape in the example in Peeters's painting, they were rolled quickly around the handle of a wooden spoon right after removal from hot iron moulds.[69] Her example also shows the engraved design of the wafer-iron. In some of her paintings, aspects of the sweets she portrayed may have carried symbolic associations, including the letter P, a cross or a heart, referencing the name of the painter, Christ or love, as discussed in the next chapter.

The rock candy in *Still Life with Gilt Goblet, Porcelain and Eatables*, as well as other paintings by Peeters, was made with sugar brought to refineries in Antwerp from Madeira, the Canaries, Cuba, Jamaica and other Caribbean islands and Brazil, and probably other overseas plantations that were not under the control of the Spanish Habsburgs, such as Barbados.[70] In Antwerp the raw sugar was whitened. Sugar was an 'extravagance for the rich', the German physician Hieronymus Bock wrote in his *New Herb Book* (1539).[71] Courts and aristocratic households employed confectioners – like they employed painters – to create sweet delights out of expensive sugar. We have already referred to the 'mountain of sugar' in a festivity organised in the Southern Netherlands in honour of Philip II.[72] In 1574 sugar sculptures based on designs by Jacopo Sansovino, the famed Venetian architect (who had died a few years earlier) were presented to King Henry III of France in a banquet held at the Doge's palace in Venice.[73] In Ferrara and Rome, a certain Luigi Fedele became renowned in the seventeenth century, primarily as the creator of sugar sculptures for Pope Innocent X (whom Diego Velázquez eternalised in a famous portrait).[74]

A large tart occupies the centre of the table of Peeters's *Still Life with Tart, Silver Tazza, Porcelain, and Oysters* (fig.42). It is decorated with artificial flowers and stems of rosemary, the central one hung with gold ornaments in the shape of strawberries; they are probably earrings. Among the celebrations that included tarts and pies were weddings, and this

may be one such case. A poem by Robert Herrick (1591–1674) shows that in England both a specific type of cake, and also rosemary, were associated with matrimony: '[…] who shal make / That Wedding-smock, this Bridal-cake […] / That done we'l draw lots, who shall buy / And guild the Baies and Rosemary […]'.[75] Strawberries, as with so many other things, could have many different associations. One of them was with fertility, because of the abundance of achenes (which were thought to be seeds) visible on their surfaces.[76] In the case of rosemary, it was used for its odour and as a condiment, and it also had many different associations.[77] The English herbalist John Parkinson (1567–1650) noted that it was commonly used as a token at both weddings and funerals, and a short poem by Herrick entitled 'The Rosemary Branch' reads: 'Grow for two ends, it matters not at all, / Be't for my bridal, or my burial'.[78]

The sugar products seen in the paintings by Clara Peeters are a reminder of the benefits that wealthy Europeans extracted from colonialism. In the seventeenth century the demand for sugar rose considerably, affecting first the Spanish and Portuguese plantations, and later others with ties to England, France, the Netherlands and other European regions. Indigenous workers, contracted Europeans and enslaved Africans provided the labour necessary to produce high quantities of sugar at low prices – slavery of Africans in the later seventeenth and the eighteenth centuries was largely the result of the taste for sugar in Europe. By the time sugar products reached an upper-class table in Antwerp, or were depicted in their painted counterpart by Peeters and others, the human cost was of little concern. What mattered to them was that luxury sweets reflected affluence and status.

FLOWERS

The early career of Clara Peeters coincides with the rise of flower still lifes. In addition to including flower

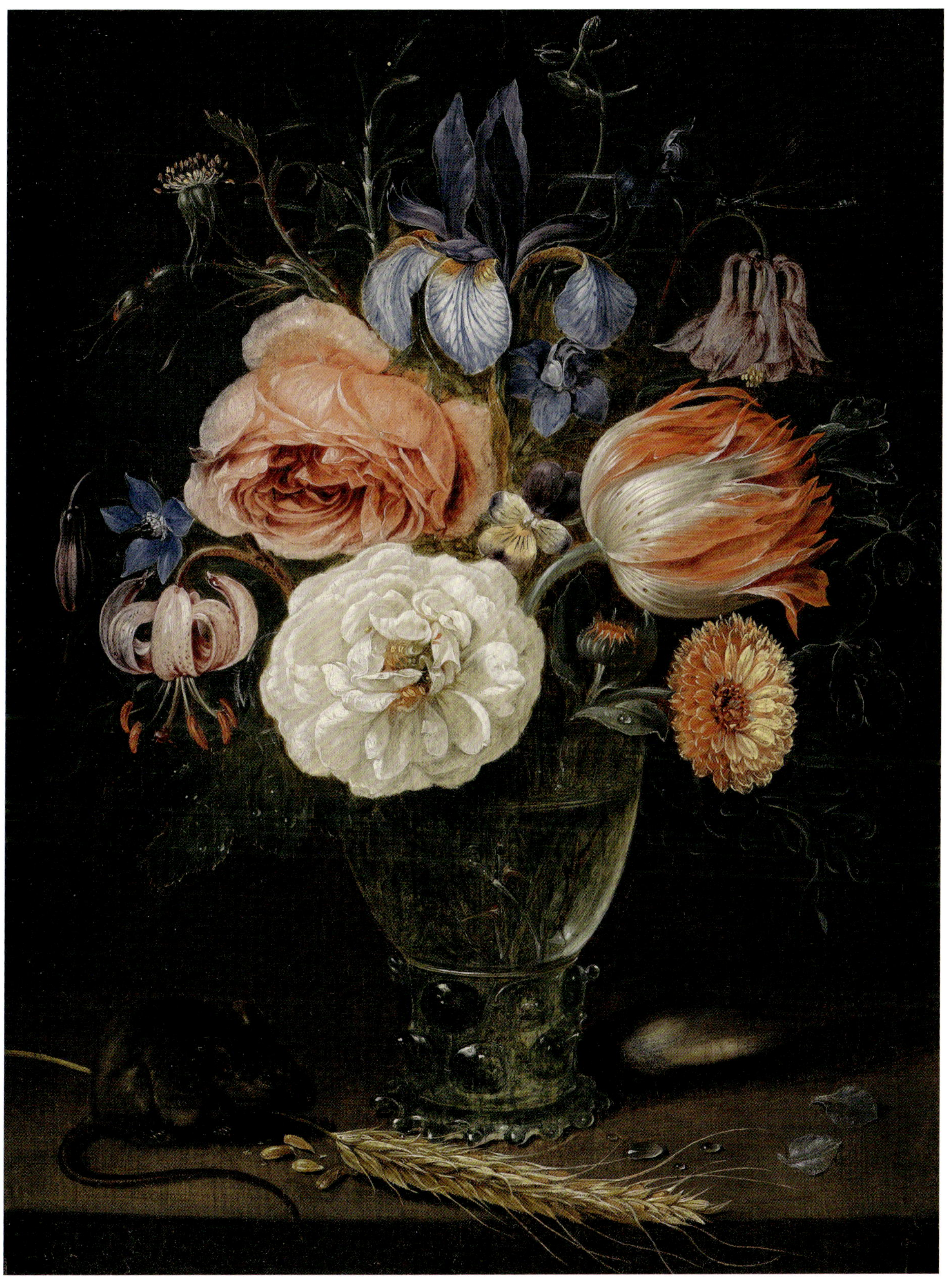

52 Clara Peeters, *Still Life of Flowers with a Mouse and an Ear of Wheat*, signed, *c.*1612–21, oil on panel, 27 × 21 cm (10 ⅝ × 8 ¼ in), private collection, sold Sotheby's London, 5 July 2012, lot 186

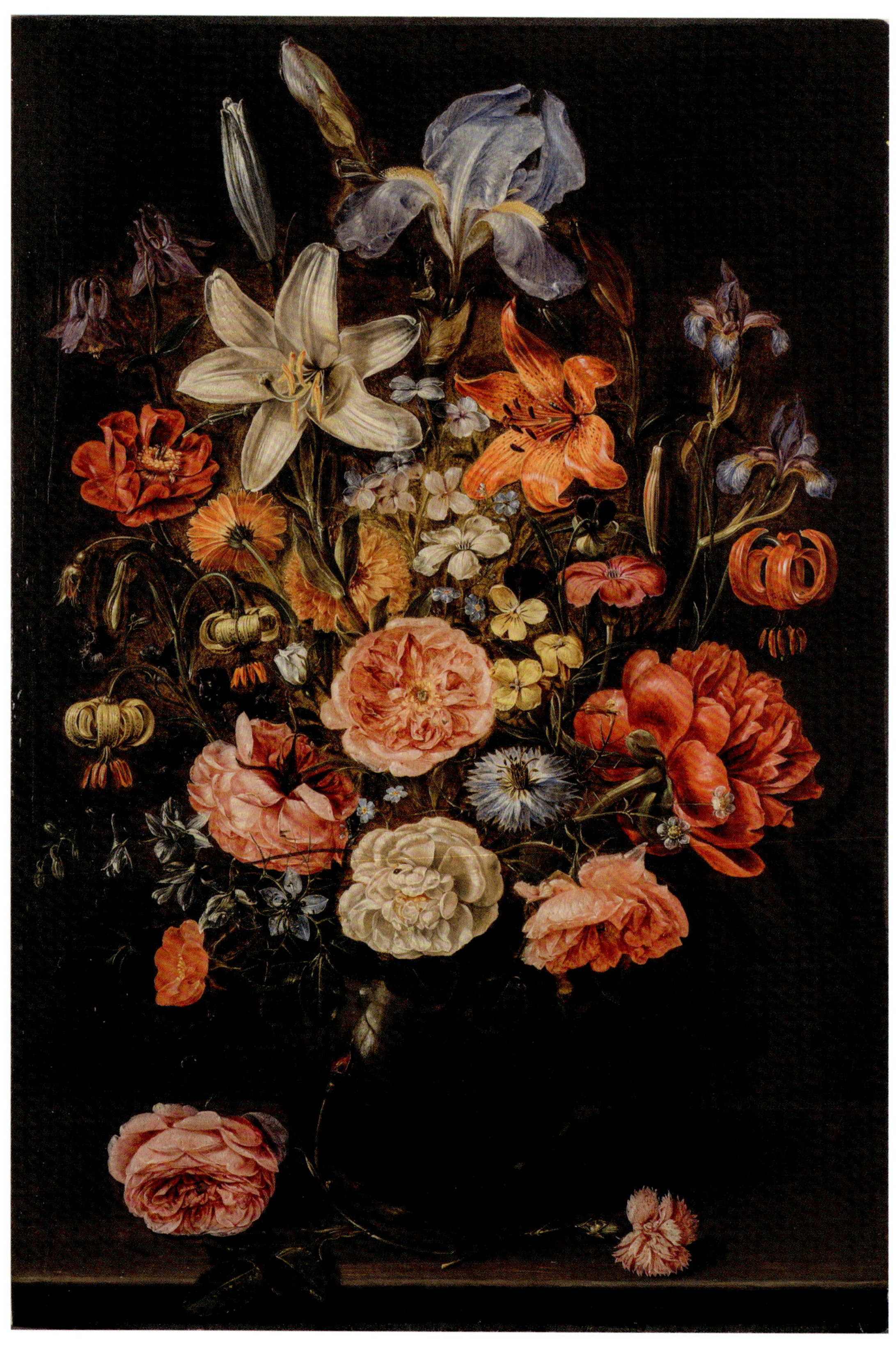

53 Clara Peeters, *A Still Life of Lilies, Roses, Iris, Pansies, Columbine, Love-in-a-Mist, Larkspur and Other Flowers in a Glass Vase on a Table Top, Flanked by a Rose and a Carnation*, c.1610, oil on wood panel, 49.5 × 33.7 cm (19 ½ × 13 ¼ in), National Museum of Women in the Arts, Washington, DC

arrangements in several of her paintings, Peeters devoted certain works exclusively to this theme. Antwerp was central to the creation of the first works of the kind, traditionally termed 'flower pieces'. Roelant Savery, who emigrated to the Northern Netherlands as a young child with his family, and Jacques de Gheyn II, Ambrosius Bosschaert and Jan Brueghel, all active in Antwerp, are usually credited with the earliest paintings of this type. The first documented flower still life, in this case representing a bouquet, was sent by Brueghel in 1606 from Antwerp to his Milanese patron Borromeo. Painted in painstaking detail and containing 102 floral varieties, the picture is in the Pinacoteca Ambrosiana, the museum founded by Borromeo in Milan. Brueghel's devotion to flower still lifes contributed to the prestige and expansion of this type in its early period, when it was not yet considered a single, unified genre. We now understand that painters who specialised in representing kitchen scenes or banquets usually also painted *vanitas* paintings or flower paintings. Peeters is a case in point. Likely encouraged by the example of Breughel and a very few others, she eventually became one of the painters who contributed to the centrality of flower still lifes in Antwerp.

The only known dated flower arrangement by Peeters is the one she included in *Still Life with Flowers, Gilt Goblet, Eatables and a Pewter Flagon* (fig.9), a painting of 1611. A very small painting on copper (fig.51) signed by Peeters (but not dated) is reminiscent of the hybrid images that Joris Hoefnagel made at the end of the sixteenth century. Several flowers in Peeters's painting emerge from a *roemer*, in this case without the typical stem. Surrounding the central oval in which the flower arrangement is shown are insects and small creatures. Their symmetrical arrangement is central to the effort of the artist, as is the descriptive precision and the display of skill.

In other flower still lifes, also undated (figs 36, 52, 53), Peeters represented all the flowers in the composition visually, combined with an organisation

that creates the impression of rich, lavish bouquets. This latter quality agrees with a general tendency of flower paintings in Europe, which evolved in the direction of more abundant and more complex overlapping of flowers. For the most part, however, these paintings fit best within the context of the first generation of flower painters in Flanders, such as Jan Brueghel. The organisation of the bouquets and other accompanying elements in these pictures, for example the flowers that have fallen on the ledge or tabletop, are reminiscent of his works. In addition, the mouse in *Still Life of Flowers with a Mouse and an Ear of Wheat* (fig.52) is very similar to the same animal as painted by Hoefnagel (fig.26), and to examples painted by Brueghel in the very early seventeenth century, just before Peeters started practising her art.

The objects described in the preceding pages give shape to the painted world of Clara Peeters, which was based in the reality of contemporary material culture and elevated the appeal of her paintings. In studying them we learn about objects that surrounded people of the time and the activities they associated them with. We learn about the interaction of Europeans with faraway lands through colonisation and commerce, and their fascination with exotica; about precious ceramics, glass and silver objects and how their display on special occasions defined the social status of their owners; and about the precedent set by scientific illustrations for the development of painting, especially in Antwerp. We also learn about dietary culture and are reminded of the significance of salt and sugar for contemporary Europeans. An important corollary that stems from studying all that is represented in the paintings of Peeters is to understand that the paintings too were luxury goods. Aside from their material value, objects in still-life paintings are often associated with symbolic meanings. We will now turn our attention to this uncertain territory.

5

Problems of Meaning and Interpretation

A quandary posed by many paintings made in Europe in the early modern period is to discern if artists intended to imbue them with symbolic meaning. This is especially true with the genre of still lifes because there are many cases where symbolism is conspicuous. Should we look for symbolism in the paintings of Clara Peeters? And if so, how?

The answer is not easy. Understanding the meaning that contemporaries assigned to paintings is one of the more vexing questions in art history. The time that has passed since the seventeenth century has separated us from cultural clues that would have been evident then but are less so today. This distance is made more problematic by the fact that the culture of Europe has become less symbolic over time. Symbols were most often used in art to represent abstract concepts that did not easily lend themselves to mimesis, and, in paintings of the time that we are concerned with, those concepts were most often associated with Christianity. For example, Peeters's first picture (fig.1) is from the same year that she became pregnant, and was painted some months before she gave birth to her first child. The objects in the painting, a burning candle, wine, jewels and other items could be an expression of hopeful expectations at the time.[1] The lit candle could signify life (in contrast with paintings where a burnt candle

near a skull signifies death), the letter P could denote the artist, the heart could refer to love, and the cross places those concepts in a Christian framework. Trying to find symbolic meaning in paintings can be like a guessing game with only very general clues. Contemporary artistic culture was often symbolic, but not always, and not always very specifically so. A first decision that must be made when interpreting paintings is whether there are elements that lend themselves to be read symbolically or whether they are simply what we see: beautiful items that people were proud to own. Or, perhaps, they could be both.

Another difficulty has to do with tacit knowledge: there are things which we all take to be so natural and obvious that they are never explained. This can be a problem when trying to interpret the past. It affects, first, the decision to try to interpret something symbolically or not and, if the answer is yes, it makes it difficult to know exactly how to interpret things. For example, is the presence of abundant food in paintings by Peeters simply something that an owner would like to see, or is it a criticism of excess, according to a concept often brought up in contemporary religious writings? Finding the right answer to these questions is important because it is to come close to how contemporaries related to the paintings of Clara Peeters.

None of the still-life paintings by Peeters include an inscription or text that could explain an explicit symbolic message. There is nothing in her work like the *Vanitas Still Life* painting of 1603 by Jacques de Gheyn II, roughly a contemporary of Peeters (fig.54). The picture includes the inscription '*humana vana*' ('human vanity') next to a skull, a bubble and a smoking urn. It follows that the meaning of these elements is related to the concept expressed: they refer to the transitory nature of all things and to human vanity in the face of this fact, a message that was important to the Christian faith. In a painting mentioned earlier, the *Allegory of Worldly Riches* (fig.20), the critical commentary on the wealth accumulated on the table is clarified by the devils that harass the dying merchant in the background.

Paintings that offer such clear evidence are useful because they demonstrate that this kind of content could be expected in paintings, and because they tell us that when these same objects appear in other paintings, even if there is no inscription, there is a high possibility that they allude to the same concept. On the other hand, in the painting *Still Life with Confectionery, Wine, Jewels and Burning Candle* (fig.1), two pieces of rock candy lean against each other to form the shape of a cross. Similar rock candy is present in a painting by Osias Beert, *Sill Life with Porcelain Vessels, Glassware and Eatables* (fig.22). The cross could not be missed by viewers, but it is unclear if the painters intended to go beyond simply representing a type of sweet that existed at the time to suggest symbolic meaning or, regardless, if beholders interpreted it in this way.

Which paintings by Peeters could have symbolic meaning? The portrait of a woman seated at a table that we have already analysed (fig.16) includes a bubble, and thus probably expresses the idea of transience. The dice in the painting also seem like an odd presence that is thus best read symbolically, perhaps as a reference to fortune. We know so little about this painting that it is hard to make sense of it.

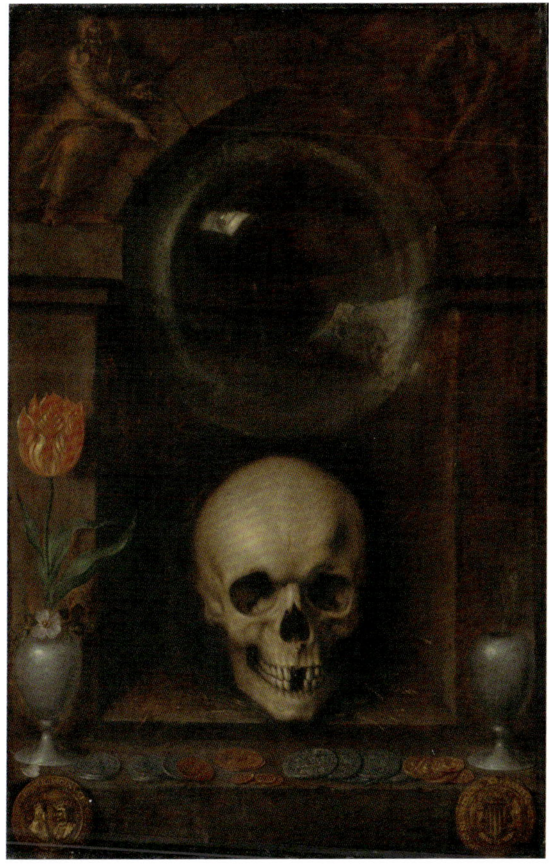

54 Jacques de Gheyn II, *Vanitas Still Life*, 1603, oil on wood, 83 × 54 cm (32 ⅝ × 21 ¼ in), The Metropolitan Museum of Art, New York

Who is the woman portrayed? For whom was it painted?

Other elements in the earliest known scene by Clara Peeters invite interpretation.[2] There is a large biscuit in the shape of a letter P that must be a reference to Peeters herself, as we have seen. The abundant signatures, reflected self-portraits and knives inscribed with her name show that she was very keen to leave signs of her authorship in her paintings. The biscuit in the shape of a heart

presumably refers to love. On the table is a branch
of rosemary from which hang several earrings in the
shape of a strawberry – some have fallen and lay on
the table – and nearby is a ring. As mentioned in
Chapter 4, strawberries were sometimes identified
with fertility, because their surface appears to be
studded with seeds (they are actually achenes),
and rosemary was sometimes carried in wedding
processions and used to decorate wedding tables, as
contemporary descriptions of such events prove. The
candle, lit or not, is a common presence in paintings
that refer to the *vanitas* theme, because the flame,
like life, will inevitably exhaust itself and die. The
wine could be a reference to a fancy import, but
also to the sacrament of the Eucharist, which was
of great importance to Catholics in the Southern
Netherlands, as elsewhere. When all these elements
are seen together there is a strong sense of a symbolic
intention – it must have been made to celebrate an
event that involved Peeters and love, under the aegis
of Christian religion, perhaps a birth or a wedding.
Without more information we can only offer a
tentative interpretation. Rosemary, strawberries,
a candle; all these elements could have various
meanings when used symbolically.

Such is also the case in *Still Life with Fish, Candle,
Artichokes, Crabs and Shrimp* (fig.30), where there is an
unlit candle to the left. It seems like an unnecessary
presence here. For that reason, perhaps it does have
a specific symbolic meaning that refers to the idea of
transience, so important to Christian culture and so
common in still-life paintings. Artichokes also carried
specific associations. They were a source of fascination
until at least the end of the sixteenth century, as
attested by Giuseppe Arcimboldo's *Allegory of Summer*
of 1573 (known in several versions), which presents
a figure made of fruits and vegetables, including an
artichoke on its chest. This food had been a rarity
until that time. Several sources inform us that they
were widely considered aphrodisiacs, including a
book by the English physician Andrew Borde, *A*

Dyetary of Health, of 1542, and in Thomas Hill's
popular *Gardener's Labyrinth*, first published in 1577.[3]
Henry Buttes wrote in 1599 in his cookbook *Dyets
Dry Dinner* that artichokes 'please the taste: provoke
urine and Venus'.[4] The Italian Bartolomeo Boldo, in
his *Libro della natura et virtu delle cose che nutriscono*,
published in Venice in 1575, described artichokes
as sexual stimulants for both women and men.[5]
Artichokes may have held a special interest at the
time because of these sexual connotations; although
modern science has not confirmed these properties,
contemporaries believed in them. But we can also
explain the presence of this eatable in paintings by
Peeters because of its unusual, interesting shape and
because, as we have seen, it had recently become
expected on at least some tables. The choice of objects
and their placement in the painting do not provide
clear evidence of symbolism. Peeters's intention here
seems to be to confront us with realistic description
and pictorial beauty.

That the mindset of early modern Europeans
was more sensitive than ours to symbolism does not
mean that Peeters had an explicit symbolic intention
every time she painted. By the early seventeenth
century a very gradual transition was underway
in European culture in which reality took priority
over metaphoric possibilities. In the art of painting,
this would substitute, very gradually, the previously
dominant idealism and the use of symbolism. The
very idea of painting still lifes that emerged in the
last few years of the sixteenth century is testimony
to this gradual shift. These are ostensibly paintings
of the surrounding reality, of nothing transcendent.
Some artists resisted this idea by incorporating
specific symbolic references to abstract notions in
the paintings. Others accepted more willingly the
novelty implied in representing material culture and
displaying pictorial ability. Clara Peeters is among
the latter. This is clear when we compare her with
De Gheyn, Hieronymus Francken or Beert, in whose
paintings we often find a more overt symbolism.

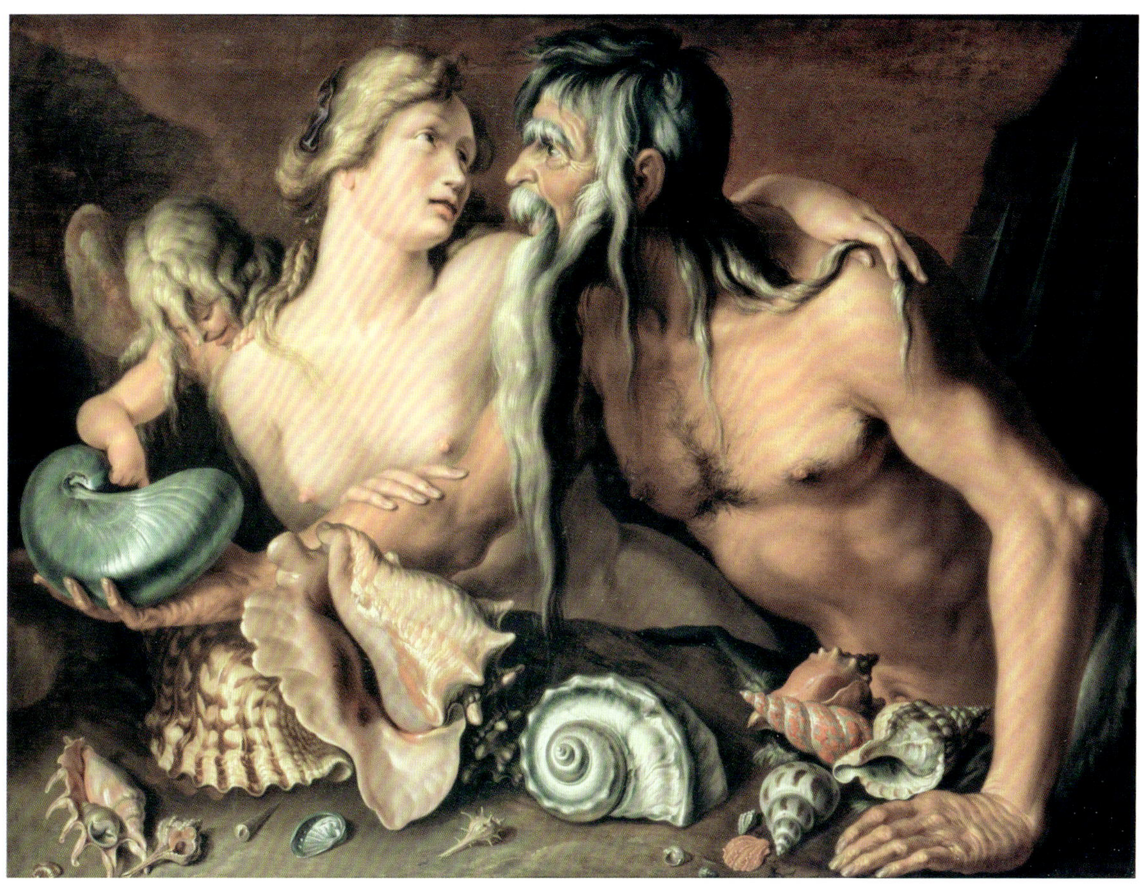

55 Jacques de Gheyn II, *Amphitrite and Cupid with a Nautilus Shell*, early seventeenth century, oil on canvas, 103 × 137 cm (40 ½ × 53 ⅞ in), Wallraf-Richartz-Museum, Cologne

Inevitably, Peeters's paintings give voice to a Eurocentric world view dominated by Christian concepts. But this subject is implicit, as exemplified in her pictures that contain shells. There is ample testimony to the idea that these objects, like beautiful flowers and exotic animals, could be seen as reflections of 'the glory of God', as conveyed in the poem *The Beach*, by the Dutch poet Philibert van Borsselen, mentioned in Chapter 4. The subtitle of the poem is *In Praise of the Creator of All Things*, which makes clear Van Borsselen's belief that earthly beauty arose from divine inspiration. Similar testimonies about other objects that Peeters painted

are abundant. For example, at about the same time of Van Borsselen's poem, Cardinal Federico Borromeo praised the fruits and vegetables that Jan Brueghel had painted in one of his religious scenes, because they 'show us the wisdom and refinement of divine providence; their profusion, abundance and great variety will open our eyes to the liberality and generous heart of this so magnanimous Creator'.[6] There is no specific, literal reference to this concept of God's creation of nature in the paintings by Peeters, but we can be sure that both she and her contemporaries shared it. Another meaning contemporaries would have been receptive to is the value of exotic shells as signifiers of worldliness and status. These are implicit meanings, and not specific symbolic messages.

This religious view overlapped with the more scientific one that valued precision in the rendering of things. An example is in the correspondence between the same patron and painter, Borromeo and Brueghel, which includes several statements that highlight the fact that animals and flowers had been painted after natural specimens. In a letter of 1606, Brueghel wrote to Borromeo that he had travelled from Antwerp to Brussels to study rare flowers through direct observation so that he could best incorporate them into his paintings. In another letter of 1621, he boasted that 'the birds and animals were done from life from several of Her Serene Highness's specimens', referring to a painting made after live animals in the zoological collection of the Brussels court.[7]

In some still-life paintings by other artists that contain shells, on the other hand, there is a very specific symbolism. Because of their shapes, certain seashells were used in some paintings as proxies for sexual organs. An example is a painting by De Gheyn, *Amphitrite and Cupid with a Nautilus Shell* (fig.55). The young Cupid sticks his finger into the nautilus, a clear reference to intercourse, and the large shell in front of the goddess Amphitrite is easily associated with her vulva. Other shells in the painting are susceptible to similar interpretations.[8] If Peeters had wanted to convey this or any other very specific symbolism in her paintings with shells, other objects painted nearby would provide clues. But this is not the case.

Further to the potential for sexual symbolism is the monkey present to the right in *Still Life with Fruit in a Basket, Dead Birds and a Monkey* (fig.56). We know that such animals could be used symbolically, as references to unbridled sensual desires, or to refer to art as the ape of nature (paintings where monkeys are seen making art were not unusual). But there is no other element in this painting that encourages a specific symbolic reading. Rather, the intention seems

to be to invoke perspectives and practices of the time. For example, monkeys were collectables, shipped to Europe from the tropical forests of Central and South America, and also from Africa, from the sixteenth century, and they were kept as pets. They are often seen in portraits of the elite of the time. Isabel Clara Eugenia, the woman who ruled the Southern Netherlands during the lifetime of Clara Peeters, was portrayed during her youth with a pet monkey in a painting by Alonso Sánchez Coello, as was her sister Catalina Micaela, in a likeness by Sofonisba Anguissola.[9] On several occasions after moving from Madrid to Brussels to take on her role as ruler, Isabel Clara Eugenia had monkeys, parrots and other exotic animals and objects sent to her from Spain.[10] In a letter of 23 November 1605 that she sent from Brussels to Madrid, she wrote to the Duke of Lerma, the King's favourite advisor, about a monkey that she had received from him, 'the best gift you could have given me'. The animal was well behaved, she stated, better than one that 'ate the organ in San Lorenzo', presumably referring to an event that she witnessed at the Escorial during her youth.[11] Because monkeys were common enough in the everyday life of the elite, their presence in a still-life painting can simply reflect a contemporary interest in exotic pets. This is probably how we should read *Still Life with Fruit in a Basket, Dead Birds and a Monkey*.

The quest for symbolism can lead to mistakes in interpretation. The four paintings by Clara Peeters that belong to the Museo del Prado (figs 9, 14, 29, 30) have been interpreted as paintings of the four elements, earth, air, fire and water, based on the fact that such series of images were somewhat common, and on the belief that the four pictures had a shared history and thus were probably made as a unified series from the start. The objects in each of the paintings do not easily lend themselves to be read as references to the elements, however. More importantly in this case, the argument that they share a common history turns out not to be

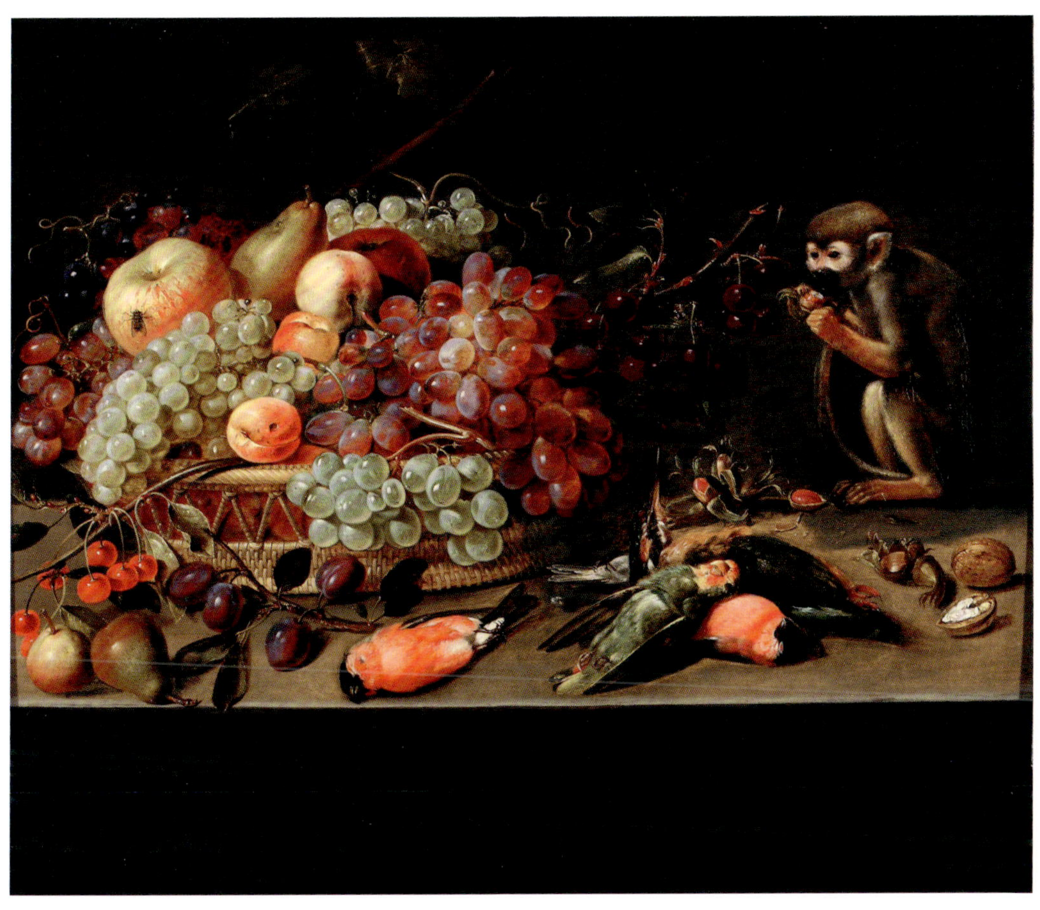

56 Clara Peeters, *Still Life with Fruit in a Basket, Dead Birds and a Monkey*, c.1612–21, oil on panel, 47 × 66 cm (18 ½ × 26 in), private collection

true. Two of the paintings, *Still Life with a Sparrow Hawk, Fowl, Porcelain and Shells* (fig.29) and *Still Life with Fish, Candle, Artichokes, Crabs and Shrimp* (fig.30), were listed in the Spanish royal collection in 1666. They hung in the King's palace in Madrid, where they were described simply as paintings, 'one of fish and the other of birds'.[12] The other two Prado paintings (figs 9, 14) have a different history. They are first documented in the royal collection in 1746, in the palace of San Ildefonso in La Granja, as part of the collection of the Queen, Isabel de Farnesio.[13] This provenance suggests that the four paintings by Peeters at the Prado were made as two pairs, and not as a single set of four. Also against an allegorical interpretation of these four paintings is the fact that they are always described in the royal collection as paintings of the objects depicted, and not as fables or allegories, as was the case with other pictures in the same collection. For example, the famous series of five paintings of the senses by Jan Brueghel and Peter Paul Rubens of 1617–18 now in the Prado (fig.43) was described as '*los cinco sentidos*' ('the five senses') in inventories of 1636, 1666 and 1686. This suggests that Peeters's four paintings were not identified as allegories of the elements. That is, they were not considered as obviously, or primarily, metaphoric.

To cite another example, Peeters, along with other artists in Antwerp that are roughly her contemporaries, such as Brueghel, Frans Snyders or, slightly later, Paul de Vos (1595–1678), often enriched her still lifes with the presence of a cat. These artists spurred each other on as they thought of ways to enhance the variety to this new genre of painting by adding elements. We know that cats were sometimes used symbolically in paintings. Samuel van Hoogstraten's *Perspective Box of a Dutch Interior* from 1663 (Detroit Institute of Arts, Michigan) shows a cat perched above a table laden with food. In the background, above the entrance to the room, is the inscription '*Memento mori*', a reminder that the end awaits us and that all things are perishable.

This immediately makes us think that some of the contents of the table will soon be gone by the agency of the cat. In ancient sources such as Aristotle's *The History of Animals*, and later in Conrad Gessner's *Historia animalium* (published in four volumes in Zurich between 1551 and 1558), cats were associated with many different concepts, including night and darkness because of their night vision and nocturnal activity, and freedom, because of their independence. They were also said to be neat and useful in the home for pest control, but also carriers of pestilence.

Does all this mean that Peeters considered the cats in her paintings, such as *Still Life with Fish and Cat* (fig.17), as symbolic? Not necessarily. The felines were common pets at the time and were also frequent visitors to food stalls in markets, and to areas of the home where food was prepared. The presence of a cat in the scene by Peeters seems perfectly natural. The animal is cautious, its ears partially pulled back as if alert to a presence – the artist's, and ours. As is often the case when observing these animals in real life, we are alert to what may suddenly unfold. The cat in the still life by Peeters is 'watchful and wary', as Edward Topsell describes these animals in his 1607 book *The Historie of Foure-Footed Beastes*.[14] It must have just jumped up on the table because it has not yet started eating the unattended food. Things will not remain as they are for long: the cat will either soon be gone, chased away by a kitchen hand, or it will dig its teeth into the fish. What the presence of the cat does here, rather than suggesting a specific symbolism, is to add a note of tension to the image, intensifying our reaction to it.

Numerous testimonies from the seventeenth century show that the skill demonstrated by the artists of still-life paintings – the quality of the images – was what was most valued. In 1604 Karel van Mander wrote about Lodewijck van den Bosch (1525–after 1568), a sixteenth-century painter of flower bouquets and fruit paintings of whom no works are known today, that he 'applied much time, patience, and precision [to

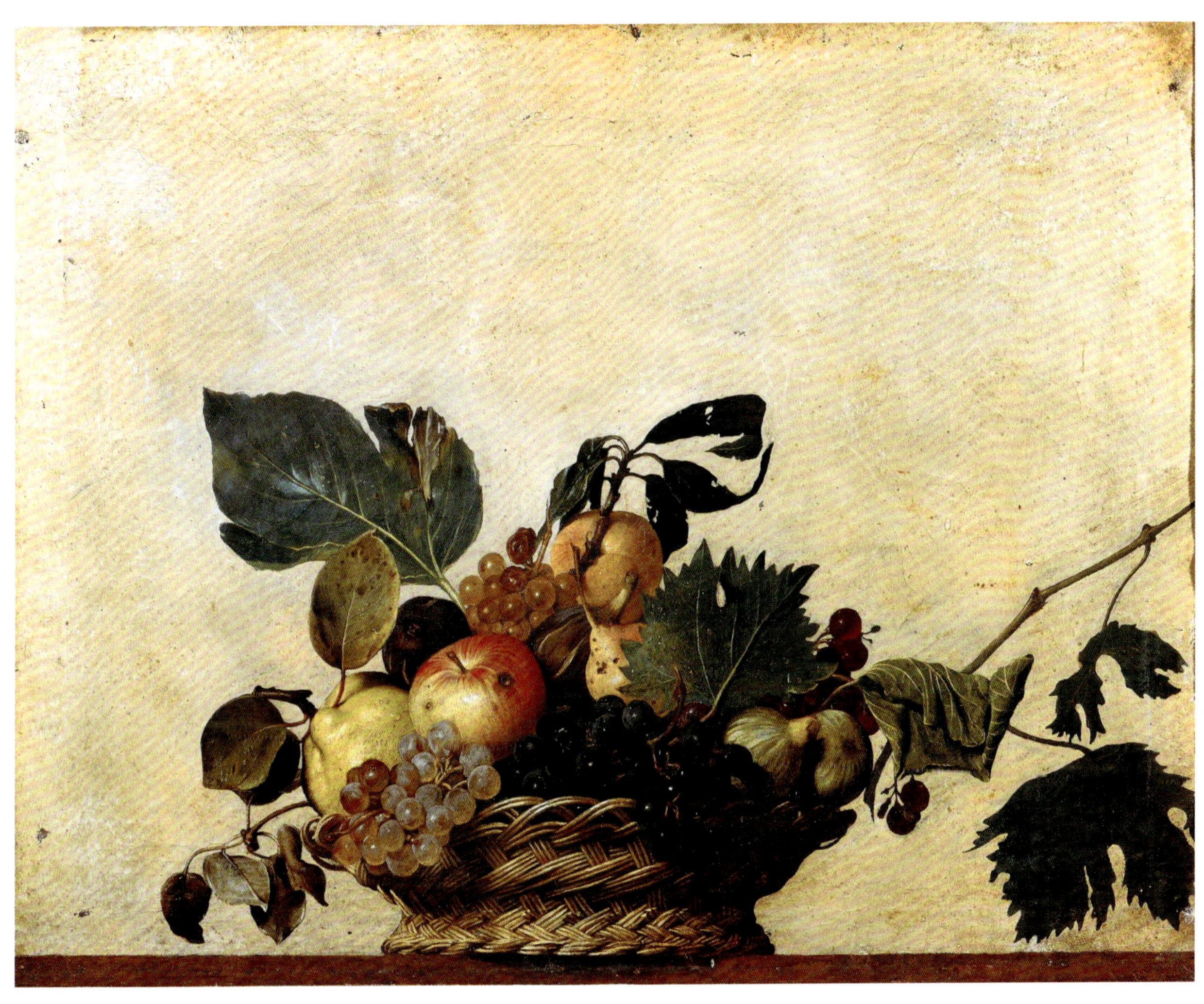

57 Caravaggio, *Basket of Fruit*, *c.*1599, oil on canvas, 46 × 64 cm (18 ⅛ × 25 ¼ in), Pinacoteca Ambrosiana, Milan

his paintings] so that everything appeared natural'.[15]
Similarly, Borromeo, who owned Caravaggio's *Basket
of Fruit* (fig.57), one of the earliest known still lifes
(it is generally dated to *c.*1599), wrote in his text
Museum of 1625 about its 'beauty and incomparable
excellence', with no mention of any possible ulterior
meaning.[16] In the same text he included a description
of a painting made jointly by Jan Brueghel and Hans
Rottenhammer (1564–1625) that displayed a striking
contrast between a winter landscape and flowers
scattered in it. Borromeo wrote that the painting
'exhibits a paradox in that flowers, which convey a
sense of comfort, and snow, which is frozen by the
cold, each represent opposite extremes of nature. [...]
That said, when I asked to have the painting done in
this way I did not have these paradoxes or symbolic
meanings in mind.'[17] Giovanni Pietro Bellori, writing
in 1672 about some still lifes by Caravaggio that are not
known to us, praised their mimetic effect, their beauty
and the painter's ability to recreate 'the transparency
of the water and the glass and the reflections from
the window of a room'.[18] Furthermore, Francisco
Pacheco wrote in his *Arte de la pintura* that the
challenge of painting pictures of flowers lay in their
'true imitation', in the mastery of depicting the glasses,
earthenware, silver and gold vessels or baskets in which
the flowers were usually placed, and in the design of
the composition.[19] In 1631, Jan Brueghel the Younger
(1601–78), son of his often mentioned namesake, stated
that his goals for a set of paintings of the senses were
to paint realistically and to depict a wide variety of
objects: 'As for the five senses, I am enjoying working
on them to do everything after the life, and the subject
is also agreeable to having all that is on earth put into
it.'[20] At the end of the seventeenth century, Gerard de
Lairesse wrote that Willem Kalf (1619–93) 'excelled
in still life above others, yet [...] he could give little
reason for his depictions, why he showed this or that;
but he only depicted what came to mind [...] without
thinking of producing something of importance that
might contain special meaning [...]'.[21]

These testimonies are revealing. We can conclude
from them that, for viewers contemplating paintings
in the seventeenth century, symbolic interpretations
could be expected, but also that making had primacy
over specific meaning in the appreciation of still-
life paintings. The art of Clara Peeters is a perfect
example of this approach.

Conclusion

Peeters's Artistry

At the beginning of this book, I wrote that Peeters had not been the focus of much scholarly attention. What have we gained after spending some time thinking about her art and about her as an artist – after 'illuminating' Clara Peeters?

Because she was a woman in early modern Europe, pursuing a career as a painter was more difficult and more constrained than it was for most men. That she managed to do so is a sign of an unusual determination. The fact that we have little secure documentation that can inform us about her life and work can be attributed to her gender: in her lifetime, the expectations of those writing about art did not lead them to focus much attention on women painters. A change is already underway in this regard. Monographic exhibitions such as the one organised by the Prado in 2016 have a great influence on where the public focuses its interest. That exhibition, the first ever devoted to Peeters, drew a disproportionate amount of attention from the local and international press, suggesting that its time was long due. Books such as this in a series titled *Illuminating Women Artists* will hopefully have a similar effect.

As the curator of the Flemish collection at the Prado I am witness to another sign of the unquestionable growth of interest in Peeters. From the time of the 2016 exhibition, the number of requests to borrow paintings by her for different kinds of exhibitions in other museums has surged. In the past we encouraged others to borrow, with the goal of giving visibility to her works. Our effort now is perforce directed at reducing loans to a minimum (our main goal in museums is to preserve the artworks and travelling can put them at risk). With their increased status, and as happens with the most prominent works in public collections, Peeters's still-life paintings will presumably travel little in the future. Members of the public interested in seeing them in person will have to make the pilgrimage to the museums that own them – none as many as the Prado, where four pictures by Peeters are kept.

When explaining the development of her style in this text, and when mapping her place within the history of still-life paintings, the aim has been to follow an evolutionary model. Her individual paintings occupy a certain place within the trajectory of her growth as an artist, and her work is representative of an early chapter in the evolution of the genre of still-life paintings. This method has been used by art historians for centuries, and it has the advantage of offering a useful tool to understand evolutionary aspects of the history of humanity. But it can be limiting. What happens when, rather than seeing the paintings of Peeters as stepping stones in a path (her own activity; the history of still-life paintings), we consider each as a final destination, an embodiment of her particular way of presenting the world to us?

Realism is a salient characteristic of the artistic language of Clara Peeters. This term can, however, mislead. Realism is a way of presenting things, but it does not mandate what objects are displayed, or how they relate to each other. Its purpose was to offer an alternative to the entrenched idealism of the Renaissance tradition. It was part of the general process of increasing materialism that was beginning to drive European culture in the early modern period. In the art of painting, it found expression in a new stylistic trend that emerged at the very end of the sixteenth century. It is usually referred to by art historians as 'naturalism' and is identified with the art of Caravaggio and his followers, and with realistic-looking landscapes, genre paintings and still lifes. This manner of painting was fundamentally different from the idealism and stylistic self-awareness that pervaded the sixteenth century, and it signified a chasm in the history of European art. Its radical character must have been especially felt in the context of Antwerp, where the arts were dominated well into the seventeenth century by the high idealism of Peter Paul Rubens. The aesthetic value of the paintings of Peeters needs to be seen in the context of this realist movement.

The literary critic Denis Donoghue, in his wonderful book *Speaking of Beauty*, wrote of idealism that it 'makes it hard to endow mere objects, the ordinary universe, with value'.[1] The goal of Clara Peeters and of artists working in a realistic vein in Europe was to do precisely this: to offer and to value an experience close to the here and now, to come close to the actual appearance of the surrounding reality. Their art offers us an example of what would eventually be referred to as 'facticity', the philosophical attitude that values reality beyond any ulterior meaning.[2] Elsewhere in the same book,

citing Nathaniel Hawthorne's story 'The Birthmark', Donoghue contrasts 'the immortal essence', which is the goal of idealism, with the 'dim sphere of half development'.[3] This is where real life takes place. One of the virtues of Peeters is that she focuses our minds on this limited sphere and its unforeseen possibilities and beauty.

The realistic representation of things brings them close to the experience of everyday life. The realism of Clara Peeters is characterised by the precise definition of form and texture, the unadorned backgrounds, which contribute to an overall impression of simplicity, and a preference for imperfections such as a crack on the edge of a table or ledge. Contours and shapes are not overly sinuous or calligraphic and thus encourage us to focus on the objects they describe. This is different from what we find, for example, in the still lifes by Frans Snyders, who is more prone to linear flourishes (fig.21). In *Still Life with Cheeses, Almonds and Pretzels* (figs 33, 58), the objects appear to be casually distributed. A few almonds and raisins have fallen out of the plate. Yet, the textures of the different surfaces are rendered with diligent care. In the upper section of the Gouda-like cheese Peeters has painted the hole that was made to assess the state of the cheese with a tester. In *Still Life with Flowers, Gilt Goblet, Eatables and a Pewter Flagon* (figs 9, 59), a half-eaten pretzel implies that someone has been at this table, contributing to make the painted illusion seem real.

A comparison between the art of Clara Peeters and Jan Brueghel is a useful way to highlight the innovative aesthetics of naturalism, one of the defining features of the art of Peeters. Brueghel's allegorical fantasies display the same type of objects that we find in the still lifes of Peeters, and they allude to the same social customs. They both lived and painted in the Southern Netherlands during the same period. Brueghel painted for the court of Isabel Clara Eugenia and Albert, and for the highest echelons of collectors. Peeters placed some of her works in very

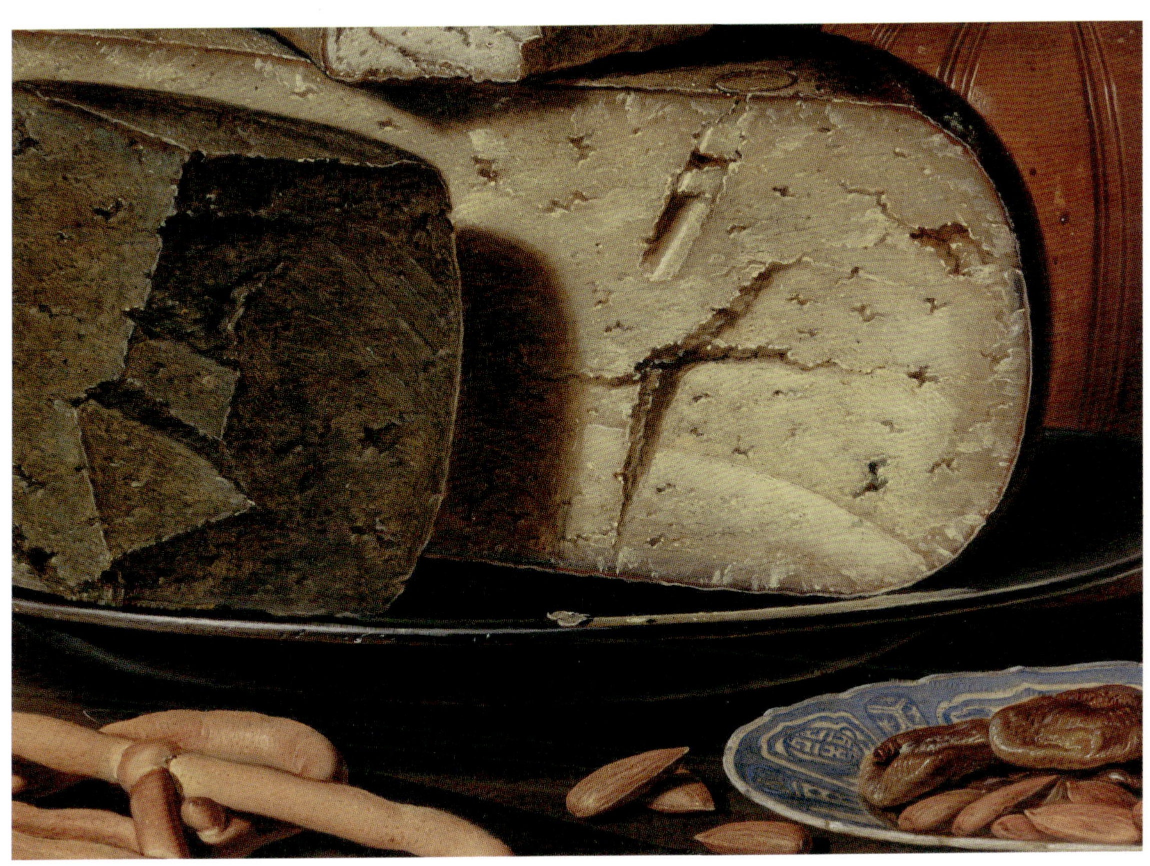

58 Detail of fig.33

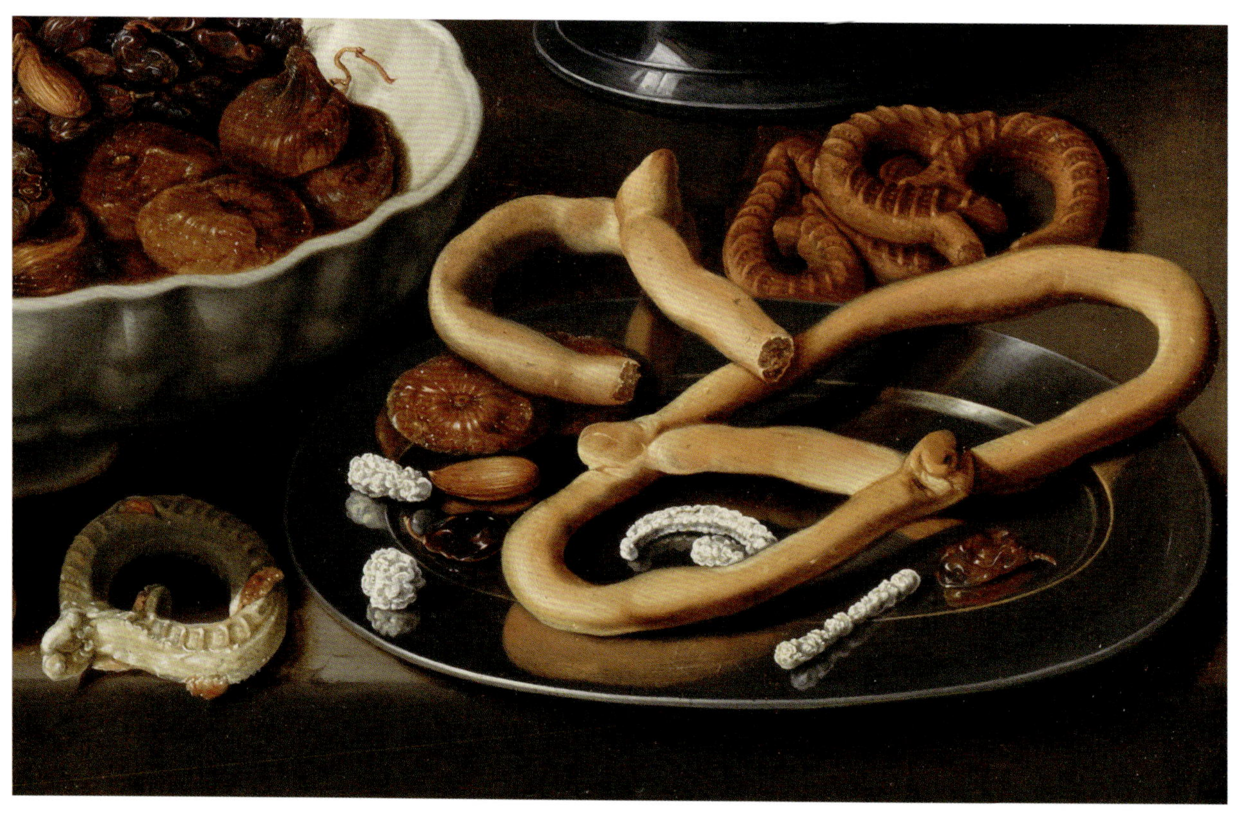

59 Detail of fig.9

elite collections but most often must have worked for a lower tier of elite clients, whether they acquired her work as patrons or, more likely, on the open market, which imitated the cultural and collecting patterns of the court. In this sense the comparison helps us to understand that she painted high-end products intended for elite collectors.

The pictorial language of Brueghel is more exuberant than what we find in Peeters. This is evident in the paintings that belong to the *Five Senses* series (fig.43). His art combines the language of miniature painting, which he learned from his maternal grandmother Mayken Verhulst in Antwerp, and the aesthetic goals of idealism. In his paintings, attention to detail is extreme. When contemplating these paintings, one feels that he not only represents but also celebrates the objects represented. In philosophical terms, the purpose of this type of art was to elevate reality, to bring before our eyes a reflection of a higher, more beautiful, ideal world. In the still lifes of Peeters the same objects – birds, shells and flowers, silver cups, goblets, porcelain, glass and eatables – appear less luscious and less celebratory. She does not surround the objects with a palatial context and her paintings are more restrained in tone.

Art collectors in the seventeenth century were aware of different stylistic options at the time. Chapter 3 discussed an event that took place in 1639, when the Duke of Aarschot, a leading Flemish aristocrat, was offered the possibility of having Jacob van Hulsdonck (fig.23) paint some still lifes for him. He rejected them, pointing to reasons of money but also of taste: 'as for the paintings by Van Hulsdonck, his work is clean, but it lacks liveliness and does not disserve the high price that is being asked and therefore I will do without it'.[4] By liveliness Aarschot must have meant the formal richness and intense colour that we find in paintings by Brueghel, Rubens, Snyders and artists close to them, who represented the prevailing elite taste in Flemish painting at the time. By contrast, the art of Peeters was more in tune with the very latest developments in still-life painting and other expressions of naturalism around Europe – it was closer to the art of Van Hulsdonck. Its description of forms is more discreet, with less calligraphic emphasis. Its colour range is limited but nuanced. Rather than intense individual colour, she favoured a harmonious variation in a few tones. One could say, finding inspiration in a sentence from Virginia Woolf (in *A Room of One's Own*), that the realist style of Peeters is more attached to life than its counterpart.

The brown hues of different objects in the still-life paintings of Clara Peeters are framed in many examples by dark brown backgrounds and lighter, glowing ledges. Brown tones are one of Peeters's specialities and contribute to the beauty of her works. The covered *façon de Venise* glass and the bread and stoneware jug in *Still Life with Cheeses, Almonds and Pretzels* (fig.33) form one of several melodies of colour within the painting, where the blue porcelain almost seems dissonant. In *Still Life with Gilt Goblet, Porcelain and Eatables* (fig.31), the carefully composed objects sing a similar tune. Here the pomegranate takes brown as close to red as it can come. The play of vertical and horizontal accents is masterful in this painting, and immensely satisfying to observe and contemplate. The rims and bodies of the goblet and the stack of porcelain bowl and plates guide us up and across simultaneously. Every other element in the painting contributes to this central tune. The painting *Still Life with Flowers, Gilt Goblets, Coins and Shells* (fig.10) can be read in the same way. Here the contrast with the vertical axis is provided by porcelain plate, shells, coins and gold chain. The geometric emphasis created by the dark background space or wall and the surface and side of the ledge in front of it is similar: it is discreet, but it asks to be noticed.

Another key aesthetic quality of the paintings of Clara Peeters is relational richness; it is a quality that she brings to her realism. This is the web of connections based on similarities and dissimilarities

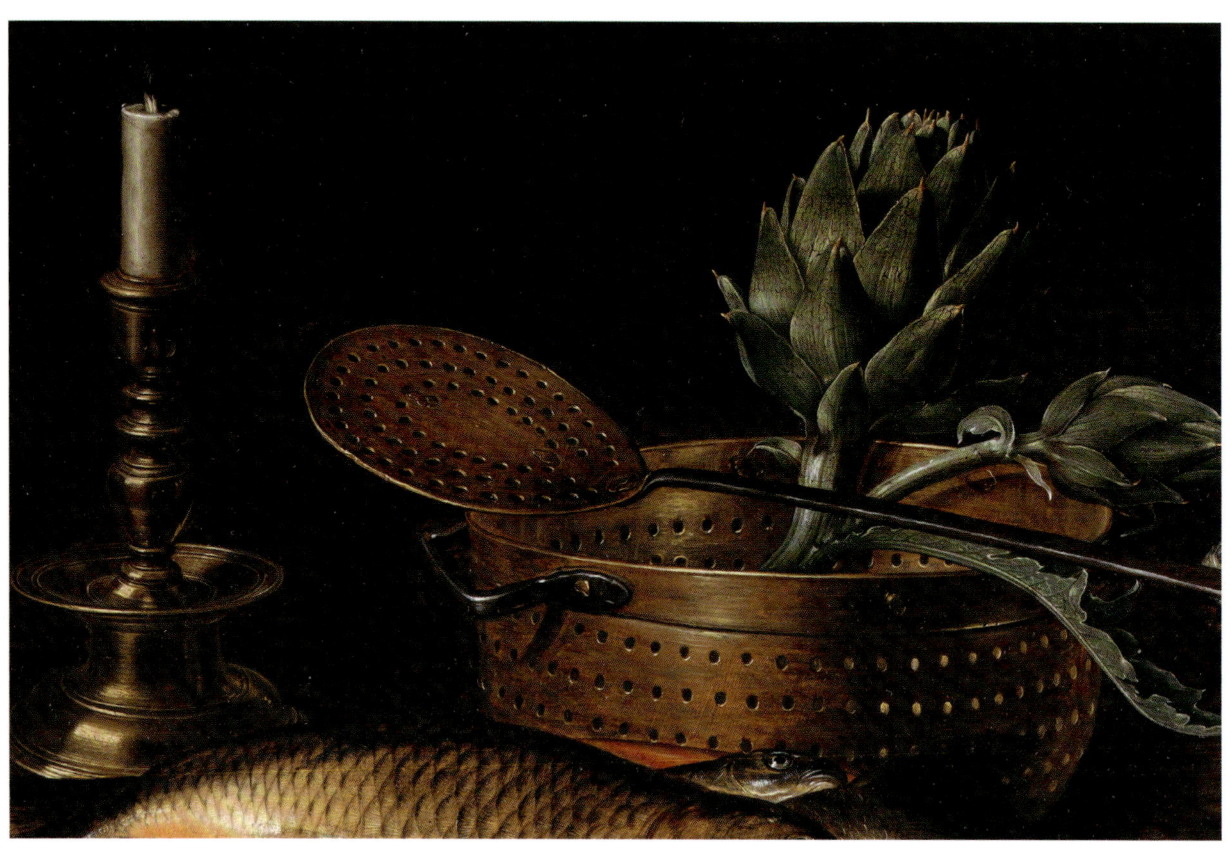

60 Detail of fig.30

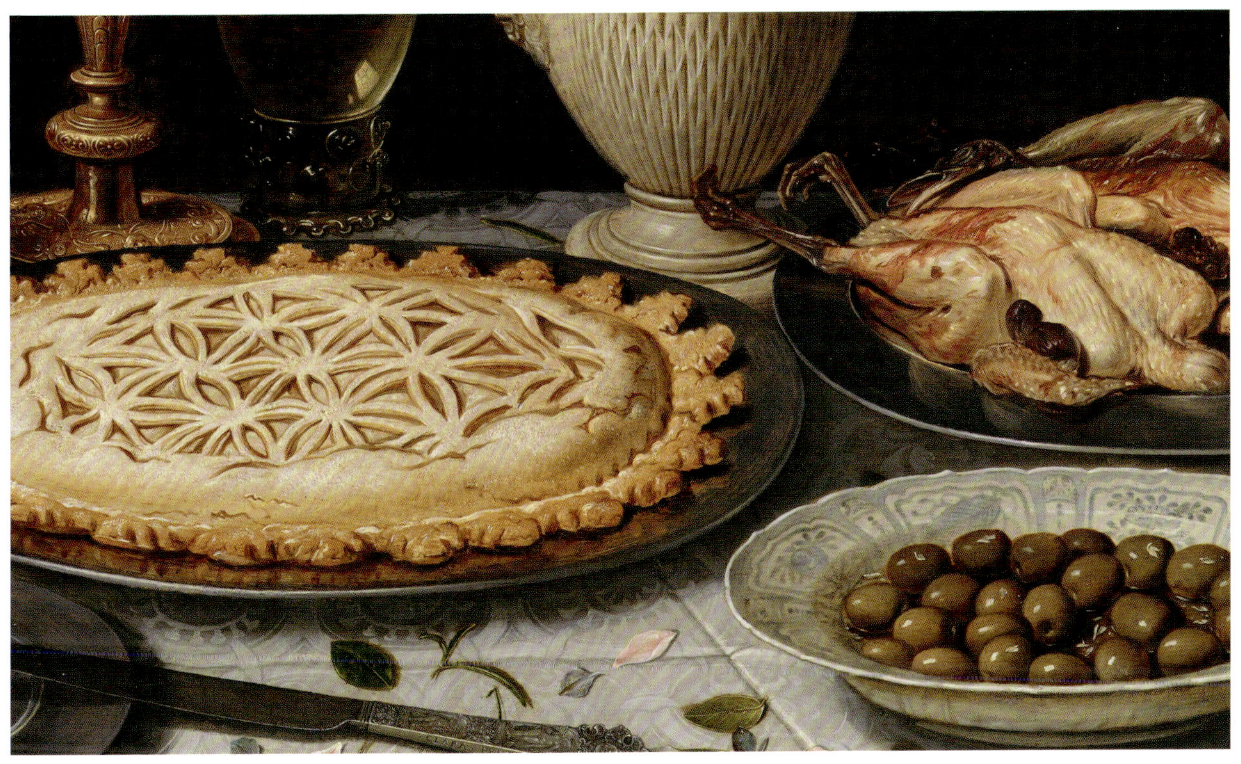

61 Detail of fig.14

of forms, colours and textures that exists between the objects in her paintings. In *Still Life with Fish, Candle, Artichokes, Crabs and Shrimp* (figs 30, 60) we find it in the variations of the rich, red tones of the copper sifter, and in the contrast between the elegant dark background and the objects that seem to glow before it. The colour is more luminous here than in the painting described previously. The painter has used the light brown tone of the preparation (*imprimatura*) layer to add chromatic drama. Relational richness also results from the rhythmic contrast that we see in this picture between rounded and jagged shapes, as in the colander and the artichoke, and between the different patterns, as in the surface decoration of the stoneware jug and the scales of the fish and holes of the colander. When painting the numerous holes in the copper colander and the skimmer she laboured so that each one of them is just slightly different. And then, as mentioned in Chapter 3, she made minute changes to some of the holes before she was satisfied with the result. This is one of Peeters's most carefully executed works. The care exemplified here is another of the characteristics that we find in her best paintings.

In the painting *Table with Cloth, Foodstuffs and Other Objects* (figs 14, 61), we again witness Peeters's penchant for creating rhythms based on similitude and dissimilitude. A pie in the centre, accentuated by a patterned top crust and an ornamental edge, lies on a round pewter plate, and nearby rounded olives are placed in a shallow porcelain bowl with a foliated rim. The comparison between variated, rounded and straight lines and shapes is a sub-theme that activates this painting. The folds of the tablecloth are a sign of a well-kept household, as described in Chapter 4, and they create another pattern of connecting lines that further enriches the composition. In *Still Life with a Sparrow Hawk, Fowl, Porcelain and Shells* (fig.29) we are encouraged to focus on the roundness of forms, from plates and baskets to the swollen bodies of the birds, and to contrast this with the flatness of the ledge below. The tendency of Clara Peeters to contrast

and compare also leads her to place the hard surfaces of shells and porcelain vessels next to the soft warmth of some of the birds, and to juxtapose the fine surface of shells and porcelains, echoing the etymological link that exists between the two (as explained in Chapter 4, the term 'porcelain' derives from an Italian word that refers to a type of white shell: *porcellana*). We recognise the same intent and care also in this painting when the artist diligently isolates the red-chested bullfinch to the right from a nearby string of birds to bring it close to the like-coloured shells, all harmonised with the green head of a large mallard. Peeters is a master at creating these relations and visual echoes. However, time has transformed the painting: the tail of the rooster in the upper left corner has lost nearly all its colour and is barely visible. It would have echoed the hue of the green head of the duck and contrasted with the reddish colour of the mallard's feet. The image is no longer complete; sometimes losing something is the best way to appreciate it.

At first sight, the realism of Clara Peeters does not call attention to itself. Her paintings offer us a window through which we come close to the material culture and social practices of the time. This world does not seem ostentatious; instead, it is one of understated luxury. It does not encourage us to covet what we see but rather to find value and beauty in looking closely at how things are. When we look carefully, however, we notice that we have been deceived. In the paintings of Peeters, we see a version of reality that is subtly but highly aestheticised. The special qualities she brings to her art are an eye sensitive to rich variations in texture and tone and an awareness of relational richness. The result is a kind of beauty that would be missed had she not managed to become a painter.

Notes

INTRODUCTION

1   The most thorough studies of the artist are Pamela
    Hibbs Decoteau, *Clara Peeters, 1594–ca.1640, and the
    Development of Still-Life Painting in Northern Europe*,
    Lingen, Luca Verlag, 1992; and Alejandro Vergara, ed.,
    The Art of Clara Peeters, Madrid, Museo del Prado, 2016.

2   Alejandro Vergara, 'Clara Peeters en el Prado: Una
    cuestión de categorías', in Ernesto Calabuig, *Un ángulo
    me basta, Visiones pedagógicas*, Madrid, editorial Tres
    hermanas, 2021, pp 22–35, on p.33.

3   Vergara, ed., *The Art of Clara Peeters*. The catalogue was
    published on the occasion of the exhibition *El arte
    de Clara Peeters* (*The Art of Clara Peeters*), which was
    developed by the Museo del Prado and held there, and
    also the Rockoxhuis museum in Antwerp (now the
    Snijders and Rockoxhuis museum), in 2016 and 2017.

I THE LIFE AND CONTEXT OF CLARA
PEETERS

1   For the extant paintings by Peeters, in addition to
    Pamela Hibbs Decoteau, *Clara Peeters, 1594–ca.1640,
    and the Development of Still-Life Painting in Northern
    Europe*, Lingen, Luca Verlag, 1992; and Alejandro
    Vergara, ed., *The Art of Clara Peeters*, Madrid, Museo
    del Prado, 2016, see the information available in the
    web page of the Rijksbureau voor Kunsthistorische
    Documentatie (Netherlands Institute for Art History:
    https://research.rkd.nl/en; search for Clara Peeters in
    the RKD Images database).

2   Gemeentearchief, Amsterdam, Notarial Archives,
    no.5075, inv.no.483, fol.563. It can be consulted in Getty
    Provenance Index (Inventory N-2206), anonymous
    collection, Amsterdam, 1635, item 4: 'Suyckerbanquet'.
    See https://www.getty.edu/research/tools/provenance/
    index.html.

3   This possibility, and the biography that derives from it,
    stems from the research published in Jean Bastiaensen,
    'Finding Clara: Establishing the Biographical Details
    of Clara Peeters (*c.*1587–after 1636)', *Boletín del Museo del
    Prado*, vol.34, no.52 (2016), pp 17–31 (which also includes
    a summary of earlier publications on the artist).

4   For a history of Antwerp at the time, see the essays in
    Jan Van der Stock, ed., *Antwerp, Story of a Metropolis*,
    Martial & Snoeck, Gent, 1993.

5   Susan Foister and Peter van den Brink, *Dürer's Journey:
    Travels of a Renaissance Artist*, London, National Gallery
    Company, 2021, p.39.

6   Alejandro Vergara, ed., *Patinir: Studies and Critical
    Catalogue*, Madrid, Museo del Prado, 2007, cat.no.14.

7   Karel van Mander, *Het Schilder-Boeck*, Haarlem,
    1604 (modern English edn *The Lives of the Illustrious
    Netherlandish and German Painters, from the First
    Edition of the Schilder-boeck* (1603–4), ed. and trans.
    Hessel Miedema, 6 vols, Doornsprijk, Davaco, 1994–9),
    vol.1, p.213.

8   ibid., vol.1, p.213.

9   Simon Schama, *The Embarrassment of Riches: An
    Interpretation of Dutch Culture in the Golden Age*, New
    York, Alfred A. Knopf, 1987, p.161.

10   Other examples are Gillian Riley, *The Dutch Table: Gastronomy in the Golden Age of the Netherlands*, Painters and Food series, San Francisco, CA, Pomegranate Artbooks, 1994, p.48; and Hanneke Grootenboer, *The Pensive Image: Art as a Form of Thinking*, Chicago, IL, University of Chicago Press, 2020, p.15. See also Alan Chong and Wouter Kloek, *Still-Life Painting from the Netherlands 1550–1720*, Zwolle, Waander Publishers, 1999; and Sam Segal, *A Prosperous Past: The Sumptuous Still Life in the Netherlands, 1600–1700*, The Hague, SDY Publishers, 1989.

11   See Dorothy M. Meads, ed., *The Diary of Lady Margaret Hoby 1599–1605*, London, Routledge, 1930.

12   Arthur J. DiFuria, 'Towards an Understanding of Mayken Verhulst and Volcxken Diericx', in Elizabeth Sutton, ed., *Women Artists and Patrons in the Netherlands*, Amsterdam, Amsterdam University Press, 2019, pp 157–77.

13   Andrea Pearson, 'Marking Female Ocular Agency in the "Medieval Housebook"', in Merry Wiesner-Hanks, ed., *Challenging Women's Agency and Activism in Early Modernity*, Amsterdam, University of Amsterdam Press, 2021, pp 229–49.

14   Manuel Parada López de Corselas, *El viaje de Jan van Eyck de Flandes a Granada*, Madrid, Ediciones de La Ergástula, 2016, pp 192, 193.

15   Linda Nochlin, 'Why Have There Been No Great Women Artists?', *Art News*, 1971 (reprinted in Linda Nochlin, *Women, Art and Power and Other Essays*, New York, Harper Collins, 1988); Anne Sutherland Harris and Linda Nochlin, *Women Artists: 1550–1950*, New York, Knopf, 1976; Whitney Chadwick, *Women, Art and Society*, London, Thames & Hudson, 1990; and Sarah Joan Moran and Amanda C. Pipkin, *Women and Gender in the Early Modern Low Countries, 1500–1750*, Leiden, Brill, 2019.

16   Edward Norgate, *Miniatura, or, The Art of Limning*, ed. Jeffrey M. Muller and Jim Murrell, New Haven, CT and London, Yale University Press, 1997, p.108.

17   Patrisia Cavazzini, *Painting as Business in Early Seventeenth-Century Rome*, University Park, PA, Pennsylvania State University Press, 2008, pp 72–80.

18   Van Mander, *Het Schilder-Boeck*, 1604, fol.5v. See also Walter S. Melion, *Shaping the Netherlandish Canon: Karel van Mander's Schilder-Boek*, Chicago, IL and London, University of Chicago Press, 1991, p.5.

19   For the ideas of these writers about still-life painting, see Guido M.C. Jansen, '"On the Lowest Level": The Status of Still Life in the Netherlandish Art and Literature of the Seventeenth Century', in Chong and Kloek, *Still-Life Painting*, 1999, pp 51–7.

20   John Loughman, 'The Market for Netherlandish Still Lifes, 1600–1700', in Chong and Kloek, *Still-Life Painting*, 1999, pp 87–102; and Jeffrey M. Muller, 'Private Collections in the Spanish Netherlands: Ownership and Display of Paintings in Domestic Interiors', in Peter Sutton, ed., *The Age of Rubens*, Boston, MA, Boston Museum of Fine Arts and Ludion Press, 1993, pp 195–206.

21   Cavazzini, *Painting as Business*, p.73.

22   ibid., p.73.

23   Katlijne van der Stighelen, ed., *Michaelina Wautier: Glorifying a Forgotten Talent*, Kontich, BAI Publishers, 2018 (for the two paintings mentioned, see cat.3, pp 166–71, and cat.13, pp 208–17).

24   Mary D. Garrard, *Artemisia Gentileschi: The Image of the Female Hero in Italian Baroque Art*, Princeton, NJ, Princeton University Press, 1989, pp 136, 357, 390, 394, 398.

25   Van der Stighelen, ed., *Michaelina Wautier*, p.89.

26   For self-portraiture in European art, see James Hall, *The Self-Portrait: A Cultural History*, New York, Thames & Hudson, 2014.

27   For Peeters's self-portraits, see Jennifer Brynn Black, 'Female Self-Portraiture in Early Modern Europe: Colonna, Anguissola, Whitney, and Peeters', PhD dissertation, Boston University, MA, 2004. Celeste Brusati also focuses on the self-portraits of Peeters, placed in the broader context of Netherlandish still-life painting, in 'Stilled Lives: Self-Portraiture and Self-Reflection in Seventeenth-Century Netherlandish Still-Life Painting', *Simiolus*, vol.20, nos 2–3 (1990–91), pp 168–82; and Frances Borzello does so in the context of self-portraits of women painters in *Seeing Ourselves: Women's Self-Portraits*, rev. edn, London, Thames & Hudson, 2016 (1st edn 1998).

28   See Joanna Woods-Marsden, *Renaissance Self-Portraiture: The Visual Construction of Identity and the Social Status of the Artist*, New Haven, CT and London, Yale University Press, 1998, pp 133–7.

29 Van Mander, *Het Schilder-Boeck*, 1604, ch.7, fols 29r–34r. For the importance of reflections in painting in the writings of Karel van Mander, see Melion, *Shaping the Netherlandish Canon*, pp 70–77.

30 Pliny the Elder, *Natural History*, Loeb Classical Library, 10 vols, Cambridge, MA, Harvard University Press, 1938–62, XL.147–8; Plutarch, *Life of Pericles*, XXXI.4–5.

31 Plato, *Alcibiades*, I.133A.

32 Foister and van den Brink, *Dürer's Journey*, pp 124–5.

33 Lorne Campbell, *The Fifteenth Century Netherlandish Schools*, London, National Gallery Publications, 1998, pp 174–211.

34 Decoteau, *Clara Peeters*, ill.37, pp 51–3; Black, 'Female Self-Portraiture', pp 155–8; Anna Bianco, 'Journey through a Painting: An Allegory of Vanitas', PhD dissertation, Universiteit Amsterdam, 2010.

35 Francisco Pacheco, *Arte de la pintura* (1649), ed. Bonaventura Bassegoda i Hugas, Madrid, Cátedra, 1990, p.517.

2 STILL-LIFE PAINTING

1 Karel van Mander, *Het Schilder-Boeck*, Haarlem, 1604, fol.5v. See also Walter S. Melion, *Shaping the Netherlandish Canon: Karel van Mander's Schilder-Boek*, Chicago, IL and London, University of Chicago Press, 1991, p.5.

2 For the early history of still-life painting in the Southern and Northern Netherlands, see Sam Segal, *A Prosperous Past: The Sumptuous Still Life in the Netherlands, 1600–1700*, The Hague, SDY Publishers, 1989; Peter Sutton, ed., *The Age of Rubens*, Boston, MA, Boston Museum of Fine Arts and Ludion Press, 1993; Alan Chong and Wouter Kloek, *Still-Life Painting from the Netherlands 1550–1720*, Zwolle, Waander Publishers, 1999; and Adriaan van der Willigen and Fred J. Meijer, *A Dictionary of Dutch and Flemish Still-Life Painters Working in Oils, 1525–1725*, Leiden, Primavera Press and RKD, 2003. For the history of still-life painting in general, a good summary is Peter Cherry, 'Introduction. In the Presence of Things: Two Centuries of Still-Life Painting', in Peter Cherry, ed., *In the Presence of Things: Four Centuries of European Still-Life Painting, Part One: 17th–18th Centuries*, Lisbon, Calouste Gulbenkian Foundation, 2010, pp 12–43.

3 Segal, *A Prosperous Past*, pp 39–45, 227; and Van der Willigen and Meijer, *A Dictionary of Dutch and Flemish Still-Life Painters*, p.85. See the Conclusion for a discussion of the term 'realistic'.

4 For the still lifes by Snyders in Rubens's collection see Jeffrey M. Muller, *Rubens: The Artist as Collector*, Princeton, NJ, Princeton University Press, 1989, pp 135–7, nos 239, 260, 261, 263 and 264. For the paintings by Snyders in the Leganés collection, see José Juan Pérez Preciado, 'El Marqués de Leganés y las Artes', 2 vols, PhD dissertation, Universidad Complutense de Madrid, 2008, vol.1, nos 195, 745–55, and, for the still lifes, vol.2, nos 102, 103, 125, 152–4, 156, 159, 321, 502, 769–71.

5 Van der Willigen and Meijer, *A Dictionary of Dutch and Flemish Still-Life Painters*, p.32; Edith Greindl, *Les peintres flamands de nature morte au XVIIe siècle*, Sterrebeek, Editions d'art Michel Lefebvre, 1983.

6 Jean Bastiaensen, 'Finding Clara: Establishing the Biographical Details of Clara Peeters (*c*.1587–after 1636)', *Boletín del Museo del Prado*, vol.34, no.52 (2016), pp 17–31, on p.24.

7 Segal, *A Prosperous Past*, pp 64–5.

8 Karolien de Clippel and David van der Linden, 'The Genesis of the Netherlandish Flower Piece: Jan Brueghel, Ambrosius Bosschart and Middelburg', *Simiolus*, vol.38, nos 1–2 (2015–16), pp 73–86.

9 Brian W. Ogilvie, *The Science of Describing: Natural History in Renaissance Europe*, Chicago, IL, University of Chicago Press, 2006; and Robert Huxley, ed., *The Great Naturalists*, London, Thames & Hudson and The Natural History Museum, 2007. The importance of scientific illustrations for a Southern Netherlandish context similar to that of Peeters is emphasised in Beatrijs Brenninkmeijer-de Rooij, *Roots of Seventeenth-Century Flower Painting: Miniatures, Plant Books, Paintings*, Leiden, Primavera Pers, 1996; and Liesbeth M. Helmus, ed., *Fish Still Lifes by Dutch and Flemish Masters, 1550–1700*, Utrecht, Centraal Museum, 2004.

10 Marrigje Rikken, 'A Spanish Album of Drawings of Animals in a South-Netherlandish Context: A Reattribution to Lambert Lombard', *The Rijksmuseum Bulletin*, vol.62, no.2 (2014), pp 107–23.

11 Marjorie Lee Hendrix, 'Joris Hoefnagel and the "Four

Elements": A Study in Sixteenth-Century Nature Painting', PhD dissertation, Princeton University, NJ, 1984.

3 ARTISTIC PRODUCTION

1   These numbers come from adding the information from the RKD website (https://research.rkd.nl/en; search for Clara Peeters in the RKD Images database) to the information in Pamela Hibbs Decoteau, *Clara Peeters, 1594–ca.1640, and the Development of Still-Life Painting in Northern Europe*, Lingen, Luca Verlag, 1992. The RKD website also lists as autograph seven paintings that do not have an inscription or a signature. The numbers are not definitive because paintings by Peeters show up in auction sales or private sales occasionally. Some are new discoveries; more often they are paintings that re-emerge (an example is a picture that remained unsold at a Christie's auction held in London on 6 July 2023 (auction number 20683). The painting had earlier been sold by Johnny van Haeften, London, and by Koller, Zurich (as indicated by the provenance given by Christie's).

2   These paintings are in private collections and inaccessible. For the one not illustrated here, see Decoteau, *Clara Peeters*, ill.1.

3   ibid., ill.19, p.180.

4   ibid., p.8.

5   See Chapter 1, n.2.

6   Getty Provenance Index (Inventory N-4049), collection of Rudolphus Mensingh and Alida Coties, Haarlem, 1685, item 8: 'Een vogel stuckie van Peeters'. See https://www.getty.edu/research/tools/provenance/index.html.

7   José Juan Pérez Preciado, 'El Marqués de Leganés y las Artes', 2 vols, PhD dissertation, Universidad Complutense de Madrid, 2008, vol.2, nos 50 and 51, pp 56–7.

8   Letter from Rubens to Pierre Dupuy, 27 January 1628, in Ruth S. Magurn, *The Letters of Peter Paul Rubens*, Cambridge, MA, Harvard University Press, 1955, p.234.

9   Jonathan Brown, *Kings and Connoisseurs: Collecting Art in Seventeenth-Century Europe*, Princeton, NJ, Princeton University Press, 1996.

10   Decoteau, *Clara Peeters*, ill.29, pp 42–3, 194.

11   Magurn, *The Letters of Peter Paul Rubens*, pp 59–61.

12   Private collection; sold Christie's New York, 22 April 2021, lot 15.

13   See RKD web page (https://rkd.nl/images/54614). That the painting, which I have not seen, is signed, is stated at the RKD link to the artist.

14   Pamela Hibbs Decoteau has cast doubts on the possibility that Cave worked with Peeters, suggesting instead that he simply emulated her; see 'The Art of Clara Peeters, by Alejandro Vergara, ed.', *Historians of Netherlandish Art Reviews* (April 2017).

15   See Decoteau, *Clara Peeters*, and the link to Clara Peeters on the RKD website (https://research.rkd.nl) for paintings that have been attributed to her circle in the past.

16   John Loughman, 'The Market for Netherlandish Still Lifes, 1600–1700', in Alan Chong and Wouter Kloek, *Still-Life Painting from the Netherlands 1550–1720*, Zwolle, Waander Publishers, 1999, pp 87–102.

17   For Arenberg's collecting in Madrid, and the specifics of this case, see Pérez Preciado, 'El Marqués de Leganés y las Artes', vol.1, pp 206–16.

4 SOCIAL PRACTICE AND MATERIAL CULTURE

1   Samuel Quiccheberg, *Inscriptiones; vel, tituli amplissimi . . .*, Munich, 1565 (trans. and ed. Mark Meadow and Bruce Robertson, Los Angeles, CA, The Getty Research Institute, 2013, pp 78, 81.

2   Giancarlo Malacarne, *Lords of the Sky: Falconry in Mantua at the Time of the Gonzaga*, Alessandria, Artiglio Editore, 2011, pp 175–6.

3   For the collection of Rudolf II, see Thomas DaCosta Kaufmann, 'Remarks on the Collections of Rudolf II: The *Kunstkammer* as a Form of Representation', *Art Journal*, vol.38, no.1 (1978), pp 22–8; Thomas DaCosta Kaufmann, *The School of Prague: Painting at the Court of Rudolf II*, Chicago, IL, University of Chicago Press, 1988; and Eliška Fučíková, ed., *Rudolf II and Prague: The Court and The City*, Prague, London and New York, Prague Castle Administration, Thames & Hudson and Skira, 1997. For the collection of Philip II, see Fernando Checa, *Felipe II, mecenas de*

las artes, Madrid, Nerea, 1992, pp 155–6 and 367–85. See also Paula Findlen, 'The Museum: Its Classical Etymology and Renaissance Genealogy', *Journal in the History of Collections*, vol.1, no.1 (1989), pp 59–78.

4   See the collection of essays in Marisa Anne Bass, Anne Goldgar, Hanneke Grootenboer and Claudia Swan, *Conchophilia: Shells, Art and Curiosity in Early Modern Europe*, Princeton, NJ, Princeton University Press, 2021.

5   Pliny the Elder, *Natural History*, Loeb Classical Library, 10 vols, Cambridge, MA, Harvard University Press, 1938–62, II.23.

6   Cicero, *De Oratore*, II.22–3.

7   Roemer Visscher, *Sinne-Poppen*, Amsterdam, Willem Jansz., 1614, no.IV. For the value of shells, see Daniel Margócsy, *Commercial Visions: Science, Trade and Visual Culture in The Dutch Golden Age*, Chicago, IL, University of Chicago Press, 2014, p.37; and S. Peter Dance, *A History of Shell Collecting*, Leiden, Brill, 1986 (1st edn Faber and Faber, 1966), both of which refer for the most part to prices of dates later than Clara Peeters.

8   Marlise Rijks, 'Defenders of the Image: Painted Collectors' Cabinets and the Display of Display in Counter-Reformation Antwerp', in Perry Chapman, Frits Scholten and Joanna Woodall, eds, *Arts of Display*, Netherlands Yearbook for History of Art, vol.65, Leiden, Brill, 2015, pp 55–82, on p.65.

9   Giovanni Crivelli, *Giovanni Brueghel, pittor fiammingo, o sue letter e quadretti esistenti presso l'Ambrosiana*, Milan, Boniardi-Pogliani, 1868, p.75.

10 In the descriptions of the cities of Zayton (present day Quanzhou) and Tingui (perhaps Dehua City). Marco Polo, *Travels in the Land of Serpents and Pearls*, trans. Nigel Cliff, London, Penguin Classics, 2015, pp 221–4, 387.

11 For porcelain in the collection of Spanish rulers, see Teresa Canepa, 'The Iberian Royal Courts of Lisbon and Madrid, and their Role in Spreading a Taste for Chinese Porcelain in 16th-Century Europe', in Jan van Campen and Titus Eliëns, eds, *Chinese and Japanese Porcelain for the Dutch Golden Age*, Zwolle, Waanders, 2014, pp 17–35; Almudena Pérez de Tudela, 'Making, Collecting, Displaying and Exchanging Objects: Archival Sources Relating to the Infanta Isabel's Personal Possessions (1566–1599)', in Cordula van Wyhe, ed., *Isabel Clara Eugenia: Female Sovereignty in the Courts of Madrid and Brussels*, Madrid and London, Centro de Estudios Europa Hispánica and Paul Holberton Publishing, 2011, pp 60–87; and especially Cinta Krahe, *Chinese Porcelain in Habsburg Spain*, Madrid, Centro de Estudios Europa Hispánica, 2016.

12 This is mentioned by the painter in his diary, in the entry for 3 September 1520: Albrecht Dürer, *Diary of His Journey to the Netherlands, 1520–1521*, Greenwich, CT, New York Graphic Society Ltd, 1971, p.65.

13 Krista de Jonge, 'Building Policy and Urbanization during the Reign of the Archdukes: The Court and Its Architects', in Luc Duerloo and Werner Thomas, eds, *Albert and Isabella, 1598–1621: Essays*, Turnhout, Brepols, 1998, pp 191–219, on p.195.

14 For all these Antwerp collections, see Canepa, 'The Iberian Royal Courts', pp 34–5.

15 For *kraak* porcelain, see Maura Rinaldi, *Kraak Porcelain: A Moment in the History of Trade*, London, Bamboo Publishing, 1989.

16 See Cynthia Viallé, 'Camel Cups, Parrot Cups and other Chinese Kraak Porcelain Items in Dutch Trade Records, 1598–1623', in Jan van Campen and Titus Eliëns, eds, *Chinese and Japanese Porcelain for the Dutch Golden Age*, Zwolle, Waanders, 2014, pp 37–51.

17 ibid., p.42.

18 The painting by Van der Hamen (1596–1631), *Still Life with Sweetmeats and Glass Vessels*, of 1622, is in the Museo del Prado, Madrid (P1164). The still life by Koets (c.1592–1654), *Still Life with Cheese and Fruits*, is dated 1625 and is in the Museum Mayer van den Bergh, Antwerp (inv.no.929).

19 Ludovicco Guicciardini, *Descrittione di tutti i Paesi Bassi*, Antwerp, W. Silvius, 1567 (1612 edn Amsterdam, Beschrijvinghe van alle de Nederlanden, anderssins ghenoemet Neder-Duytschlandt, 1612), p.89.

20 Sven Dupré, 'The Value of Glass and the Translation of Artisanal Knowledge in Early Modern Antwerp', in Christine Göttler, Bart Ramakers and Joanna Woodall, eds, *Trading Values in Early Modern Antwerp*, Netherlands Yearbook for History of Art, vol.64, Leiden, Brill, 2014, pp 138–61, on pp 142–4.

21 Claudia Goldstein, *Pieter Bruegel and the Culture of*

the Early Modern Dinner Party, Burlington, VT and Farnham, Ashgate, 2013, p.58.

22 Bartolomeo Scappi, *The Opera of Bartolomeo Scappi (1570): L'arte et prudenza d'un maestro cuoco. The Art and Craft of a Master Cook*, trans. with commentary Terence Scully, Toronto, Toronto University Press, 2008.

23 For the section 'Book IV. Preparing Meals: For the Sideboard', see ibid., pp 421–4.

24 Juan Cristóbal Calvete de Estrella, *El felicíssimo viaje del muy alto y muy poderoso príncipe Don Phelippe . . .*, Antwerp, Martin, Nucio, 1552 (modern edition by Oaloma Cuanca Muñoz and José María de Francisco Olmos, Madrid, Turner Libros, 2001), p.72.

25 ibid., pp 352–3.

26 Diederik Lanoye, 'Structure and Composition of the Household of the Archdukes', in Duerloo and Thomas, eds, *Essays*, 1998, pp 107–19.

27 For this painting, see *La Moda Española en el Siglo de Oro*, Toledo, Junta de Comunidades de Castilla-La Mancha, 2015, pp 208–9 (text by Joanna Kilian Michieletti).

28 Sam Segal, *A Prosperous Past: The Sumptuous Still Life in the Netherlands, 1600–1700*, The Hague, SDY Publishers, 1989, pp 69–70.

29 Bart Ramakers, 'Sophonisba's Dress: Costume, Tragedy and Value on the Antwerp Stage (c.1615–1630)', in Göttler et al., eds, *Trading Values in Early Modern Antwerp*, pp 298–347, on pp 330–31.

30 Peter Brears, *Cooking and Dining in Tudor and Early Stuart England*, London, Prospect Books, 2015, p.463.

31 For the use of knives, see ibid., pp 446–9, 463.

32 For the use of forks, see ibid., pp 448–9.

33 See Ken Albala, *Eating Right in the Renaissance*, Berkeley, CA and London, University of California Press, 2002. Other books that I have relied on for information on food that is relevant to the paintings of Clara Peeters are Gillian Riley, *The Dutch Table: Gastronomy in the Golden Age of the Netherlands*, Painters and Food series, San Francisco, CA, Pomegranate Artbooks, 1994; Ken Albala, *Food in Early Modern Europe*, Westport, CT, Greenwood Press, 2003; Scappi, *The Opera of Bartolomeo Scappi*; J. Timothy Tomasik and Ken Albala, eds, *The Most Excellent Book of Cookery. Livret fort excellent de Cuysine* (1555), London, Prospect Books, 2014; Brears, *Cooking and Dining*; and Quentin

34 Buvelot, *Slow Food: Dutch and Flemish Meal Still Lifes, 1600–1640*, The Hague, Mauritshuis, 2017.

35 Albala, *Eating Right in the Renaissance*, p.197.

36 ibid., p.256.

37 For this matter, see Jane O'Hara-May, *Elizabethan Dyetary of Health*, Lawrence, KS, Coronado Press, 1977; and Albala, *Eating Right in the Renaissance*, especially pp 7, 17–21, 30–31, 48–114.

38 Alan Davidson, *The Oxford Companion to Food*, 3rd edn, ed. Tom Jaine, Oxford, Oxford University Press, 2014, p.322.

39 Scappi, *The Opera of Bartolomeo Scappi*, pp 421–2.

40 For fish still lifes, see Liesbeth M. Helmus, ed., *Fish Still Lifes by Dutch and Flemish Masters, 1550–1700*, Utrecht, Centraal Museum, 2004.

41 Ludovicus Nonnius, *Diaeteticon sive de re cibaria*, Antwerp, 1627 (2nd edn, Antwerp, 1645), pp 362, 366, 372, 412.

42 Eddy Stols, 'Gustos y disgustos en la confrontación y el intercambio alimenticios entre España y Flandes (siglos XVI y XVII)', in Ana Crespo Solana and Manuel Herrero Sánchez, *España y las 17 provincias de los Países Bajos: Una revisión historiográfica (XVI–XVIII)*, 2 vols, Córdoba, Universidad de Córdoba, 2002, vol.2, pp 585–614, on p.589.

43 Bernardo J. García García, 'Bruselas y Madrid: Isabel Clara Eugenia y el duque de Lerma', in Duerloo and Thomas, eds, *Essays*, 1998, pp 67–77, on p.73; and Antonio Rodríguez Villa, ed., *Correspondencia de la Infanta Archiduquesa Isabel Clara Eugenia de Austria con el duque de Lerma y otros personajes*, Madrid, Fortanet, 1906, p.134.

44 For the history of hawking, see Robin S. Oggins, *The Kings and Their Hawks: Falconry in Medieval England*, New Haven, CT and London, Yale University Press, 2004; and the very stimulating Helen Macdonald, *H is for Hawk*, New York, Grove Press, 2014. For falconry and art, see Christian Antoine de Chamerlat, *Falconry and Art*, London, Sotheby's Publications, 1987. I have also benefitted from the knowledge of this subject shared by José Manuel Rodríguez Villa.

45 Bernardo García García, 'Los regalos de Isabel Clara Eugenia y la Corte Española: Intimidad, gusto, devoción', *Reales Sitios*, no.143 (2000), pp 16–27, on pp 21, 26, n.15.

45   Alan Chong, 'Contained Under the Name of Still Life: The Associations of Still-Life Painting', in Alan Chong and Wouter Kloek, *Still-Life Painting from the Netherlands 1550–1720*, Zwolle, Waander Publishers, 1999, pp 11–37, on p.23 (original quote in Gerard de Lairesse, *Groot schilderboek, waar in de schilderkonst in al haar deelen grondig werd onderweezen*, 2 vols, Haarlem, 1740 (1st edn Amsterdam, 1707; reprint Doornspijk, Davaco, 1969), vol.2, p.260).

46   For this legislation, see Victor Brants, *Recueil des ordonnances des Pays-Bas: Règne d'Albert et Isabelle, 1597–1621, Tome 2, contenant les actes*, Brussels, Gemaere, 1912, pp 186–96. For the subject of the hunt in art at the time of the archdukes, and in game still-life paintings, see Susan Koslow and Frans Snyders, *The Noble Estate: Seventeenth-Century Still Life and Animal Painting in the Southern Netherlands*, Antwerp, Fonds Mercator, 1995, pp 98–9, 102, 224, 332–3, nn 75–80, with further bibliography.

47   See Anne Lenders, 'Clara Peeters Lays the Table: Objects and Foods through the Eyes of Seventeenth-Century Viewers', in Alejandro Vergara, *The Art of Clara Peeters*, Madrid, Museo del Prado, 2016, pp 49–65.

48   Calvete de Estrella, *El felicíssimo viaje*, p.180.

49   Alonso Vázquez, 'Los sucesos de Flandes y Francia del tiempo de Alejandro Farnese por el capitán Alonso Vázquez, sargento mayor de la milicia de Jaén y su distrito, escrito en diez y seis libros', in Marqués de la Fuensanta del Valle, José Sancho Rayón and Francisco de Salbalburu, *Colección de documentos inéditos para la historia de España*, vol.72, Madrid, Viuda de Calero, 1879, pp 14, 15, 25. This chronicle was written between 1610 and 1614.

50   Juan Cabrera, *Bosque de Doña Ana a la presencia de Felipo Quarto . . .: demonstraciones que el Duque VIII de Medina Sidonia, don Manuel Alonso Perez de Guzman el Bueno*, Seville, 1624; see http://bdh-rd.bne.es/ viewer.vm?id=0000177606&page=1.

51   Stols, 'Gustos y disgustos', p.601.

52   Pliny the Elder, *Natural History*, Loeb Classical Library, XV.30.

53   Rodríguez Villa, ed., *Correspondencia de la Infanta Archiduquesa Isabel Clara Eugenia*, p.334.

54   The following information comes from Guicciardini, *Descrittione di tutti i Paesi Bassi*, pp 120–25.

55   Brears, *Cooking and Dining*, pp 375–6, 544.

56   ibid., pp 347–8.

57   Pliny the Elder, *Natural History*, Loeb Classical Library, XXXV.65–6.

58   ibid., XXXV.66.

59   Stols, 'Gustos y disgustos', p.600.

60   ibid., p.602.

61   Brears, *Cooking and Dining*, p.466.

62   Cited in Albala, *Eating Right in the Renaissance*, p.55.

63   For the former, see Tomasik and Albala, eds, *The Most Excellent Book of Cookery*, pp 241, 253, 255. For Scappi's book, see Scappi, *The Opera of Bartolomeo Scappi*, recipes II, 264, 270, and VI, 189.

64   Brears, *Cooking and Dining*, pp 535–6.

65   Stefania Macioce, *Michelangelo Merisi da Caravaggio: Documenti, fonti e inventari 1513–1875*, 2nd rev. and enlarged edn, Rome, Ugo Bozzi Editore, 2010, pp 163–4, doc.584.

66   Lancelot de Casteau, *Ouverture de cuisine*, Liège, 1604, section 'Herbs'.

67   Scappi, *The Opera of Bartolomeo Scappi*, pp 421–2.

68   Brears, *Cooking and Dining*, pp 214–15, 530.

69   ibid., pp 576–7.

70   For all pertaining to sugar, see Darra Goldstein, ed., *The Oxford Companion to Sugar and Sweets*, Oxford, Oxford University Press, 2015.

71   See the entry on 'Sugar and Health' in ibid.

72   Calvete de Estrella, *El felicíssimo viaje*, pp 352–3.

73   Ewa Kociszewska, 'Displays of Sugar Sculpture and the Collection of Antiquities in Late Renaissance Venice', *Renaissance Quarterly*, vol.73 (2020), pp 441–88.

74   Luigi Fedele is mentioned as an outstanding court confectioner in *The Oxford Companion to Sugar and Sweets*, in the entry on 'Court Confectioners'.

75   Brears, *Cooking and Dining*, pp 404–5. See also p.134.

76   Miriam Milman, 'The Mysterious "Mejlikan" Revisited: Some Thoughts about the Symbolism of the Carnation', *Konsthistorisk tidskrift*, vol.65, no.2 (1996), pp 115–34.

77   For rosemary, see Jeanne d'Andrea, *Ancient Herbs*, Los Angeles, CA, The J. Paul Getty Museum, 1982, pp 73–5; and George R. Keiser, 'Rosemary: Not Just for Remembrance', in Peter Dendle and Alain Touwaide, eds, *Health and Healing from the Medieval*

Garden, Woodbridge, Suffolk, The Boydell Press, 2008, pp 180–204.

78 Robert Herrick, _The Poetical Works of Robert Herrick_, 2 vols, London, William Pickering, 1825, vol.2, p.46.

5 PROBLEMS OF MEANING AND INTERPRETATION

1 As suggested in Jean Bastiaensen, 'Finding Clara: Establishing the Biographical Details of Clara Peeters (_c_.1587–after 1636)', _Boletín del Museo del Prado_, vol.34, no.52 (2016), pp 17–31, on p.26.

2 For the interpretation of this painting, see Miriam Milman, 'The Mysterious "Mejlikan" Revisited: Some Thoughts about the Symbolism of the Carnation', _Konsthistorisk tidskrift_, vol.65, no.2 (1996), pp 115–34, pp 128–9; and Katlijne van der Stighelen and Mirjam Westen, eds, _Elk zijn waerom: Vrowelijke kunstenaars in België en Nederland 1500–1950_, Ghent, Ludion Press, 1999, pp 141–3.

3 Andrew Borde, _A Compendyous Regyment or A Dyetary of Health_, 1542 (republished London, Early English Text Society and Trübner and Co., 1870), p.280. Thomas Hill, _Gardener's Labyrinth_, London, Henry Bynneman, 1577, p.127.

4 Cited in Peter Brears, _Cooking and Dining in Tudor and Early Stuart England_, London, Prospect Books, 2015, p.284.

5 Bartolomeo Boldo, _Libro della natura et virtu delle cose che nutriscono_, Venice, Domenico and Gio. Battista Guerra, 1575, p.66.

6 Pamela M. Jones, _Federico Borromeo and the Ambrosiana: Art Patronage and Reform in Seventeenth-Century Milan_, Cambridge, Cambridge University Press, 1993, p.86.

7 Giovanni Crivelli, _Giovanni Brueghel, pittor fiammingo, o sue letter e quadretti esistenti presso l'Ambrosiana_, Milan, Boniardi-Pogliani, 1868, pp 63, 272.

8 Anna Grasskamp, 'Shells, Bodies, and the Collector's Cabinet', in Marisa Anne Bass, Anne Goldgar, Hanneke Grootenboer and Claudia Swan, _Conchophilia: Shells, Art and Curiosity in Early Modern Europe_, Princeton, NJ, Princeton University Press, 2021, pp 49–71, on pp 52–8.

9 The painting by Alonso Sánchez Coello is at the Museo del Prado, Madrid. The portrait of Catalina Micaela belongs to Rafael Valls Ltd.

10 Santiago Martínez Hernández, 'Significación y trascendencia del género epistolar en la política cortesana: la correspondencia inédita entre la infanta Isabel Clara Eugenia y el marqués de Velada', _Hispania_, no.217 (2004), pp 467–514, on p.485. For the collecting of exotic birds in Madrid and Brussels at this time, see Eddy Stols, 'De tromf van de exotica of de bredere wereld in de Nederlanden van de aartshertogen', in Luc Duerloo and Werner Thomas, eds, _Albert and Isabella, 1598–1621: Essays_, Turnhout, Brepols, 1998, pp 291–301.

11 Antonio Rodríguez Villa, ed., _Correspondencia de la Infanta Archiduquesa Isabel Clara Eugenia de Austria con el duque de Lerma y otros personajes_, Madrid, Fortanet, 1906, pp 141–2.

12 Alejandro Vergara, ed., _The Art of Clara Peeters_, Madrid, Museo del Prado, 2016, p.98.

13 ibid., p.72.

14 Edward Topsell, _The Historie of Foure-Footed Beastes_, London, 1607, p.80.

15 Karel van Mander, _Het Schilder-Boeck_, Haarlem, 1604 (modern English edn _The Lives of the Illustrious Netherlandish and German Painters, from the First Edition of the Schilder-boeck_ (1603–4), ed. and trans. Hessel Miedema, 6 vols, Doornsprijk, Davaco, 1994–9), vol.1, p.126 (and p.127 for the original text in Dutch).

16 Federico Borromeo, _Museum_, ed. and trans. Kenneth S. Rothwell Jr, intro. and notes Pamela M. Jones, Cambridge, MA, Harvard University Press and The I Tatti Renaissance Library, 2010, p.193.

17 ibid., p.181.

18 I take the Bellori quotes from Mina Gregori, _The Age of Caravaggio_, New York, Metropolitan Museum, 1985, pp 262–5.

19 Francisco Pacheco, _Arte de la pintura_ (1649), ed. Bonaventura Bassegoda i Hugas, Madrid, Cátedra, 1990, pp 517, 511.

20 Jean Denucé, _Brieven en documenten betreffend Jan Briueghel I en II (Bronnen voor de geschiedenis van de Vlaamnse Kunst)_, no.3, Antwerp and The Hague, De Sikkel and Martinus Nijhof, 1934 (I take the

translation from Eddy de Jongh, ed., *Still-Life in the Age of Rembrandt*, Auckland, Auckland City Gallery, 1982, p.34).

21   See Alan Chong, 'Contained Under the Name of Still Life: The Associations of Still-Life Painting', in Alan Chong and Wouter Kloek, *Still-Life Painting from the Netherlands 1550–1720*, Zwolle, Waander Publishers, 1999, pp 11–37, on, p.17 (the original in Gerard de Lairesse, *Groot schilderboek, waar in de schilderkonst in al haar deelen grondig werd onderweezen*, 2 vols, Haarlem, 1740 (1st edn Amsterdam, 1707; reprint Doornspijk, Davaco, 1969), vol.2, p.268).

CONCLUSION: PEETERS'S ARTISTRY

1   Denis Donoghue, *Speaking of Beauty*, New Haven, CT and London, Yale University Press, 2003, p.65.

2   Martin Heidegger, *Ontology: The Hermeneutics of Facticity*, Bloomington, IN, Indiana University Press, 1999 (first published in German as *Gesamtausgabe*, vol.63, Frankfurt am Main, Vittorio Klostermann, 1988); and Lesley Chamberlain, *A Shoe Story: Van Gogh, the Philosophers and the West*, Chelmsford, Essex, Harbour Press Books, 2014.

3   Donoghue, *Speaking of Beauty*, p.16.

4   José Juan Pérez Preciado, 'El Marqués de Leganés y las Artes', 2 vols, PhD dissertation, Universidad Complutense de Madrid, 2008, vol.1, p.208.

Bibliography

Albala, Ken, *Eating Right in the Renaissance*, Berkeley, CA and London, University of California Press, 2002.

—, *Food in Early Modern Europe*, Westport, CT, Greenwood Press, 2003.

D'Andrea, Jeanne, *Ancient Herbs*, Los Angeles, CA, The J. Paul Getty Museum, 1982.

Bass, Marisa Anne, Anne Goldgar, Hanneke Grootenboer and Claudia Swan, *Conchophilia: Shells, Art and Curiosity in Early Modern Europe*, Princeton, NJ, Princeton University Press, 2021.

Bastiaensen, Jean, 'Finding Clara: Establishing the Biographical Details of Clara Peeters (*c.*1587–after 1636)', *Boletín del Museo del Prado*, vol.34, no.52 (2016), pp 17–31.

Bianco, Anna, 'Journey through a Painting: An Allegory of Vanitas', PhD dissertation, Universiteit Amsterdam, 2010.

De Bie, Cornelis, *Het gulden cabinet van de edel vry Schilder-Const*, Antwerp, 1662.

Black, Jennifer Brynn, 'Female Self-Portraiture in Early Modern Europe: Colonna, Anguissola, Whitney, and Peeters', PhD dissertation, Boston University, MA, 2004.

Boldo, Bartolomeo, *Libro della natura et virtu delle cose che nutriscono*, Venice, Domenico and Gio. Battista Guerra, 1575.

Borde, Andrew, *A Compendyous Regyment or A Dyetary of Health*, 1542 (republished London, Early English Text Society and Trübner and Co., 1870).

Borromeo, Federico, *Museum*, ed. and trans. Kenneth S. Rothwell Jr, intro. and notes Pamela M. Jones, Cambridge, MA, Harvard University Press and The I Tatti Renaissance Library, 2010.

Borzello, Frances, *Seeing Ourselves: Women's Self-Portraits*, rev. edn, London, Thames & Hudson, 2016 (1st edn 1998).

Brants, Victor, *Recueil des ordonnances des Pays-Bas: Règne d'Albert et Isabelle, 1597–1621, Tome 2, contenant les actes*, Brussels, Gemaere, 1912.

Brears, Peter, *Cooking and Dining in Tudor and Early Stuart England*, London, Prospect Books, 2015.

Brenninkmeijer-de Rooij, Beatrijs, *Roots of Seventeenth-Century Flower Painting: Miniatures, Plant Books, Paintings*, Leiden, Primavera Pers, 1996.

Brown, Jonathan, *Kings and Connoisseurs: Collecting Art in Seventeenth-Century Europe*, Princeton, NJ, Princeton University Press, 1996.

Brusati, Celeste, 'Stilled Lives: Self-Portraiture and Self-Reflection in Seventeenth-Century Netherlandish Still-Life Painting', *Simiolus*, vol.20, nos 2–3 (1990–91), pp 168–82.

Buvelot, Quentin, *Slow Food: Dutch and Flemish Meal Still Lifes, 1600–1640*, The Hague, Mauritshuis, 2017.

Cabrera, Juan, *Bosque de Doña Ana a la presencia de Felipo Quarto . . .: demonstraciones que el Duque VIII de Medina Sidonia, don Manuel Alonso Perez de Guzman el Bueno*, Seville, 1624.

Calvete de Estrella, Juan Cristóbal, *El felicíssimo viaje del muy alto y muy poderoso príncipe Don Phelippe . . .*, Antwerp, Martin, Nucio, 1552 (modern edition by Oaloma Cuanca

Muñoz and José María de Francisco Olmos, Madrid, Turner Libros, 2001).

Campbell, Lorne, *The Fifteenth Century Netherlandish Schools*, London, National Gallery Publications, 1998.

Canepa, Teresa, 'The Iberian Royal Courts of Lisbon and Madrid, and their Role in Spreading a Taste for Chinese Porcelain in 16th-Century Europe', in Jan van Campen and Titus Eliëns, eds, *Chinese and Japanese Porcelain for the Dutch Golden Age*, Zwolle, Waanders, 2014, pp 17–35.

Cavazzini, Patrisia, *Painting as Business in Early Seventeenth-Century Rome*, University Park, PA, Pennsylvania State University Press, 2008.

Chadwick, Whitney, *Women, Art and Society*, London, Thames & Hudson, 1990.

Chamberlain, Lesley, *A Shoe Story: Van Gogh, the Philosophers and the West*, Chelmsford, Essex, Harbour Press Books, 2014.

De Chamerlat, Christian Antoine, *Falconry and Art*, London, Sotheby's Publications, 1987.

Checa, Fernando, *Felipe II, mecenas de las artes*, Madrid, Nerea, 1992.

Cherry, Peter, 'Introduction. In the Presence of Things: Two Centuries of Still-Life Painting', in Cherry, ed., *In the Presence of Things*, 2010, pp 12–43.

—, ed., *In the Presence of Things: Four Centuries of European Still-Life Painting, Part One: 17th–18th Centuries*, Lisbon, Calouste Gulbenkian Foundation, 2010.

Chong, Alan, 'Contained Under the Name of Still Life: The Associations of Still-Life Painting', in Chong and Kloek, *Still-Life Painting*, 1999, pp 11–37.

Chong, Alan, and Wouter Kloek, *Still-Life Painting from the Netherlands 1550–1720*, Zwolle, Waander Publishers, 1999.

De Clippel, Karolien, and David van der Linden, 'The Genesis of the Netherlandish Flower Piece: Jan Brueghel, Ambrosius Bosschart and Middelburg', *Simiolus*, vol.38, nos 1–2 (2015–16), pp 73–86.

Crivelli, Giovanni, *Giovanni Brueghel, pittor fiammingo, o sue letter e quadretti esistenti presso l'Ambrosiana*, Milan, Boniardi-Pogliani, 1868.

Dance, S. Peter, *A History of Shell Collecting*, Leiden, Brill, 1986 (1st edn Faber and Faber, 1966).

Davidson, Alan, *The Oxford Companion to Food*, 3rd edn, ed. Tom Jaine, Oxford, Oxford University Press, 2014.

Decoteau, Pamela Hibbs, *Clara Peeters, 1594–ca.1640, and the Development of Still-Life Painting in Northern Europe*, Lingen, Luca Verlag, 1992.

—, 'The Art of Clara Peeters, by Alejandro Vergara, ed.', *Historians of Netherlandish Art Reviews* (April 2017).

Denucé, Jean, *Brieven en documenten betreffend Jan Briueghel I en II (Bronnen voor de geschiedenis van de Vlaamnse Kunst)*, no.3, Antwerp and The Hague, De Sikkel and Martinus Nijhof, 1934.

DiFuria, Arthur J., 'Towards an Understanding of Mayken Verhulst and Volcxken Diericx', in Sutton, ed., *Women Artists and Patrons*, 2019, pp 157–77.

Donoghue, Denis, *Speaking of Beauty*, New Haven, CT and London, Yale University Press, 2003.

Duerloo, Luc, and Werner Thomas, eds, *Albert and Isabella, 1598–1621: Catalogue*, Turnhout, Brepols, 1998.

—, *Albert and Isabella, 1598–1621: Essays*, Turnhout, Brepols, 1998.

Dupré, Sven, 'The Value of Glass and the Translation of Artisanal Knowledge in Early Modern Antwerp', in Christine Göttler, Bart Ramakers and Joanna Woodall, eds, *Trading Values in Early Modern Antwerp*, Netherlands Yearbook for History of Art, vol.64, Leiden, Brill, 2014, pp 138–61.

Dürer, Albrecht, *Diary of His Journey to the Netherlands, 1520–1521*, Greenwich, CT, New York Graphic Society Ltd, 1971.

Findlen, Paula, 'The Museum: Its Classical Etymology and Renaissance Genealogy', *Journal in the History of Collections*, vol.1, no.1 (1989), pp 59–78.

Foister, Susan, and Peter van den Brink, *Dürer's Journey: Travels of a Renaissance Artist*, London, National Gallery Company, 2021.

Fučíková, Eliška, ed., *Rudolf II and Prague: The Court and The City*, Prague, London and New York, Prague Castle Administration, Thames & Hudson and Skira, 1997.

García García, Bernardo, 'Bruselas y Madrid: Isabel Clara Eugenia y el duque de Lerma', in Duerloo and Thomas, eds, *Essays*, 1998, pp 67–77.

—, 'Los regalos de Isabel Clara Eugenia y la Corte Española: Intimidad, gusto, devoción', *Reales Sitios*, no.143 (2000), pp 16–27.

Garrard, Mary D., *Artemisia Gentileschi: The Image of the Female Hero in Italian Baroque Art*, Princeton, NJ, Princeton University Press, 1989.

Goldstein, Claudia, *Pieter Bruegel and the Culture of the Early Modern Dinner Party*, Burlington, VT and Farnham, Ashgate, 2013.

Goldstein, Darra, ed., *The Oxford Companion to Sugar and Sweets*, Oxford, Oxford University Press, 2015.

Grasskamp, Anna, 'Shells, Bodies, and the Collector's Cabinet', in Bass et al., *Conchophilia*, 2021, pp 49–71.

Gregori, Mina, *The Age of Caravaggio*, New York, Metropolitan Museum, 1985.

Greindl, Edith, *Les peintres flamands de nature morte au XVIIe siècle*, Sterrebeek, Editions d'art Michel Lefebvre, 1983.

Grootenboer, Hanneke, *The Pensive Image: Art as a Form of Thinking*, Chicago, IL, University of Chicago Press, 2020.

Guicciardini, Ludovicco, *Descrittione di tutti i Paesi Bassi*, Antwerp, W. Silvius, 1567 (1612 edn Amsterdam, Beschrijvinghe van alle de Nederlanden, anderssins ghenoemet Neder-Duytschlandt, 1612).

Hall, James, *The Self-Portrait: A Cultural History*, New York, Thames & Hudson, 2014.

Harris, Anne Sutherland, and Linda Nochlin, *Women Artists: 1550–1950*, New York, Knopf, 1976.

Heidegger, Martin, *Ontology: The Hermeneutics of Facticity*, Bloomington, IN, Indiana University Press, 1999 (first published in German as *Gesamtausgabe*, vol.63, Frankfurt am Main, Vittorio Klostermann, 1988).

Helmus, Liesbeth M., ed., *Fish Still Lifes by Dutch and Flemish Masters, 1550–1700*, Utrecht, Centraal Museum, 2004.

Hendrix, Marjorie Lee, 'Joris Hoefnagel and the "Four Elements": A Study in Sixteenth-Century Nature Painting', PhD dissertation, Princeton University, NJ, 1984.

Herrick, Robert, *The Poetical Works of Robert Herrick*, 2 vols, London, William Pickering, 1825.

Hill, Thomas, *Gardener's Labyrinth*, London, Henry Bynneman, 1577.

Huxley, Robert, ed., *The Great Naturalists*, London, Thames & Hudson and The Natural History Museum, 2007.

Jansen, Guido M.C., '"On the Lowest Level": The Status of Still Life in the Netherlandish Art and Literature of the Seventeenth Century', in Chong and Kloek, *Still-Life Painting*, 1999, pp 51–7.

Jones, Pamela M., *Federico Borromeo and the Ambrosiana: Art Patronage and Reform in Seventeenth-Century Milan*, Cambridge, Cambridge University Press, 1993.

De Jonge, Krista, 'Building Policy and Urbanization during the Reign of the Archdukes: The Court and Its Architects', in Duerloo and Thomas, eds, *Essays*, 1998, pp 191–219.

De Jongh, Eddy, ed., *Still-Life in the Age of Rembrandt*, Auckland, Auckland City Gallery, 1982.

Kaufmann, Thomas DaCosta, 'Remarks on the Collections of Rudolf II: The *Kunstkammer* as a Form of Representation', *Art Journal*, vol.38, no.1 (1978), pp 22–8.

—, *The School of Prague: Painting at the Court of Rudolf II*, Chicago, IL, University of Chicago Press, 1988.

Keiser, George R., 'Rosemary: Not Just for Remembrance', in Peter Dendle and Alain Touwaide, eds, *Health and Healing from the Medieval Garden*, Woodbridge, Suffolk, The Boydell Press, 2008, pp 180–204.

Kociszewska, Ewa, 'Displays of Sugar Sculpture and the Collection of Antiquities in Late Renaissance Venice', *Renaissance Quarterly*, vol.73 (2020), pp 441–88.

Koslow, Susan, and Frans Snyders, *The Noble Estate: Seventeenth-Century Still Life and Animal Painting in the Southern Netherlands*, Antwerp, Fonds Mercator, 1995.

Krahe, Cinta, *Chinese Porcelain in Habsburg Spain*, Madrid, Centro de Estudios Europa Hispánica, 2016.

De Lairesse, Gerard, *Groot schilderboek, waar in de schilderkonst in al haar deelen grondig werd onderweezen*, 2 vols, Haarlem, 1740 (1st edn Amsterdam, 1707; reprint Doornspijk, Davaco, 1969).

Lanoye, Diederik, 'Structure and Composition of the Household of the Archdukes', in Duerloo and Thomas, eds, *Essays*, 1998, pp 107–19.

Lenders, Anne, 'Clara Peeters Lays the Table: Objects and Foods through the Eyes of Seventeenth-Century Viewers', in Vergara, ed., *The Art of Clara Peeters*, 2016, pp 49–65.

Lomazzo, Paolo, *Trattato dell'arte della pittura*, Milan, 1584.

Loughman, John, 'The Market for Netherlandish Still Lifes, 1600–1700', in Chong and Kloek, *Still-Life Painting*, 1999, pp 87–102.

Macdonald, Helen, *H is for Hawk*, New York, Grove Press, 2014.

Macioce, Stefania, *Michelangelo Merisi da Caravaggio: Documenti, fonti e inventari 1513–1875*, 2nd rev. and enlarged edn, Rome, Ugo Bozzi Editore, 2010.

Magurn, Ruth S., *The Letters of Peter Paul Rubens*, Cambridge, MA, Harvard University Press, 1955.

Malacarne, Giancarlo, *Lords of the Sky: Falconry in Mantua at the Time of the Gonzaga*, Alessandria, Artiglio Editore, 2011.

Van Mander, Karel, *Het Schilder-Boeck*, Haarlem, 1604 (modern English edn *The Lives of the Illustrious Netherlandish and German Painters, from the First Edition of the Schilder-boeck* (1603–4), ed. and trans. Hessel Miedema, 6 vols, Doornsprijk, Davaco, 1994–9).

Margócsy, Daniel, *Commercial Visions: Science, Trade and Visual Culture in The Dutch Golden Age*, Chicago, IL, University of Chicago Press, 2014.

Martínez Hernández, Santiago, 'Significación y trascendencia del género epistolar en la política cortesana: la correspondencia inédita entre la infanta Isabel Clara Eugenia y el marqués de Velada', *Hispania*, no.217 (2004), pp 467–514.

Meads, Dorothy M., ed., *The Diary of Lady Margaret Hoby 1599–1605*, London, Routledge, 1930.

Melion, Walter S., *Shaping the Netherlandish Canon: Karel van Mander's Schilder-Boek*, Chicago, IL and London, University of Chicago Press, 1991.

Milman, Miriam, 'The Mysterious "Mejlikan" Revisited: Some Thoughts about the Symbolism of the Carnation', *Konsthistorisk tidskrift*, vol.65, no.2 (1996), pp 115–34.

La Moda Española en el Siglo de Oro, Toledo, Junta de Comunidades de Castilla-La Mancha, 2015.

Moran, Sarah Joan, and Amanda C. Pipkin, *Women and Gender in the Early Modern Low Countries, 1500–1750*, Leiden, Brill, 2019.

Muller, Jeffrey M., *Rubens: The Artist as Collector*, Princeton, NJ, Princeton University Press, 1989.

—, 'Private Collections in the Spanish Netherlands: Ownership and Display of Paintings in Domestic Interiors', in Sutton, ed., *The Age of Rubens*, 1993, pp 195–206.

Nochlin, Linda, 'Why Have There Been No Great Women Artists?', *Art News*, 1971 (reprinted in Linda Nochlin, *Women, Art and Power and Other Essays*, New York, Harper Collins, 1988).

Nonnius, Ludovicus, *Diaeteticon sive de re cibaria*, Antwerp, 1627 (2nd edn, Antwerp, 1645).

Norgate, Edward, *Miniatura, or, The Art of Limning*, ed.

Jeffrey M. Muller and Jim Murrell, New Haven, CT and London, Yale University Press, 1997.

Oggins, Robin S., *The Kings and Their Hawks: Falconry in Medieval England*, New Haven, CT and London, Yale University Press, 2004.

Ogilvie, Brian W., *The Science of Describing: Natural History in Renaissance Europe*, Chicago, IL, University of Chicago Press, 2006.

O'Hara-May, Jane, *Elizabethan Dyetary of Health*, Lawrence, KS, Coronado Press, 1977.

Pacheco, Francisco, *Arte de la pintura* (1649), ed. Bonaventura Bassegoda i Hugas, Madrid, Cátedra, 1990.

Parada López de Corselas, Manuel, *El viaje de Jan van Eyck de Flandes a Granada*, Madrid, Ediciones de La Ergástula, 2016.

Pearson, Andrea, 'Marking Female Ocular Agency in the "Medieval Housebook"', in Merry Wiesner-Hanks, ed., *Challenging Women's Agency and Activism in Early Modernity*, Amsterdam, University of Amsterdam Press, 2021, pp 229–49.

Pérez Preciado, José Juan, 'El Marqués de Leganés y las Artes', 2 vols, PhD dissertation, Universidad Complutense de Madrid, 2008.

Pérez de Tudela, Almudena, 'Making, Collecting, Displaying and Exchanging Objects: Archival Sources Relating to the Infanta Isabel's Personal Possessions (1566–1599)', in Cordula van Wyhe, ed., *Isabel Clara Eugenia: Female Sovereignty in the Courts of Madrid and Brussels*, Madrid and London, Centro de Estudios Europa Hispánica and Paul Holberton Publishing, 2011, pp 60–87.

Pliny the Elder, *Natural History*, Loeb Classical Library, 10 vols, Cambridge, MA, Harvard University Press, 1938–62.

Polo, Marco, *Travels in the Land of Serpents and Pearls*, trans. Nigel Cliff, London, Penguin Classics, 2015.

Quiccheberg, Samuel, *Inscriptiones; vel, tituli amplissimi . . .*, Munich, 1565 (trans. and ed. Mark Meadow and Bruce Robertson, Los Angeles, CA, The Getty Research Institute, 2013).

Ramakers, Bart, 'Sophonisba's Dress: Costume, Tragedy and Value on the Antwerp Stage (*c.*1615–1630)', in Christine Göttler, Bart Ramakers and Joanna Woodall, eds, *Trading Values in Early Modern Antwerp*, Netherlands Yearbook for History of Art, vol.64, Leiden, Brill, 2014, pp 298–347.

Rijks, Marlise, 'Defenders of the Image: Painted Collectors' Cabinets and the Display of Display in Counter-Reformation Antwerp', in Perry Chapman, Frits Scholten and Joanna Woodall, eds, *Arts of Display*, Netherlands Yearbook for History of Art, vol.65, Leiden, Brill, 2015, pp 55–82.

Rikken, Marrigje, 'A Spanish Album of Drawings of Animals in a South-Netherlandish Context: A Reattribution to Lambert Lombard', *The Rijksmuseum Bulletin*, vol.62, no.2 (2014), pp 107–23.

Riley, Gillian, *The Dutch Table: Gastronomy in the Golden Age of the Netherlands*, Painters and Food series, San Francisco, CA, Pomegranate Artbooks, 1994.

Rinaldi, Maura, *Kraak Porcelain: A Moment in the History of Trade*, London, Bamboo Publishing, 1989.

Rodríguez Villa, Antonio, ed., *Correspondencia de la Infanta Archiduquesa Isabel Clara Eugenia de Austria con el duque de Lerma y otros personajes*, Madrid, Fortanet, 1906.

Scappi, Bartolomeo, *The Opera of Bartolomeo Scappi (1570): L'arte et prudenza d'un maestro cuoco. The Art and Craft of a Master Cook*, trans. with commentary Terence Scully, Toronto, Toronto University Press, 2008.

Schama, Simon, *The Embarrassment of Riches: An Interpretation of Dutch Culture in the Golden Age*, New York, Alfred A. Knopf, 1987.

Segal, Sam, *A Prosperous Past: The Sumptuous Still Life in the Netherlands, 1600–1700*, The Hague, SDY Publishers, 1989.

Van der Stighelen, Katlijne, ed., *Michaelina Wautier: Glorifying a Forgotten Talent*, Kontich, BAI Publishers, 2018.

Van der Stighelen, Katlijne, and Mirjam Westen, eds, *Elk zijn waerom: Vrowelijke kunstenaars in België en Nederland 1500–1950*, Ghent, Ludion Press, 1999.

Van der Stock, Jan, ed., *Antwerp, Story of a Metropolis*, Martial & Snoeck, Gent, 1993.

Stols, Eddy, 'De tromf van de exotica of de bredere wereld in de Nederlanden van de aartshertogen', in Duerloo and Thomas, eds, *Essays*, 1998, pp 291–301.

—, 'Gustos y disgustos en la confrontación y el intercambio alimenticios entre España y Flandes (siglos XVI y XVII)', in Ana Crespo Solana and Manuel Herrero Sánchez, *España y las 17 provincias de los Países Bajos: Una revisión historiográfica (XVI–XVIII)*, 2 vols, Córdoba, Universidad de Córdoba, 2002, vol.2, pp 585–614.

Sutton, Elizabeth, ed., *Women Artists and Patrons in the Netherlands*, Amsterdam, Amsterdam University Press, 2019.

Sutton, Peter, ed., *The Age of Rubens*, Boston, MA, Boston Museum of Fine Arts and Ludion Press, 1993.

Tomasik, J. Timothy, and Ken Albala, eds, *The Most Excellent Book of Cookery. Livrer fort excellent de Cuysine (1555)*, London, Prospect Books, 2014.

Vázquez, Alonso, 'Los sucesos de Flandes y Francia del tiempo de Alejandro Farnese por el capitán Alonso Vázquez, sargento mayor de la milicia de Jaén y su distrito, escrito en diez y seis libros', in Marqués de la Fuensanta del Valle, José Sancho Rayón and Francisco de Salbalburu, *Colección de documentos inéditos para la historia de España*, vol.72, Madrid, Viuda de Calero, 1879.

Vergara, Alejandro, ed., *Patinir: Studies and Critical Catalogue*, Madrid, Museo del Prado, 2007.

—, *The Art of Clara Peeters*, Madrid, Museo del Prado, 2016.

—, Vergara, Alejandro, 'Clara Peeters en el Prado: Una cuestión de categorías', in Ernesto Calabuig, *Un ángulo me basta, Visiones pedagógicas*, Madrid, editorial Tres hermanas, 2021, pp 22–35.

Viallé, Cynthia, 'Camel Cups, Parrot Cups and other Chinese Kraak Porcelain Items in Dutch Trade Records, 1598–1623', in Jan van Campen and Titus Eliëns, eds, *Chinese and Japanese Porcelain for the Dutch Golden Age*, Zwolle, Waanders, 2014, pp 37–51.

Visscher, Roemer, *Sinne-Poppen*, Amsterdam, Willem Jansz., 1614.

Van der Willigen, Adriaan, and Fred J. Meijer, *A Dictionary of Dutch and Flemish Still-Life Painters Working in Oils, 1525–1725*, Leiden, Primavera Press and RKD, 2003.

Woods-Marsden, Joanna, *Renaissance Self-Portraiture: The Visual Construction of Identity and the Social Status of the Artist*, New Haven, CT and London, Yale University Press, 1998.

Image Credits

Allen Phillips/Wadsworth Atheneum: fig.20
Art Collection 2 / Alamy Stock Photo: fig.40
© Ashmolean Museum / Bridgeman Images: fig.44
Bridgeman Images: figs 46, 55
Photo © Bonhams, London, UK / Bridgeman Images:
    fig.16
© Brussels, RMFAB/photo: J. Geleyns – Art
    Photography: fig.18
Creative Commons: figs 10, 11
Private collection, by courtesy of the Hoogsteder Museum
    Foundation, The Hague: fig.1
Courtesy of J. Paul Getty Museum: fig.23
Photo by Lee Stalsworth: figs 17, 53
Courtesy Los Angeles County Museum of Art. Gift of
    Mr. and Mrs. Edward W. Carter (M.2003.108.8):
    fig.34
Metropolitan Museum of Art, New York. Charles B.
    Curtis, Marquand, Victor Wilbour Memorial, and
    The Alfred N. Punnett Endowment Funds, 1974:
    fig.54
Metropolitan Museum of Art, New York. Purchase, Lila
    Acheson Wallace, Howard S. and Nancy Marks,
    Friends of European Paintings, and Mr. and Mrs. J.
    Tomilson Hill Gifts, Gift of Humanities Fund Inc.,
    by exchange, Henry and Lucy Moses Fund Inc. Gift,
    and funds from various donors, 2020: fig.36
MMFA, Christine Guest: fig.41
Copyright © Museo Nacional del Prado: figs 6, 9, 12, 14,
    15, 19, 24, 29, 30, 43, 50, 59, 60
© 2025 Museum of Fine Arts, Boston: figs 7, 21

Courtesy National Gallery of Art, Washington. The Lee
    and Juliet Folger Fund Accession Number 2013.141.1:
    figs 13, 51, 61
North Carolina Museum of Art, Raleigh Purchased with
    funds given in honor of Harriet Dubose Kenan Gray
    by her son Thomas S. Kenan III, and from Arthur
    Leroy and Lila Fisher Caldwell, by exchange, 98.3:
    fig.47
Penta Springs Limited / Alamy Stock Photo: figs 3, 4, 5
piemags/rmn / Alamy Stock Photo: fig.26
Courtesy of Rijksmuseum: fig.25
Sotheby's: figs 22, 52
Wikimedia Commons: fig.2

Index

Note: italic page numbers indicate figures; Clara Peeters is abbreviated to CP in headings and subheadings.

Aarschot, Duke of 64, 105
Adoration of the Magi (Mantegna, *c*.1500) 71
Aertsen, Pieter 14, 32, 54, 80
Albert VII of Austria 15, 46, 76, 82, 83, 102
Allegorical Banquet of Habsburg Rulers (Anonymous, 1596) 75, 76–8, 79
allegorical painting 32–3
Allegory of Summer (Arcimboldo, 1573) 94
Allegory of Worldly Riches (Frans Francken the Younger, 1600) 34, 35, 92
Amphitrite and Cupid with a Nautilus Shell (de Gheyn II, early 17th century) 67, 95, 96
Amsterdam (Netherlands) 11, 67, 71
Anguissola, Sofonisba 20–21, 96
Self-Portrait Holding a Medallion (*c*.1556) 20
Antwerp (Netherlands) 11, *13*, 15–17, 96
    as art centre 12–14, 15–16, 19, 32, 39, 41, 43, 45, 65–6, 102
    art industry in 52
    art market in 13–14, 39, 57
    collaborative painting practices in 12–13
    De Violeren (civic association) 78
    economy of 12, 15
    fishing industry in 82
    and flower paintings 91
    food culture in 85, 86, 88
    iconoclasm in 14, 68
    and international trade 12, 88
    printing industry in 14
    shell collecting in 68
    still life painting in 32, 33, 34–9, 41–3
    and Twelve Years' Truce (1609–21) 43
Antwerp painters' guild 11, 12, 39

apprenticeship system 19
Archdukes of Netherlands 5, 46, 51, 76, 83, 84
Archetypa studiaque patris Georgii Hoefnageli (Hoefnagel, 1592) *42, 43*
Arcimboldo, Giuseppe 86, 94
Aristotle 41, 66, 98
Arnolfini Portrait (van Eyck, 1434) 26
art dealers 64
art market 13–14, 39, 57, 64
art patrons/collectors 21, 33–4, 35, 43, 51, 57, 63–4, 65–6, 71, 105
artichokes 52, 61, 80, 86, 94
artistic style/language of CP 9, 16–17, 45, 101
    and alterations 54, 108
    and artistic trends 34, 43, 46
    attention to detail 57, 58, 85, 91
    axis lines/mechanical aids 52–4
    evolution of 45–52
    and figures in paintings 46–51
    foreshortening/spatial depth 31, 45, 46
    illusionism 22, 46, 61, 102
    imprimatura technique 54, 108
    influence of other painters on 39–41, 43
    innovations in 22, 28, 61, 65
    and materials/processes 52–7
    naturalism/realism 34, 39, 43, 46, 102, 105, 108
    and proportion/colour 58, 105, 108
    and relations between objects 106–8
    repetition of elements 54–7
    textures of surfaces 28, 39, 58, 61, 85
    and tiers of paintings 57–8
    viewpoint 39, 45, 46, 52, 105
    and workshop system 61–4

Basket of Fruit (Caravaggio, *c.*1599) *99*, 100
Basket of Grapes, a Goldfinch, Game and a Squirrel (*c.*1612–21) *60*,
    61, 85
beach, The (van Borsselen, 1611) 66, 95
Beert, Osias *37*, *39*, 74, 86, 93, 94
Belgium 12, 15, 84
Bellini, Giovanni 52, 71
Belon, Pierre 41, 80
Bessemers, Mayken Verhulst 18
Beuckelaer, Huybrecht 32, *33*, *33*, 34, 86
Beuckelaer, Joachim 13, 14, 32, 54, 80
biscuit, heart-shaped 93–4
biscuit as identifier in CP's paintings *10*, 28, *50*
Borromeo, Cardinal Federico 46, 64, 68, 91, 95, 96, 100
Bosch, Hieronymus 14, 63
Bosschaert, Ambrosius, the Elder 41, 43, 91
Bouquet of Flowers, A (*c.*1612) *5*, *57*, 61
Bruegel, Pieter, the Elder 14, 15
Brueghel family 19, 57
Brueghel, Jan, the Elder 13, 15, *16*–17, 19, 33, 41, 43, 54, 71, 95,
    102–5
    Five Senses series (1618) 46, 68, *70*, *76*, 98, 105
    Hunting Party with the Archdukes (*c.*1611) *82*, *83*
    and patron (Federico Borromeo) 46, 64, 68, 91, 96
    van Dyck's portrait of (1632) *16*
Brueghel, Jan, the Younger 100
Bruges (Netherlands) 12, 26
Brussels (Netherlands) 12, 18, 21, 41, 64, 68, *82*, 85, 96

Calvete de Estrella, Juan Cristóbal 75
candles 61, 80, 92, 94
Caravaggio 86, *99*, 100, 102
Catholicism 41, 46, 68, 85, 94
Cave, Nicolaes *62*
Charles V 71, 76, 78
Christianity 19, 41, 78, 85, 92, 94, 95
    see also Catholicism; Protestantism
Cicero 66
Claesz, Pieter *26*, 28
classical world 25, 32, 41, 66, 79
Cock, Hieronymus 14
collaborative painting practices 12–13, 35, 39, 57
Collaert, Adriaen 41, *42*, 43, 80
colonialism 12, 66–8, 88, 91
constkamer paintings 33–4, *34*, 65–6, 68
cookbooks/dietaries 79–80
Counter-Reformation 15, 46
culinary rituals 74–9

cutlery 79
    see also knife as identifier in CP's paintings

Daffodils (Collaert, 1587–9) *42*, 43
d'Arenberg, Philippe-Charles (Duke of Aarschot) 64
David, Gerard *40*, 41
de Bry, Theodor/de Bry, Johann Theodor 79
de Casteau, Lancelot 86
de Estrella, Calvete 75, 84
de Gheyn, Jacques, II 39–41, 43, 67, 91, 94, *95*, *96*
de Lairesse, Gerard 83, 100
de Smytere, Anna 19
De Violeren (Antwerp civic association) 78
de Vos, Cornelis *77*, 78
Diericx, Volcxken 14
Donoghue, Denis 102
Dürer, Albrecht 12, 14, 17, 26, 71

Elisabeth of Valois 20, 78
Europe, early modern
    changes in 65
    and colonial imports 12, 66–8, 88, 91
    conflict in 14
    and materialism/naturalism 32, 102
    symbolism in art of 92, 94
    trade/travel in 66–7, 71–4
    women painters in 8–9, 11, 19, 21, 101

falconry 83–4
Faydherbe, Maria 21
Feast of the Gods, The (Bellini, 1514) 71
fish in still life painting 79–82
Five Senses series (Brueghel/Rubens, 1618) 46, 68, 70, 76, 98, 105
Flegel, Georg *39*, 86
Florilegium series (Collaert, 1587–9) *42*, 43
flower paintings 41, 43, 88–91, 96, 98–100
food in still life painting 74–88
    cheese/butter 84
    and cookbooks/dietaries 79–80
    and culinary rituals 74–9
    and cutlery *see* cutlery
    fish/game 80–84
    fruit/vegetables 84–6
    sweets 86–8
Fortuny Delphos gown 8
France 67, 78, 85, 88
Francis of Sales, Saint 17
Francken, Frans, the Younger 33, *35*, 68, 93

Francken, Hieronymus, the Younger 34, 94
fruit/vegetables in still life painting 84–5, 84–6, 94, 95

Garland of Flowers with a Madonna and Child (1621) 46, *47*, 51
Gentileschi, Artemisia 21
Germany 58, 75, 78, 85
Gessner, Conrad 41, 80, 98
Ghent (Netherlands) 12, 63
Gillis, Nicolaes 39, 41, 84
glassware 74, 91
Goltzius, Hendrick 66
Gonzaga, Vincenzo 66, 75, 78
Grapheus, Abraham *77*, 78
Guicciardini, Ludovico 74, 189
Guild of Saint Luke 11, 39

Haarlem (Northern Netherlands) 14, 41, 51, 84
Habsburgs 9, 14, 46, 68, 76–8, 79, 88
Hawthorne, Nathaniel 102
Herrick, Robert 88
history painting 19, 21
Hoby, Lady Margaret 17
Hoefnagel, Joris 41–3, *42*, 66, 91
Horenbout, Susanna 14, 17
Hunting Party with the Archdukes (Brueghel, *c.*1611) *82*, 83
hunting theme 83–4

Iaia 25
idealism 35, 94, 102, 105
imprimatura technique 54, 108
Isabel Clara Eugenia, Archduke 15, 20, 46, 68, 76–8, 82, 83, 84–5, 96, 102
Isabel (wife of Philip the Good) 18
Italy 19, 35, 39, 46, 51, 75, 85

knife as identifier in CP's paintings 11, *27*, 28, *53*, *69*, *72*, *73*, 93

Lambert, Jan 39
Lamberts, Nicasius (CP's father) 11, 12, 19, 39
landscape painting 32, 46
Landscape with the Temptation of Saint Anthony (Patinir/Massys, *c.*1520) 13
lapis lazuli 52
Leganés, Marquis of (Diego Mexía) 35, 51
Linard, Jacques *67*
Lisbon (Portugal) 18, 71
Lomazzo, Paolo 21–2

Madrid (Spain) 20, 64, 96
    royal collection in 51–2, 58, 66, 68, 98
Mantegna, Andrea 52, 71
Mantua, Duke of (Vincenzo Gonzaga) 66
Margaret of Austria 26, 71
Massys, Quentin 13, 14, 43, 46
materialism 32, 102
Mechelen (Netherlands) 11, 12, 26
Mexía, Diego (Marquis of Leganés) 35, 51
Middelburg (Northern Netherlands) 39, 41, 71
Milan (Italy) 46, 64, 68, 75, 85, 91
Moreels, Clara (later Lamberts, CP's mother) 11–12
Moulins, Master of 28

Natural History (Pliny) 25, 66, 85
naturalia 65, 66
naturalism 32, 34, 39, 43, 46, 102, 105, 108
Negrin, Adèle Henriette 8
Netherlands 64, 68, 75, 84
    Archdukes of 15, 46, 51, 76, 83, 84
    see also Northern Netherlands; Southern Netherlands; *and see specific cities*
Nonnius, Ludovicus 82, 85
Northern Netherlands 14, 15, 22, 39, 41, 51
Núñez de Oria, Francisco 79

Ommegang in Brussels: Procession of Guilds (van Alsloot/Sallaert, 1616) 18, *18*, 82

P (letter) in CP's paintings 28, 88, 92, 93
Pacheco, Francisco 31, 100
painting genres 19–21
Parmigianino 22
Pasquetti, Jacomo 74
Patinir, Joachim 12–13, 14, 32, 43, 46
Pausias and Glycera (Rubens/Beert, *c.*1615) 39
Peeters, Clara, self-portraits of 21, 22–8
Peeters, Clara (née Lamberts/Lambrechts)
    and Antwerp art scene 14, 15
    artistic status/reputation of 35–9, 51, 52, 64, 65, 101
    artistic style of *see* artistic style/language of CP
    artistic training of 11, 12
    children of 12
    and collectors 17, 33–4, 51, 63–4, 65–6
    as Dutch/Flemish 15
    exhibition of (Museo del Prado, 2016) 9, 101
    family of 11–12
    and flower paintings 41

and genres of painting 20–21
  paintings attributed to 11, 45
  research gaps for 8, 19
  self-portraits of 21, 22, 28–31, 45
  signature of 21, 28, 45, 93
  still lifes of *see* still life painting
  as woman artist 8, 9, 11, 19, 20–21, 43
Peeters, Henrick (CP's husband) 11, 12, 39
Perspective Box of a Dutch Interior (van Hoogstraten, 1663) 98
Phideas 25
Philip II of Spain 14, 20, 66, 71, 75, 76, 82, 88
Philip III of Spain 51, 71, 83
Philip IV of Spain 51, 64, 84
Pisium vivae icones (Collaert, *c.*1610) 80
Pliny the Elder 25, 32, 41, 66, 84, 85
Polo, Marco 68
porcelain 68–74, 78, 108
Portrait of Abraham Grapheus (Cornelis de Vos, 1620) 77, 78
portraiture 20, 21–2, 66
Portugal 12, 18, 66, 71
Prado, Museo del (Madrid) 8–9, 57, 96–8, 101
Prodigal Son, The (Huybrecht Beuckelaer, *c.*1565) 33, 33
Protestantism 14, 68

Quiccheberg, Samuel 65

Raphael 46, 57
reflected self-portraits 22–6, 45, 58, 61, 93
reflections in painting 22–8
Renaissance 32, 57, 74–5, 102
Renaissance Interior with Banquet (van Bassen, *c.*1620) 76
Rome (Italy) 21, 46, 86, 88
  ancient 32, 78, 79, 85
rosemary 78, 88, 94
Rossi, Properzia de' 19
Rubens, Peter Paul 13, 14, 15–16, 19, 20, 35, 51, 54, 57, 84, 85, 102, 105
  Five Senses series (1618) 46, 68, 70, 76, 98
  Pausias and Glycera (*c.*1615) 39
  van Dyck's portrait of (1632) 16

Saint Michael (Master of Zafra, *c.*1495–1500) 25, 26
Sallaert, Antoon 18, 18, 82
salt cellars 54, 75, 78–9
Savery, Roelant 43, 91
Scappi, Bartolomeo 75, 78, 79, 80, 86
Schama, Simon 15
science 41, 65
Sciences and the Arts, The (van Stalbent, *c.*1650) 34, 66, 68

scientific illustrations 41–3, 42, 91
Self-Portrait in a Convex Mirror (Parmigianino, 1524) 22
self-portraits 20, 21, 22–8, 45
shell gold 52
shells 66–8, 95–6
Snyders, Frans 15, 35, 36, 64, 71, 98, 102, 105
Southern Netherlands 8, 12, 14, 15, 17, 20, 39, 46, 64, 71, 75, 78, 82, 83, 84, 85, 88, 102
  see also specific cities
Spain 26, 64, 85
  royal collection of 51–2, 58, 66, 68, 98
Still Life with Cheeses, Almonds and Pretzels (*c.*1612–15) 53, 57, 58–61, 74, 84, 102, 103, 105
Still Life with Cheeses, Artichoke, and Cherries (*c.*1625) 54, 55, 57
Still Life with Cheeses, Shrimp and Crayfish (*c.*1612–21) 73, 74
Still Life with Confectionery, Wine, Jewels and Burning Candle (1607) 10, 11, 22, 45, 74, 93–4
Still Life with Crystal Ball (Claesz, *c.*1628) 28
Still Life with Fish 80–82, 81
Still Life with Fish, Candle, Artichokes, Crabs and Shrimp (1611) 49, 51–2, 54, 57, 61, 80, 94, 96–8, 106, 108
Still Life with Fish and Cat (*c.*1610–20) 30, 31, 82, 98
Still Life with Flowers, Gilt Goblet, Eatables and a Pewter Flagon (1611) 22, 23, 43, 45–6, 57, 74, 91, 96–8, 102, 104
Still Life with Flowers, Gilt Goblets, Coins and Shells (1612) 6, 24, 25, 45–6, 54, 57, 58, 105
Still Life of Flowers with a Mouse and an Ear of Wheat (*c.*1612–21) 89, 91
Still Life with Flowers Surrounded by Insects and a Snail (*c.*1610) 87
Still Life with Fruit in a Basket, Dead Birds and a Monkey (*c.*1612–21) 85, 96, 97
Still Life with Fruit, Wanli Porcelain and Squirrel (Snyders, 1616) 35, 36, 102
Still Life with Fruits and Flowers (1612–13) 72, 85
Still Life with Game (*c.*1612–21) 61–3, 62
Still Life with Gilt Goblet, Porcelain and Eatables (*c.*1612) 50, 54, 86–8, 88, 105
Still Life with Herring, a Porcelain Dish with Butter and Other Eatables (1612) 44, 46, 51, 83
Still Life with Lemons, Oranges, and a Pomegranate (van Hulsdonck, *c.*1620–30) 38, 39
Still Life of Lilies, Roses, Iris, Pansies, Columbine, Love-in-a-Mist, Larkspur and Other Flowers in a Glass Vase on a Table Top, Flanked by a Rose and a Carnation (*c.*1660) 57, 91
still life painting 16–17, 20, 21, 22, 28531 32–44, 64
  allegorical/symbolic *see* symbolism in still lifes
  and *constkamer* paintings 33–4, 34, 65–6, 68
  flower paintings 41, 43, 88–91

foodstuffs in *see* food in still life painting

imported tableware in 68–74

letter P in 28, 88, 92, 93

naturalistic *see* naturalism

reflections in 22–8, 45, 58, 61, 93

salt cellars in 54, 75, 78–9

and scientific illustrations 41–3, 91

shells in 66–8

squirrels in 35, *36, 60*, 61, 76

and *vanitas* theme 31, 34, 91

and women artists 45

see also specific still life paintings

Still Life with Peacock Pie (Claesz, 1627) *26*, 28

Still Life with a Peregrine Falcon and its Prey (c.1612–21) 61–3, *62*

Still Life with a Peregrine Falcon and its Prey (Cave, c.1625) *62*, 63

Still Life with Porcelain Vessels, Glassware and Eatables (Beert, c.1610) *37*, 39, 93

Still Life with Shellfish, Salt Cellar, Artichoke and Cherries (c.1612–21) 54, *56*, 74

Still Life with Shells and Coral (Linard, 1640) *67*, 67

Still Life with a Sparrow Hawk, Fowl, Porcelain and Shells (1611) *48*, 51–2, 54, 57, 58, 61, 67, 83, 96–8, 108

Still Life with Tart, Silver Tazza, Porcelain and Oysters (c.1612–13) 67–8, *69*, 88

strawberries 88, 94

sweets in still life painting 39, 52, 86–8

symbolism in still lifes 32–3, 41, 68, 91, 92

  and animals 96, 98

  and Christianity 92, 94, 95

  and foodstuffs 93–4

  and mimetic quality 98–100

  and problems with interpretation 92, 93, 96–8

  sexual 94, 96

  and shells 95–6

Table with Cloth, Foodstuffs and Other Objects (c.1611) *27*, 54, 57, 78, 83, 85, 96–8, *107*, 108

Teerlinc, Levina 19

Teniers, David 15

Topsell, Edward 98

Ulysses Recognising Achilles among the Daughters of Lycomedes (Francken the Younger, after 1620) 68

van Aelst, Pieter Coecke 18, 19

van Alsloot, Denis 18, *18*, 82

van Bassen, Bartholomeus *76*

van Borsselen, Philibert 66, 95

van den Bosch, Lodewijck 96–8

van der Aar, Jan Govertsz. 66, 67

van Dijck, Floris Claesz. 39, 84

van Dyck, Anthony 14, 15, *16*, 19

  self-portrait (1632) *17*

van Eyck, Jan 25–6

van Hemessen, Catharina 19, 20–21, 22

van Hemessen, Jan Sanders 14, 19

van Hoogstraten, Samuel 20, 98

van Hulsdonck, Jacob *38*, 39, 41, 64, 105

van Mander, Karel 13, 14, 20, 22–5, 98–100

van Oosterwijck, Maria 28

van Stalbent, Adriaen *34*, 66, 68

van Winghe, Jeremias 39, 41

vanitas theme 31, 34, 91, 94

Vanitas Still Life (de Gheyn II, 1603) 93, *93*

Vasari, Giorgio 19, 20, 22, 25

ven Dijck, Floris Claesz. 39

ven Reymerswale, Marinus 14

Verhulst, Mayken 19

Virgin and Child with Canon van der Paele (van Eyck, 1436) 26

Virgin and Child, The (David, c.1520) 40, 41

Wautier, Michealina 9, 21

  Self-Portrait (1649) *21*, 22

Woman Seated at a Table with Precious Objects (c.1607–11) 28–31, *29*, 46, 63, 93

women 17–19

  and class 18–19

  clothing of 22

  and entrepreneurship 17, 19

  public activities of 18

  restrictions on 17, 20

women artists 8–9, 17, 19–22, 101

  and genres of painting 19–20, 45

  and human anatomy 19, 31

  training of 11, 19, 31

workshop system 15, 19, 43, 57, 61–4

Ykens, Catarina II 9

Zafra, Master of *25*, 26

Zeuxis 85